A PILGRIM'S CONFESSION

A PILGRIM'S CONFESSION

(We Propose; God Laughs)

WILLIAM GRAF

RESOURCE *Publications* • Eugene, Oregon

A PILGRIM'S CONFESSION
We Propose; God Laughs

Copyright © 2024 William Graf. All rights reserved. Except for brief quotations in critical publications or reviews, no part of this book may be reproduced in any manner without prior written permission from the publisher. Write: Permissions, Wipf and Stock Publishers, 199 W. 8th Ave., Suite 3, Eugene, OR 97401.

Resource Publications
An Imprint of Wipf and Stock Publishers
199 W. 8th Ave., Suite 3
Eugene, OR 97401

www.wipfandstock.com

PAPERBACK ISBN: 979-8-3852-3409-7
HARDCOVER ISBN: 979-8-3852-3410-3
EBOOK ISBN: 979-8-3852-3411-0
VERSION NUMBER 12/13/24

Excerpt from THOUGHTS IN SOLITUDE by Thomas Merton. Copyright © 1958 by the Abbey of Our Lady of Gethsemani. Copyright renewed 1986 by the Trustees of the Thomas Merton Legacy Trust. Reprinted by permission of Farrar, Straus and Giroux. All Rights Reserved.

TO MY DAD, MOM, AND SISTER

Contents

Acknowledgments | ix

Where Do I Begin? | 1

A Key Moment (1960-1965) | 3

But Where Did My Story Begin? (1935-1960) | 13

Back Home with My Best Teachers | 18

A Significant Six Years (1954-1960) | 21

A Brief Interlude (Summer of 1959) | 26

End of the Interlude and the Final Year (1959-1960) | 28

The Month of June (1960) | 30

Then Came Ithaca (1965-1971) | 32

A Dream Come True (1966-1971) | 39

Drugs and Alcohol | 43

My Last Year at Ithaca | 48

A Different Kind of Life (1971-1972) | 50

Student to Professor (1972-1978) | 55

A Month of Prayer (Summer 1975) | 63

A Five Month Change of Venue (Spring 1976) | 66

Back to the "Rock" | 69

My Year at Nazareth College (1978) | 73

Then Came the Church of the Annunciation (1979-1988) | 79

My Sabbatical (Fall 1982) | 85

Extra Parish Opportunities | 91

Back to the Parish | 94

Surprise (1988) | 101

Most Precious Blood Parish (1988-1998) | 103

And, Meanwhile | 112

Again, Surprise | 119

Church of the Resurrection (1998-2008) | 121

Pastor for Priests | 131

My Saint John Fisher College (now University) Days (2001-2020) | 135

Me, as a Teacher | 150

My Life at the Legacy (2008-Present) | 163

BIRTHDAY #88: It Has Been a Wonderful Life (And Still Is) | 173

An Aside | 180

Working toward a Conclusion | 183

Acknowledgments

A MULTITUDE OF CARING PEOPLE have enriched my life. As extended family, friends, teachers, colleagues, students, communities of faith, and protagonists/antagonists, they have given me the life, encouragement, and talents to pursue my dreams in good times and in challenging times.

I am grateful to those who have helped me with the ideas and editing of this set of memories. Dr. Tim Madigan, Professor of Philosophy at Saint John Fisher University and friend, read and re-read the copy with many words of encouragement and suggestions. Fionnuala Regan, on the faculty of English as well as a tutor in the Writing Center, gently offered much help to help clarify my ideas. Fr. John Colacino, a colleague in the Religious Studies Department (now retired), offered suggestions about the material (what might be omitted) but also might better to be said. Mark Latona, a staff writer for the *Catholic Courier* (the Diocese of Rochester's newspaper) read, corrected, and suggested changes. Millie Lewis, a friend, caught some mistakes in spelling and punctuation which others missed. My final editing and feedback support came from three priests from the Jesus Caritas group that gathers monthly for a meal, prayer, and conversation about our ministry as we share how we encountered Jesus in our daily lives. Father Kevin McKenna, an author himself and pastor of a large suburban parish, Fr. Dan Holland, retired and part time chaplain at Saint Ann's Home for assisted living and rehabilitation, and Fr. Bob Schrader who is also retired and the author of over one thousand book reviews offered some ideas and some substantive editing. All three encouraged me to share my memories with others. I am grateful to all those who have helped to bring this book to its conclusion.

Acknowledgments

P.S., I need to mention the Wiktorski family who reviewed the text and brought a glaring error to my attention. I forgot to mention Mark's talented daughter. That mistake cost me! I have remedied the omission and have humbly apologized more than once. She is a winner!

For all other omissions and mistakes, I take full responsibility.

Where Do I Begin?

IN A PIVOTAL SCENE in the movie *Amistad* a perplexed lawyer goes to visit John Quincy Adams seeking much needed advice. His African client had led a revolt on the Portuguese slave ship Amistad that accidently landed on Connecticut shores. At the time a sagacious Adams, once President, had been elected to the House of Representatives. He gently urges the inexperienced lawyer to learn his client's story. The wise elder suggests that knowing one's story helps to explain why and how a person acts. That bit of advice has remained with me over the years when I dealt with those struggling with any number of personal issues. As a college professor, following Adams' wisdom, I could better understand a student's failure to meet a deadline, my expectations about the quality of an assignment, or why a student failed to show up for class.

My life has been a series of conversion moments. I believe my stories are a progression of events reflecting much change ("looking at things differently") yet also with much continuity. My journeys to different lands like China, Japan, Russia, Ireland, Italy, and the Holy Land presented me with new insights and renewed opportunities to examine current events with a bigger lens. Life is a journey but like any journey we need a spirit of adventure mixed with an opportunity to try something new even if only the food: like pickled sheep brains or sweetened sparrow, and even the local beer. I have come to believe that life's stories are a thread of key discoveries not only of places but also of oneself. As I have grown older, I have grown newer. Even as I begin this reflection, I am excited to revisit the times and places that have encouraged me to explore new ideas while still considering the old ones: sometimes they challenged me and sometimes they comforted me. I am excited about this project that has been written over the past 88 years, but now is put on paper.

As I write I will be using some fictitious names (sometimes, only pronouns) and inexact times to avoid violating any confidentiality. On the other hand, I will mention names and dates of some significant people who have since died or who would not be compromised if I mentioned them. If I do offend anyone, I am sorry. These are my memories; others might remember them differently.

A Key Moment (1960-1965)

TUESDAY, JUNE 28, 1960, pops into my head as a place to begin. I had moved my books, clothes, and tennis racket into the top floor of Holy Family rectory in Rochester, NY. It was my first assignment as a priest ordained but 24 days before. I mention the tennis racket because I tried to hide it as I walked up the stairs. I did not want the pastor to think that I was going to play games rather than work.

That same night I had dinner with him. I was a bit scared because there were just the two of us. The other two assistant pastors (we now call them parochial vicars) were with the altar boys (no altar girls in those days) for the servers' annual appreciation picnic. "Father" George was a monsignor, but he preferred to be called "Father" rather than the more honorary title, "Monsignor." I think he enjoyed it more when he wore his monsignor's red cassock on feast days. The memory of that meal has remained with me these many years. At the conclusion of the dinner punctuated with much small talk, "Father" George picked up the remaining dishes from the table. He whispered that it is one way to help the cook when we take them to the kitchen. As he started to move towards the kitchen, he turned to me and said "Remember, Bill, why you are ordained: to serve the people." He quickly added, "Now I will show what lights to turn on when you celebrate morning Mass." Even to this day I try to remember why I was ordained a priest: "to serve and not to be served."

In many ways Father George acted as a father as he modeled what he asked of us three assistants, reminding us to visit the five hospitals weekly; teach a class in the grade school each week (we had 17 classrooms: 2 each K-8 with one of the kindergartens meeting in the morning and the other in the afternoon; conduct a weekly class for high school and grade school students who attended the public schools; take Holy Communion to the sick and shut-ins at least once a month; and work with at least one of the various organizations (Boy/Girl Scouts, Legion of Mary, Holy Name Society, Rosary Society, Youth Group to name a few). Of course there were the priestly expectations of celebrating daily Mass (one of them for the 20 nuns in the convent chapel), hearing confessions for one and a half hours on Saturdays and before special feasts both in the afternoon and in the evening, meeting with couples preparing for marriage, baptizing babies every Sunday afternoon, meeting individually with those who wished to become Catholic (we called them "convert classes" in those days), be present at all the Masses on Sundays to help distribute Holy Communion (no Eucharistic ministers in those times) and then greeting the parishioners at the different doors as they exited Mass. There were the wakes with the rosary at one of the calling hours with grieving family and friends and then the funerals with a committal service. One of us was available 24-7 to administer Extreme Unction (now referred to as the Anointing of the Sick) as we took turns each day to be "on duty." Each week one of us was charged to run off the weekly bulletin on the mimeograph machine. I often wondered why we were not trained in the seminary to thread a movie projector or run a machine that needed cranking five hundred times to produce the parish events of the week. In between these varied tasks there were the more casual encounters with the people of the neighborhood as we walked the streets and visited homes.

You might wonder why I remember all that. The staff had heard that one of our newly- minted lay teachers had told her students that all the priests did was "say Mass on Sundays." In one of my visits to her class, I played the role of the innocent inquisitor when I asked the students, "What do you think the priest does all week?" As I wrote their answers and added my own, they were amazed that we did more than just "say Mass on Sunday." I admit that I walked out of the classroom with a devilish smile that masked a "that-will-fix-you-young lady" look. At times telling a story can painlessly educate.

I am a textbook case of an introvert although I hide it well. Meeting new people challenges me. Visiting patients in the hospitals meant seeing parishioners I had never met before and at a time when they were not at their best. Growing up I had often heard someone say, "I will pray for you." My seminary education often spoke of the power of prayer. Lessons, like prayer, were often discussed in the abstract. Reality changed that.

It was a sweltering day a month after Father George and I had our first dinner together. Still eager to impress him I chose to visit all the hospitals in one day. By the time I arrived at the last hospital on the list, I muttered a prayer that no parishioner would be there, and I could triumphantly return to the dinner table that night to report on the various patients in ALL the hospitals I had visited that day. I checked the list of patients at the main desk (we could do this before the HIPAA rules were promulgated) with the hope that none of our parishioners would be there. Unfortunately for me there was one listed. As I made my way to the hospital room, I was still praying that he would be out of his room. Again, no luck! I introduced myself. He seemed surprised at my visit because he was planning to be home later that day. We talked in generalities about the weather and his stay in the hospital. As I was leaving, I said that tomorrow would be the First Friday and I would gladly stop by his house to bring him Holy Communion. His whole demeanor changed as he muttered that he would like that possibility, but it had been a while since he went to confession or attended Mass. "Well, why not go to confession now and I will bring you Holy Communion tomorrow?" I suggested. And so he did. The next day I went to his home; his wife pointed me to the upstairs bedroom where he was resting. We prayed and he received the Eucharist. When I came down the stairs his wife had tears running down her cheeks as she whispered "I have prayed for him to return to the sacraments for 32 years. My prayers are finally answered." As I drove away, I began to understand more fully about prayer: the kind that got me to the hospital and asked a question that answered the longings of a caring wife.

On a lighter side that same month I was summoned to anoint a man who was seriously ill. This was a first time for me. When I arrived, he was sitting in a chair with a smile on his face. I was imagining to myself that sick people should be in bed gasping for breath. Here he was fully clothed, sitting in a comfortable chair, smiling, and speaking in full sentences. I mumbled to myself, aloud apparently, "What do I do now?" The man said, "Well, the other five times this happened the priests started with hearing my confession, then they anointed me, and finally gave me Holy Communion." I laughed as I headed back to the rectory. It was great to be coached by a pro!

My five years at Holy Family parish were formative. Ministry revolved around the seven sacraments and educating parishioners, young and old, the need for the Church in their life. But there were other ways, I believed, that we could minister. Looking back, I did things that today would be condemned as foolish and dangerous or not permitted at all. One chaperone and I took the Youth Group, numbering about 90-100 teenagers, to Buffalo (to visit Our Lady of Victory Basilica), and then lunching at an Italian restaurant on the way to Niagara Falls. There the kids were allowed to explore the Falls on their own, both on the American and Canadian side. A time was set for them to return to the two buses (*one* chaperone for each bus). Before they set out, I would prompt them gently to remember: "Who you are! Where you are! *And* What you represent!" In the four trips we made there was never any trouble unless one counts the firecrackers purchased legally in Canada but discreetly hidden under their jackets.

I taught a half dozen teenagers how to drive using my stick-shift drive Ford to prepare them for their driving license. One of them was so grateful that I never had to worry about washing my car or getting the oil changed. I taught four or five how to play tennis and others how to play handball. There were trips to New York City to see the sites and attend Broadway plays (some of the guys continued to do this well into their married life). The parish had about ten seminarians studying to be priests. We camped out for a week at a cottage owned by one of our parishioners for an annual time on the beach just for them. We prepared meals together, prayed, and enjoyed sessions for informal sharing of our calling to ministry. Home visits were important to get to know families and enjoy a meal away from the rectory. One family, a few houses from the rectory, served pasta every Wednesday night. How could I miss a meal like that?

Usually when a new priest arrives at a parish the pastor or the oldest associate would ask him which group(s) he would like to work with. In many cases, the new associate was told what groups he would monitor. Nothing like that happened to me. I did not think much about it but was aching for something of my own to do. After a few weeks, still a bit anxious, I noticed a pile of index cards on a table. I asked Father George their purpose. He casually mentioned that these were people who didn't use their Sunday envelopes or didn't go to church: "sort of lost souls." That had me thinking. I decided to count off a few each day and visit the homes of these "souls." So, every day I would head out, often walking, to call on the various individuals or families to see how I could help. In those days there was usually someone home, often a weary mother with two or three children running around the house (inside or outside). I would introduce myself, talk about the weather and current events, and eventually tell them that we miss them on Sundays. "Is there anything that is keeping you from Mass?" Then I would listen to their stories: sickness, work, embarrassment for one reason or another (usually about a member of the family, their own marriage issues, or they just got out of the habit). I made no judgment, nor did I threaten them with hell and brimstone. I just listened. As I left, I would express my gratitude for them and their story, offering to help in any way I could. Over the summer I visited about seventy-five such homes.

Towards the end of August, the pastor asked me if I would like to help him with the upcoming fund drive to build two new Catholic high schools (eventually named to honor Cardinal Mooney and Bishop Kearney). In early September the pastor, a layman who chaired the committee, and I attended mandatory meetings at the diocesan headquarters. Later we would meet in our own parish hall with volunteers for training to raise the money needed to meet our parish's assigned goal close to $90,000. That was a large amount of money at the time and for the financial status of most parishioners. We did meet the goal. I learned the names and addresses of people in the parish because I had to assign and review donation cards almost every day. That task later served me well because I would be able to connect names with faces and had a sense of their address within the parish boundaries. Working with the volunteers forced me to remember names but also hear their stories about their involvement with the parish over the years. Initially the parish was predominantly German in origin (including the Sunday sermons). Many of the founders moved to the suburbs and were replaced with younger Italian families. That bit of history helped me to understand the organization of the older committees and possibilities for the newer committees (e.g., a School Parents Association for the younger Italian members of the parish). At the conclusion of the drive (just before Thanksgiving) the pastor proudly announced that we had met our goal and even went over it by a few hundred dollars. He thanked the people, the volunteers, and me. Privately he told me that he watched to see what I would do with my time during the summer. I showed initiative visiting homes and spending time with others who were on the fringes. He liked that. "That is why I chose you to be part of the Fund Drive. I needed a go-getter to make it a success. Now what group would you like to work with?" I chose the Youth Group and training the altar servers.

My initiative helped me in a few other ways. I proposed that we sponsor a boys' basketball team and a team of girl cheerleaders. The pastor was against using our auditorium for basketball but supported the idea of the two teams. We found a place to practice. One of our men had a connection with a coach from another team who had room for our team to practice. It was easy to recruit young people for both teams. All we needed was team uniforms. We ran a candy drive (much like the Girl Scouts' cookie drive) to raise the necessary funds to purchase the uniforms and some practice balls. The candy drives and later the Christmas tree sales helped fund many of our Youth Group trips and fun nights. The team never won any championships, but we all had a great deal of spirit and bonding.

The School Sisters of Notre Dame staffed our thriving school. Sister Eva taught the first grade for over 50 years in the same classroom. She taught the grandmothers and grandfathers of some of her present students. The Sisters reflected a sense of dedication and care that was beyond anyone's expectation. Some of the changes in their Order's rule of life and their religious dress came about at the time of the Second Vatican Council. When I arrived, the Sisters' headdress was such that they could not see much to the right or left (much like blinders). I will never forget the first morning they attended Mass with their new and simpler headdress. Some of them hung their heads in fright or embarrassment (I wasn't sure which). The good news was that they could now drive a car if they had one. Two or three of the younger Sisters brushed up on their driving skills. The principal and I decided to raise money to buy a car for the convent's use. At the time "Green Stamps" were often the reward for purchases in a variety of stores. The stamps could then be redeemed for a variety of prizes. Why not a car? We invited members of the parish to contribute the Green Stamps they had earned. Volunteers counted and cataloged them towards the purchase. Still short of the necessary money we decided to have a spaghetti dinner. Some mothers volunteered to cook the sauce. We procured free pasta from a nearby dealer. The Youth Group served as hosts and waiters for the meal. The men set up table and chairs. It was a monumental group project. In the course of the preparations the principal (who was of German origin) informed me that she would provide the recipe for making the pasta sauce. "Sister," I said, "these are Italian mothers who have been making sauce their whole lives. I think it might be insulting to suggest that you were going to provide the recipe for the sauce. Sauce is their pride and joy." She relented. The dinner was a great success. The proceeds from the dinner plus the stamps paid for a new car. When I blessed it, I put some extra holy water on its four fenders quipping, "This should help keep you out of accidents."

About 50 years later, when I was teaching at Saint John Fisher College, I was driving through the neighborhood now divided by an expressway when I decided to stop by to visit one of the chaperones who helped me with the trips to Niagara Falls. She was living in the same house where she was born and raised. Always a caring person, Fran had taken care of her mother for many years, raised five children, was married and divorced from an alcoholic husband, and then had happily remarried only to bury her second husband a few decades later. During my time in the parish, she did not go to church. She took care of her sickly mother whom I visited every First Friday to bring Holy Communion. It had been my final Communion call (I had already visited 15 other shut-ins) so I brought some fresh donuts; Fran provided a pot of fresh coffee. The conversation usually revolved around the children. Over the 50 years one was murdered, another endured a long and painful disease, still another was schizophrenic and froze to death on a park bench alone as a street person. Like her father, another suffered from alcoholism. One of her troubled grandchildren died in a fiery car crash.

As we caught up on the events of the many years since we first met, Fran's eyes teared up. She looked at me and said, "I have been so lucky in my life. I give thanks to God every day for His many blessings." I was completely taken off guard. It was an awesome moment. I still see her smile and hear her voice even now as I type her words. Here was a woman who had every reason to be sour on life and complain, yet she was grateful for the memories and the blessings. Her faith was much stronger than many of the people I met during my life. She was grateful for so much. When I left the house and drove away, I had tears in my eyes. I had just left the house of a saint. Fran taught me an important lesson about gratitude.

One of the added responsibilities we assistants assumed on Fridays was covering the State Mental Hospital in Rochester. I could relate many memorable stories from my experiences from those Fridays. On one of my visits, I stopped at one of the independent resident cottages to see a patient. As I was leaving, I met a friendly resident who regularly introduced himself as Saint Michael the Archangel. On each of my visits he would walk me to the door usually with his arm around my shoulder. One time he turned to me and looked me straight in the eye. "You know, Father," he whispered, "you and I are the only sane ones in this place." As I got into my car to return to the rectory, I smiled to myself, "Well, you were finally accepted as an equal."

On a more serious note, there were two formative visits that are etched into my memory. I was called to anoint a young woman with serious heart issues. She was in her early thirties and though she looked rather healthy to me, she wanted to be anointed because she thought she was going to die. We talked a bit and then she changed the subject rather abruptly. "Do you think I look pretty or ugly?" she asked. Then with tears in her eyes she continued, "You know no one has ever told me that they loved me. I hope that you will tell people they are beautiful and that you love them. They should tell others the same thing. I wished someone would have told me that they loved me." I called the charge nurse on the floor the next day to check on the patient's health. She had died during the night. So many people go through life never hearing the words "I love you. You are a beautiful person." Another lesson learned that has formed my relationships.

On another visit the hospital called me to anoint one of the patients who had died while eating. The staff put his body in a small room off the main recreation center to avoid upsetting the other patients. As I left the smaller temporary morgue, I needed to pass through the larger recreation room. I looked around and I noticed the residents sitting along the four walls looking into space, not talking or moving. I asked the nurse what was going on. She smiled, "It's recreation time. Do you notice anything?" "They don't seem very happy," I remarked. She offered an insight that has remained with me during some difficult times. "Mentally healthy people are able to laugh." That is why I have tried to laugh as I deal, sometimes unsuccessfully, with the craziness of dysfunctional institutions.

"Serving the people" of the community became a frequent mantra as I went about my ministry over those five formative years. I would be amiss however if I did not remember those initial exciting years when the Second Vatican Council was in session. I remember as a student when Pope John XXIII first made the announcement. I spent a few hours looking up "Council" in the theological and historical textbooks to see what to expect. One of our professors dismissed it as he grumbled that it would probably be a Convocation along the line of "an event in which the bishops would assemble in Rome to accept proposed documents already prepared by members of the Roman Curia. They would vote and then peacefully return home." The contrary happened! "They came; they saw; they conquered." Four years of heated and many collegial discussions produced a set of sixteen documents that are still being discussed, evaluated, and, in some places, implemented.

I remember small gatherings of priests discussing newly published books giving a theological foundation for understanding the Council or else the reports dealing with heated arguments that were taking place (some factual and others wishful possibilities). For example, building on the "dialog Masses" in Latin, we looked forward to celebrating the various sacraments in the vernacular. An older priest pointed out during one of our sessions that the document concerning the Church would be most important because it would broaden the idea of Church to include the "people of God on pilgrimage who are called to holiness."

During our seminary training the study of the Scriptures played a secondary role to the study of moral theology, canon law, and dogmatic theology (now referred to as systematic theology). I was part of a gathering of at least thirty-eight priests from our diocese who went to the Maryknoll Seminary in Glen Ellyn outside of Chicago during the summer of 1964. Our purpose was to study Scripture for a week led by newly educated Roman Catholic Scripture scholars. What an experience! We were the largest solitary group from any diocese in the United States. About the same time Father Charlie Curran, a priest of the diocese and newly appointed faculty member at our diocesan seminary, invited Father Bernard Haring to conduct a week's workshop on a newer approach to moral theology: the use of scripture. Over 50 priests from our diocese eagerly participated in lectures and discussions that opened our minds (and hearts) to a scriptural approach to pastoral issues that surfaced during our ministry of hearing confessions and pastoral counseling. It was my experience, then and over the years, that our Rochester diocesan priests as a group are well-read and eager to understand whatever documents come from Rome. We do not always agree with each other in their interpretation. Those four years when the Second Vatican Council met were the most positive and exciting in my life and, I dare say, of my generation of priests and religious. Speaking of "religious" I need to mention the great example of the women religious of our diocese who put some of us to shame. They studied the Council's documents and acted on them eagerly and wisely.

Upon reflection I recognize a major problem for most of us: neither those who sat in the pews nor those of us who stood in the pulpit had a sufficient background fully to understand the theological/scriptural foundation for the documents. Often, we were told something we could now "do" but not "why." In fact, we were treated like children: "Do as I tell you and don't ask questions." The leaders forgot that we could read (be literate), think (critically), and have good questions (curious). Asking questions seemed to be an insult to those in charge. This is not meant to be a criticism but an observation. We could now pray the Mass in the vernacular but also wanted to know what the words meant. We were looking for their deeper and, at times, simpler theological and scriptural meanings. As children we memorized the Baltimore Catechism. As seminarians, we often memorized the approved manuals and printed lectures for our final examinations. Before ordination we signed a printed oath (written in Latin) that required us to be obedient to the teachings of the Church as if they were all equally important.

Later the ordaining bishop would ask us to swear obedience to him and to his successors. If we said "yes," the ceremony would continue with the solemn "laying on of his hands" in silence to ordain us as priests. Too often during and after Vatican II we priests did what we were told because we had sworn an oath of obedience. Some of us did so because we saw the value in the new practice; others did it grudgingly and mechanically. I remember one week celebrating Mass in three different locations each a bit differently because that is what the pastor/bishop demanded. We changed willingly and unwillingly. Some more quickly than others. No matter, the changes were forcing us to reeducate, rethink, and act accordingly.

Often when priests gather, they fondly reminisce about their first assignment and its impact on their subsequent assignments. Even those who were not as lucky as I speak of its impact both positive and negative. I remember reading about successful students in their high school and college years reflecting on their first experience in grade school who report the same thing. My five years at Holy Family parish flew by for many reasons. There were plenty of opportunities to serve the people, but they also allowed me the time to pursue a master's degree in history. It had always been a dream of mine to study history and maybe teach it. When the bishop in charge of personnel called me to see "What's the gimmick for pursuing the degree,"

I said it was a productive way to spend my day off rather than play golf. That ended that conversation. In June of 1965 I was scheduled to celebrate the weekday 6:30 a.m. Mass. Piously I prayed before Mass that wherever I would be serving next year, it would be where I would do the most good. At 9:15 I received an unexpected call from the same bishop to meet with him at the cathedral rectory the next day. Little did I know that my graduate degree would make me a candidate for a position at Ithaca College located on the south hill overlooking Cornell University. The bishop told me that I was to become the Newman Chaplain (now called "Campus Minister") with the added advice "To act prudently." I cried as I drove all the way to my next assignment. What could be better than the one I already fully enjoyed!

But Where Did My Story Begin?
(1935-1960)

I WAS LUCKY. I GREW up in a small town in Upstate New York. Brockport was home to a canning factory. In late August trucks loaded with tomatoes would line the street leading to the huge factory. The smell of catsup permeated the air, and so I knew that the school year was just around the corner. At one time my dad worked at Alderman's box factory not too far from the canning factory. We knew when he was coming home because the 5:00 whistle would blow. My sister and I would run to the end of the street where we lived so we could ride home (down about six houses on the street) with him. Sometimes he would let one of us ride on the running board holding the lucky one with his free hand as the car crept down the street. Another industry was the General Electric plant which manufactured food mixers. It became the place where I set up a lunch counter when I was in high school. I would prepare the hamburgers, sprinkle some pepper on the grill, open the doors, and let the smell go out into the assembly room. It helped business. The State college was much smaller in those days. It added a sense of educational sophistication to the village. Brockport was an easy drive to Rochester where there were more than enough industries (Kodak, Bausch and Lomb, Xerox) with good jobs to support a family. Because it was a small village of about 2500 residents, it could "take a village to raise a child." On more than one occasion by the time I got home my mother would know what mischief I had been up to; one of the neighbors had already telephoned her.

The Greyhound bus line went through town into the heart of Rochester. We could buy a round-trip ticket for a dollar and see a movie at the Palace Theater where someone entertained the audience on a giant grand organ before and after the double feature. Our local movie theater was my sister's and my favorite haunt on Saturday afternoons when we were quite young. Usually it was a cowboy movie (Gene Autry or Roy Rogers) preceded by a cartoon film and the news of the day all for a nickel. I remember the horror when the theater began to charge six cents (inflation!). Movies played an important part in my life and still do. Gregory Peck's character in *The Keys of the Kingdom* greatly influenced my calling to the priesthood and the accompanying desire to be a missionary. His kindness, openness to others, and ability to be himself impressed me deeply. That same year Bing Crosby played the role of a priest in the movie *Going My Way*, who worked with some wayward boys to form a choir. His gentle care for the elderly pastor modelled care for others who acted differently. I believe that arts like music, theatre, stained glass windows, mosaics, and paintings are powerful ways to teach young people. It can stimulate their imaginations to greatness. I know they both challenged and encouraged me.

My mother told me that when it was time to begin my schooling, she had talked with the pastor. He told her that he did not want any troublemakers in his school. At times I could be cast as one who caused trouble. Not dissuaded from letting me start school, my mother called a friend who taught kindergarten in the public school system. So I went to public school for kindergarten and first grade before transferring to the Catholic school. Over the years I often told people that the public school straightened me out so I could attend the local parish school. One of my memories of my year in kindergarten was attending a showing of the movie *King of Kings* at the high school (yes, in the public school system!). The school summoned my mother to come and pick me up. I was crying towards the end of the movie so one of the teachers took me to the principal's office. My Mom and the teacher wanted to know why I was crying. I wanted to know "what that guy on the cross did to deserve that kind of punishment." Even then I was asking good questions of authority figures. I eventually learned more fully the answer to my question when I attended second grade preparing for my first time going to confession and then my first Holy Communion.

When I transferred to the Catholic School, my life changed. We began each day with prayer followed by the Pledge of Allegiance to the flag and then singing "God Bless America." I became an altar boy memorizing Latin responses and learning the proper times to ring the bells during Mass. One of my fondest memories and the most influential was Friday afternoon "story time." If we had behaved all week, Sister (we were taught by nuns) would read us stories. The stories revolved around great men and women saints and/or historical figures. They were factual or legendary narrations that taught us how to live: models to be emulated. To this day my favorite books (and movies) are those of great people. I know they were the men and women who had been models for my calling as a priest and as a person wanting to do good. I think back to Saints Francis of Assisi, Francis Xavier, the North American Martyrs, John Bosco, Mother Cabrini, Damian of Molokai, Therese of Lisieux, to name a few. Abraham Lincoln has to head the list of great men in history that inspired me (and still do). Like many of the real-life characters I admired, I have not succeeded in everything I did. My consolation? Like them, I am flawed but at least I tried.

Because I lived in a small town my social life was limited to biking around town or to Hamlin Park (about 8 miles away) to go fishing, hunting for frogs in a nearby creek, raising a Victory garden during World War II, playing pickup baseball games that could go on for twenty or more innings, working at my dad's restaurant (short order meals) that he purchased from a friend so he could be his own boss, visiting one of my aunts on her farm for a week playing in the barnyard, pumping well water to wash, and using the outhouse. Ice skating and tobogganing made our winters more enjoyable. Our family dog, Duke, enjoyed riding down the hills on our sled or toboggan as much as we did. With all those outdoor activities there was still another that played the most important and key part in my life: the frequent trips to the local library to find new books as well as the classics to read and ponder. I have always been a reader. As I would turn the pages of books about history and (auto)biographies, I was introduced to great leaders and to far-off places and I imagined being there as part of an historical event or of visiting the exotic places to live out my dreams. Later in life I walked the great wall in China, climbed Mount Sinai, visited the tombs of the Pharaohs, lived briefly in Jerusalem, Rome, Assisi and so many more places. When I had trouble with my eyes a few years ago, I came to realize how dependent I am on reading not just for intellectual stimulation but for my mental health.

As I journeyed through those years of elementary school, I wanted to be a doctor, or a lawyer, or a teacher when I grew up. But somehow I also wanted to be a priest who was also a doctor, lawyer, or teacher. I did not know for sure which way to turn until I was in the eighth grade when I heard stories about missionary priests who could become teachers in places like Africa or China. I often share the story about that eighth grade Christmas when I gave my girlfriend a card, a bottle of perfume (total cost twenty-five cents) and a kiss. When we returned to school after our Christmas vacation, to my dismay Patti had moved out of town. I never saw her again. I applied and then was accepted into the Maryknoll Minor Seminary program in Buffalo. There is no connection between Patti's move and my decision to go to the Seminary, but it is a great story.

There were about fifteen possible "future missionaries" living on Jewett Parkway in Buffalo near the zoo and park where we played baseball or football on Sunday afternoons. We attended classes at the Buffalo "Little Seminary" (a daily walk to and from no matter the weather) where I had some of the most memorable priest-teachers that I could imagine. To this day I can see their faces and hear their voices especially as they taught me Latin, Math, and English over three years. One of our teachers had worked on the railroad from age 14 until he started high school at the age of twenty-one. Fr. Baumgarten spoke often of the difficulty of learning Latin and showed us all sorts of tools to master the language. Another of our teachers would come to class to tell us how he had read one of Cicero's letters the night before. "What a windbag that Cicero was," he would report. Fr. Marnon also taught us English. His style of teaching was so lively, he could make simple grammar lessons exciting. I remember vividly closing my eyes as he read *Macbeth* playing the roles of the different characters. Only one of those teachers, now in his nineties, was alive when I took a long-overdue (by 50 years) trip to a priests' retirement home in the suburbs of Buffalo. I wanted to thank him personally for the wonderful and best educational experience of my life. The trip was truly rewarding. Our conversation was filled with stories and laughter. Both of us seemed to be grateful for our time together.

I remember vividly a conversation I had with the rector of the Maryknoll House of Studies. Fr. Joseph Gibbons had been a missionary in Korea just prior to World War II when Japan invaded Korea. Like many missionaries in Asia at the time, the young Father Gibbons spent some time in a Japanese prisoner of war camp. After the war, he returned to the United States in need of some time to recuperate. He replaced Fr. Charles Cappell, formerly a missionary in Peru, who was finishing his last year earning a degree in biology at Canisius College in Buffalo. Fr. Cappell was the rector during my first year at the House of Studies. The year before he died, I had reached out by phone to thank him for helping me through that first year away from home.

Fr. Gibbons succeeded him. Our relationship was not as positive although I did learn about the early Christian martyrs of Korea (his master's thesis). I not only learned their lives but some French. The first priest in Korea was Fr. Andrew Kim. He sent letters, written in French, to his former teachers in Macao. These helpful letters recorded the challenges of life as a Christian in the "Hermit Kingdom" because travel in and out of Korea, by order of the emperor, was extremely limited. Fr. Gibbons shared some of the information with me as I assisted him with some amateur secretarial skills. One day, after one of our "confrontations," he advised me that if I were to ever take another name, it should be Peter the Apostle. Peter was known for his impulsive behavior and utterances. I got the point and have spent my life working on that advice.

But Where Did My Story Begin? (1935-1960)

When I became a Third Order Franciscan during my early college years, I did take the name of Peter. For the rest of my life, I found myself in trouble because I am too impulsive. It is an on-going challenge. Many times, my impulsive behavior has made a positive contribution to solving a problem. Oftentimes though my impulsive utterances have brought about some hurt to an unsuspecting person that later required an apology. In recent years, students would laugh when I responded to a touchy issue or question with my often-used expression, "I don't know. I will have to pray about that." Saint Paul says that he prayed to be delivered from his "thorn in the flesh." I can relate to that prayer. My impulsiveness is my thorn, but this thorn has also been a gift. It has kept me humble.

After three years of high school in Buffalo, I transferred to the Rochester seminary, Saint Andrew's, for my final year of high school and first two years of college. This change allowed me to live at home, get my driver's license, and commute (forty miles round trip) to school each day. Over those three years I served Mass every morning (the pastor insisted on it) at the parish church. He told me at least once a week, "Sentire cum Eccclesia." I must admit that I have spent my academic life trying to understand and follow his advice "to think with the Church." The big question has been: Who, not What, is the Church?

Back Home with My Best Teachers

WHEN I WAS ABOUT 12 years of age, my dad purchased a restaurant (it had been a pool hall at one time). I helped wait on customers, refill their cups of coffee, learned to cook "short orders," clean the toilets, sweep the floor, sell cigarettes and tobacco, and tidy up the comic book section of the store. I had my pick of free comic books the day they arrived at the store. When I was fourteen and had a worker's permit, I took a job at a nearby dry goods store. My dad demanded that I learn and exercise a good work ethic. My new job at the dry goods store was a chance to put into practice what I had learned, both by word and example, from my dad. I would sweep the two floors of the store as well as the sidewalk in front of the store, stock the shelves, learned how to use the rope-operated elevator between floors, wait on customers, decorate the front showcase windows, assemble toys at Christmas time, pin price tags on the clothes (before the invention of scanning): all with a commitment to do my best and to show initiative. Between the two jobs I was able to have some pocket money and put money into a savings account before I left for the major seminary. More importantly, I learned the importance of showing initiative, being prompt, and exercising respectful customer service.

Mom and dad modeled a way of life that influenced my sister and me. My mom stood up for her beliefs. She belonged to a religious organization of women who met monthly. One of the women's daughters became pregnant out of wedlock. The organization voted the woman out of the group. My mother protested and quit in protest. "Where was the understanding and the compassion that religion was supposed to show?" She also played the upright piano that stood in our parlor. Later, both my sister and I took piano lessons (at least learning the scales and the basics). The church organist fell ill so the pastor asked my mother to fill in for two weeks until she recovered. Thirty-two years later my mom retired from the job. During those years she engaged in more than a few battles with the gruff pastor over her choice of music ("No Protestant hymns or secular music in my church!") or her mispronunciation of a Latin word. Each year she would play "Danny Boy" on Saint Patrick's Day to the joy of one of the nuns of Irish heritage who taught in the school.

My dad was not much of a churchgoer but fed every homeless person the pastor would send to the restaurant for a free meal. Mom and dad "adopted" one of them. Together they taught him how to read, write, and drive a truck so he could get his driver's license. They bought him a battered, used truck for $75 dollars (I wish I had a picture to show you; "battered" is being polite). He began his own business collecting garbage and lived with us for about 5 years before he married. During one of my Easter vacations, "Cowboy" (his nickname) hired me to work for him collecting garbage. That was a challenging experience. I learned a great deal from other difficult jobs (hustling refreshments at ball games and air shows, mopping and waxing floors on weekends for a few local businesses, working a refreshment stand at the annual firemen's carnival, e.g.) which helped solidify my educational goals. On another occasion my dad took another homeless person, an African American, into his store. He gave him a job and provided a small room with a bed and comfortable chair. My mom taught him how to read. After about a year, he moved back to Rochester. I have often wondered what happened to him.

Another key event has lived on in my memory and I have often spoken about it. During the summer months some of Rochester's street-people would take the bus to Brockport and then walk or hike to the farms near Lake Ontario to pick fruits and vegetables. They wore the same clothes every day and did not have a place to bathe on a regular basis. One hot late afternoon in June during supper time one of them came into the restaurant. I could see the customers at the lunch counter and others sitting at their tables spy the ragged customer with faces that said, "I hope he does not sit next to me." My dad took his order when he sat down at the counter. My dad usually had a cup of coffee in front of him all day long. Between customers my dad would go grab his cup and spend time talking with the disheveled man over the next thirty or so minutes. The man stood up at the end of his meal and asked my dad for the bill. I heard my dad tell him, "No charge! I am sure you had a tough day." I was tending the cash register near the front door and as he was leaving the man turned to me and said, "That has been the first time that I have been treated like a human being in a long time." Later, I quizzed my dad, "What was that all about?" He looked at me in a way that I had not seen before, "Don't forget that you could be that person someday." The poignant beginning of an important lesson!

My sister and I call each other every night. She lives in Florida vowing never to come north again because of the cold (she wears a sweatshirt if the temperature goes down to 70 degrees). Her first husband (of 17 years) died from a hunting accident; her second husband (of 32 years) died a few years ago from some medical issues. Jeannie is more athletic and artistically talented than I am. Over the years she taught dancing at Arthur Murray's, had an exercise program which aired on local TV, taught ballet to youngsters, coached the high school band's baton twirling group, managed a bar to support her children after their dad died, became a hair stylist and ran her own business, wrote a book, and raised four children (two of whom she adopted). At the age of eighty-seven she continues to decorate her home, cook, and bake. The neighbors, her two sons, and the local pharmacists regularly receive her freshly baked cookies. Recently, she caulked and painted the tool shed, the back porch, and the kitchen, raked twenty bags of mulch around her home, still feeds five to seven feral cats (and their occasional guests) in the neighborhood, and waits on her two indoor cats and a caged dove. The postal employees, garbage crew, and anyone who stops by are served coffee in the cold weather and Coca Cola in the warm weather. The postal workers and garbage crew receive curbside services. We often speak of the influence Mom and Dad had on our work ethic and awareness of those people who are taken for granted. Growing up we grumbled. Now we give thanks because they encouraged us to show initiative, try new things, watch out for others who have less, and speak out when we see an injustice.

A Significant Six Years (1954-1960)

WITH GRADUATION FROM SAINT ANDREW'S, I moved on to Saint Bernard's Major Seminary (the last 2 years of college studying Philosophy plus 4 years studying Theology). These pre-Vatican II years were challenging times for me. The courses in our major were taught in Latin with Latin textbooks and final examinations in Latin. Most of the courses were lectures without any questions, I laugh about it now, but could you imagine going to classes on Saturday afternoon (the last class was at 4:30)?

The schedule was rigorous: rise at 5:30 a.m. and the lights automatically went off at 9:40 p.m. every day of the year except for Good Friday when we were allowed to sleep until 6:00 a.m. We had no days off except holy days, Thanksgiving, and Easter Monday. Our Christmas break was about two weeks long (December 23rd until January 6th); summer vacations from the first Saturday of June (the traditional day for Ordinations to the priesthood) until the first Tuesday after the feast of the Holy Cross (9/14). The same schedule continued for six years because "we have always done it that way." One year there was a horrendous snowstorm that closed the entire city; we still had class. Tuesday and Friday afternoons ("Walk Days") we were free to visit an assigned church or stay at the seminary to play sports (never football). Many of those afternoons, without permission and under pain of some sanction, some students could be found at a restaurant or someone's parental home for a meal. Parents would park on a nearby street to take us to and from our own homes. We were not permitted to have cars on campus.

Using the library was looked upon with suspicion. In my six years I could count on two hands the number of students I even saw in the library at the same time. However, I spent at least an hour a day there (after the daily 8:00 class) until the next one at 10:10. One of my projects during that hour was to read the writings of the Latin and Greek Fathers of the Early Church (collected and edited by J.P. Migne) with a later set of translations into English. I started with Volume One. This introduced me to a required course, Introduction to Patrology, during my first year of Theology. I remember the final exam in the course. Because I enjoyed the text we were using, I even read the footnotes. The exam had four questions, all four from the footnotes. Only four of us passed.

Because I was a regular in the library, the librarian occasionally asked me to help him move books around. I suggested the possibility of getting a subscription to *Time* magazine for the periodical rack because the Rule did not allow us to read the paper or listen to the radio. The magazine would allow us (me) to find out what was going on in the world. It worked! Our only source of information was the evening news on a black and white 24-inch TV located in the "Smoke Shack" (the name says it all) where students also played cards and could buy ice cream and snacks after dinner. Our recreation hour was followed by a study time, night prayer and the Grand Silence (no talking until breakfast the next day).

I worked hard my first two years at the "Rock" (the nickname for Saint Bernard's after the famous prison Alcatraz) to get good grades. As hard as I tried, I did not make the Dean's List. It became an obsession with me, so much so that around Easter of my second year of philosophy (senior year of college) I had to go home to see my doctor because of my weight loss (entering high school I weighed 152 pounds; I now weighed 143 pounds) and having trouble sleeping. The family doctor, who knew me from birth, wrote out a prescription and suggested emphatically to take it easy "or else you will either die or be committed to a mental hospital." I returned to the seminary, struggled through the rest of the semester, then went home to do a great deal of serious thinking. As the summer progressed, I found a job as a day camp counselor for one of the Settlement Houses, which was really relaxing. It would be a position I returned to every summer until I was ordained. The permanent staff dedicated themselves to working for the people in the neighborhood and providing a summer program that would take kids to the beach, museums, campouts, and city parks. The open air and the exercise from playing ball and swimming, taking the lively youngsters on bus rides to the museums, teaching camp songs, and telling stories to teach them lessons about God and great men/women was just what I needed to take a second look at my own life. I needed to relax and enjoy the moment.

I returned to the seminary to begin my first year of theology. I had a different attitude about studies: do the best I could without worrying about grades. For the rest of my academic studies, even when pursuing further graduate work after ordination, I did not check out my grades. I figured that if I were doing poorly, I would be dropped from whatever program I entered. I chose to learn to play handball on our outside courts which meant that during the winter we had to shovel off the snow before we could play. We used two balls during the winter: one we played with, the other rested on a heater so we always had at least one ball that bounced. I also volunteered to do some janitorial work shoveling snow, raking leaves, cleaning out a pond, and with some classmates ("the infamous class of 1960") built our class circle out of lumber and rocks under some trees overlooking the Genesee River. This was "our" place to sit, tell jokes, complain about the food, course work, and dream together what we would do with our lives. All the exercise kept me healthy.

I mentioned that I had joined the Third Order of Saint Francis when I was in high school. I renewed my membership at Saint Bernard's, becoming its leader by my final year. One of our projects was visiting the sick at the County Home and at Saint Ann's Home. I oversaw enlisting our members for a weekly visit to one of these places on one of our Walk Days each week. At one of the meetings, the faculty-moderator asked me to make a pitch for volunteers for these visitations. Unfortunately, I was overzealous at one meeting. I suggested that we were learning a great deal about Jesus' care for the lonely and the sick so this would be a wonderful way to put our words into action. I added, "and if you go to Saint Ann's Home, the Sisters will give you some pie and milk that will supplement our meals here." I was summoned to the office of the faculty-moderator to explain myself: criticizing the seminary's curriculum and the food like I did was not appropriate. He assured me the conversation was just between the two of us and would go no further. I explained that it was not a criticism but only a way of suggesting that we learn about care of others in our various classes on scripture, theology, and church law. Visiting the sick was a way of living out what we were learning in the classroom. As far as the remark about "pie and glass of milk" went, it merely meant that we would be rewarded for our service (sort of like a tip for good service). I thought that was the end of the matter. A few years later I discovered that the same faculty member suggested to the faculty that I was leading the students to "revolution and rebellion." This led to holding me back from receiving major orders (subdiaconate and diaconate) with my classmates. Now I look back at the consequences of my remarks made at the meeting and the subsequent discussion with the faculty member with no regret. Suggesting "putting your money where your mouth is" can lead to an authentic way of life. The faculty member's violation that assurances our conversation would go no further has tainted my trust of authority figures to this day. However, it also made me very aware of keeping private any conversations I had with my students in my office concerning issues about their classroom behavior, other private matters they needed to get off their chest, or just vent.

Perhaps another reason I was suspected of "revolution and rebellion" was the study groups I led (with permission, but "never done before") about two encyclicals promulgated by Pope Pius XII. One dealt, in part, with the use of the sciences (natural and social) for a wider interpretation of the Scriptures (*Humani Generis*); the other was a ground-breaking encyclical that played a role in the laity's active participation in the liturgy (*Mediator Dei*). Both letters proved to be important when the Second Vatican Council met a few years later. The faculty would certainly have accepted the Pope's two letters. The problem seemed to be that students were discussing them and asking questions. The theory of evolution and the possibility of praying the Mass or any of the sacraments in the vernacular were viewed as radical, even to discuss the idea. Our group discussions were not radical; all we did was ask questions and wonder about possibilities. We were too young and inexperienced to "lead the charge." However, it was a chance to dream and affirm those dreams safely in a small group.

When it comes to food, I am not very fussy even to this day. Our breakfasts over the six years I was a student were the same: Wheaties and Shredded Wheat every day. We sat in the same seat alphabetically at the same table according to our class year as we gradually moved closer to the kitchen. At one point during my student years, we had a "thrifty" procurator who tended to the physical needs of the building and students. For a few winters heating the buildings was a challenge. My room was about 50 degrees one morning. Some of my classmates asked the Prefect of Discipline if they could sleep in the hall where it was warmer. I remember at the end of one of the hallways was a statue of the Nativity scene. Someone put a blanket around the figures with a sign reading: "It was not this cold in the cave at Bethlehem."

One year on Holy Saturday we had scrambled eggs and ham. What a treat! At our main meal we had ham with small white onions (scallions) along with the usual fare; at our evening meal we had cold ham for sandwiches. On Easter Sunday we had more scrambled eggs with ham for breakfast. No surprise, for our Easter dinner we had the traditional Easter ham along with more scallions. You guessed it! That night we had delicious cold ham sandwiches. Monday morning more scrambled eggs and ham for breakfast (no Wheaties or Shredded Wheat). Our main meal was more ham diced with scallions. We found out later that a trainload of ham and scallions had broken down in the city. Both items were on sale at a bargain price: first come-first served. Guess who was one of the first in line to make a purchase.

One of the lessons I learned during those six years was the need to create one's own happiness and laughter. Criticism from some faculty members could get me thinking. For example, "I was too happy so there must be something wrong with me" was one of my favorites. Another time, commenting on the laugher at our end of the dining table, we were referred to as "the snake pit." I had to make up my mind that if I were to survive, I had to laugh. I had to find ways to deal with situations that could send me into depression and anger. When I was finishing my final year at Saint Andrew's, one of our teachers spoke about making the Stations of the Cross daily during his time at Saint Bernard's. That comment stuck with me, so I set my mind to do the same. Over the six years I made the Stations of the Cross every day, usually when I arrived at the chapel at 5:30 each morning. (I was usually up before the morning bell rang.) Over the years my three favorite stations were the three times Jesus fell. He always got back up on his feet only to be nailed to the cross. I was determined not to let things get to me. I might fail, but I could also decide to get up, keep moving, and keep laughing.

Another way I survived was by reading. I read the textbooks and listened to the lectures, but I found them dull and uninviting. I decided to read as much as I could. I read the Bible from Genesis to the book of Revelation. I challenged myself (and succeeded) to read all of Shakespeare's plays. Each semester during my four years of theology I chose a topic and read as much as I could to learn about it. I reviewed all the math courses I had taken and tried a few new math topics (math was not my favorite subject in school, but I wanted to try to understand its concepts). Another year I was thinking that the Gospel message is worth sharing with others much like selling a worthwhile product. That encouraged me to read as much as I could about sales techniques, conducting conversations, personal self-development, and leadership. I also realized that I would be working with people, be it in the confessional or in an office rectory, so I spent the years reading as much as I could about psychology and counselling. At the time Carl Rogers' client-centered theory about possible counselling techniques was roundly criticized by one of the faculty. We were forbidden to read his book. Naturally, that's all I needed to hear. I found the book's theory extremely helpful then and now.

A Brief Interlude (Summer of 1959)

During my third year of theology, I realized that the following summer would be my last full summer off for a long time. I spent much of the year planning a trip across the United States visiting historical spots, camping out in national parks, walking the streets of famous cities, going to Disneyland in California, experiencing the drive through the desert, and some time in Mexico: Acapulco, Guadalupe, a bull fight. I mapped out the trip and read about the different places along the way with no set timeline except the day my co-pilot (one of my best friends) and I were to begin.

A few memories of the trip still linger. There was the visit to Montana where George Custer fought and died fighting a coalition of Lakota tribes. Near the monument was a restaurant appropriately called "Custer's Last Stand." We had breakfast there: a huge 8-ounce steak, eggs, potatoes, toast, and coffee. The cost? $2.00 plus tip. About the same time, we camped out at Yellowstone Park. In those days there was no entrance fee, and we could camp wherever we wished. One of the inconveniences of camping out was washing with cold water except, of course, there. The creeks flowing from the geysers were warm and depending on how hot we wanted the water we moved closer to the geyser. I remember standing in the water shaving when a car of tourists passed by, stopping to take our picture.

We drove through Salt Lake City and on to Las Vegas where I gambled twenty-five cents. Our next night out in the open was the Grand Canyon. We chose a high bluff with no one else around us. I looked at the stars as I relaxed in my sleeping bag thinking how beautiful the skies are when we are away from the cities' night lights. The next morning I sat on the ledge to watch the sun rise, Wow! We headed out to travel the length of California from San Francisco down to Disneyland where we went on a ride before going back through Arizona and into Mexico. We were at the shrine of Our

Lady of Guadalupe on August 14th. A statue of Mary was laid out in a casket to represent her death; a vendor was selling blessed apples in honor of Mary, the new Eve, who did not eat the forbidden fruit. When we returned the next day, the statue was hanging from the ceiling to celebrate her Assumption into heaven. Struck by the beauty of the feast I decided to dedicate myself as a celibate in service to others no matter what happened when I returned to the seminary for my last year before possible ordination. A few days later I attended my first (and last) bull fight. One of the locals sat near us and explained what was going on and how one went about killing the bull. In one instance the toreador failed. Our tutor told us we have witnessed a seldom experienced event. Because the bull outsmarted the toreador, the bull won its freedom and would be put out to pasture.

From Mexico my friend and I drove back though Texas and on to New Orleans. During my five years in the seminary, one of my classmates and I would buy *Time* magazine (10 cents) on Fridays before we finished our assigned walk. We dared to buy our own and then hid it in our rooms for our own leisurely reading. It was a Friday, so I stopped by a drugstore to pick up a copy of *Time*. Lo and behold who did I meet but that same classmate who was traveling back to Rochester after a similar trek to Florida and the southeast. Some habits can't be broken but it added another story to our forty-day journey. From New Orleans my traveling companion and I wound our way through the hills and mountains of the south through Washington, D.C. and then to Providence, Rhode Island where I dropped off my friend, Bob Lavallee, with the promise to see each other when the fall semester would begin. When we finished the journey, I counted the time it took us: forty days and forty nights at the cost of about $325 apiece. I laughed at the symbolic number; rejoiced at the reasonable cost.

End of the Interlude and the Final Year (1959-1960)

RETURNING TO THE SEMINARY for my last year had its challenges. I was not ordained to Major Orders with my class in September despite my daily prayers all summer (especially to Saint Jude, patron of the impossible) with the hope that the Rector would change his mind. He did not; I tossed the book of prayers to Saint Jude into the wastebasket and never prayed to him again. I need to add very quickly that I am extremely happy, in retrospect, that I went through this difficult experience. To this day I give thanks for my disappointment at the time. It has helped me to be more conscious of the plight of others who deal with unreasonable (at least in my eyes) decisions some authorities make.

The semester went along quickly. I played lots of handball to distract me from my disappointment and continued to read as much as I could. Over the entire two semesters I read over one hundred books. I am not bragging but letting you know that I did not waste my time feeling too sorry for myself. I was hoping that the three of us who were not in Major Orders would be ordained before Christmas so I would not have to tell my parents or the pastor I would not be able to act as a deacon at Christmas Midnight Mass in my home parish. I prayed to Saint Francis Xavier, one of my heroes, who had inspired me to pursue my dreams. My prayers took the form of my annual novena going back to the days when I was hoping to be a missionary. The day after I finished the Novena in December, the rector told the three of us to prepare for ordination by making our six-day required retreat: we would be ordained later in the month just before vacation. Naturally, I was ecstatic. The private retreat was one of the best I ever made. Besides, it meant I did not have to go to classes.

End of the Interlude and the Final Year (1959-1960)

Bishop Lawrence Casey, the auxiliary to Bishop Kearney, ordained Bob, Lou, and me in the Sisters' chapel at Sacred Heart Cathedral on Flower City Parkway during the week of our final exams for the semester. The Prefect of Discipline drove us to and from in some rather heavy snow. I was so excited I think that I could have flown back to the seminary at the conclusion of both ordination ceremonies. The big one was ordination to the diaconate on December 21st: and the promise to be celibate and the right to sing (proclaim) the gospel. Later that morning I was walking away from class when I heard one of the faculty calling out my name. I pretended not to hear him, given our history. He caught up to me, tapped my shoulder, and with a smile informed me, "The whole faculty is so happy for you and how you have changed." I thanked him and said to myself, "Like hell, I am the same as I have always been."

The second semester went by very quickly preparing for ordination, designing the chalice I wanted made for my use as a priest, and choosing the holy cards to function as remembrances of the big day: June 4th, 1960. I had the classwork to finish, continued with my reading, and played handball. The day before ordination I went to my confessor for the last time. He had served in that role for all 6 years of my stay (I almost wrote "incarceration") at Saint Bernard's. At the end of the prayers, he stood up and shook my hand. "Bill," he said, "Of all your classmates you have had it the toughest, but I also think you will be the happiest."

Later in the evening my other six classmates for the diocese followed a tradition. We went from one faculty suite to the other to express our thanks to each of our professors. The last room was that of the Rector. He greeted us with the words, "Quid dicam vos? Laudo vos?" ("What can I say? Praise you?"). One of my braver classmates spoke up. "You have not done it over the past six years. No need to start tonight." He gave us his blessing and we left with a sigh of relief. The Rector had called us the worst class in the history of the school (and I was the worst in the class). Years later I was serving as the archivist for the diocese. I came across a letter that he had sent the bishop which noted, "…this same class (of 1960), from their First Philosophy year were regarded by other students as a most unusual assortment of odd-balls, individualists, neurotics, malcontents, to be assembled in a single class." In another letter, when speaking about our class ordained for the Diocese of Rochester, he ranked us from the best to the worst. Guess who was noted as the worst.

Bishop James Kearney ordained our class of "misfits" the next morning, June 4th, at 10:00 in Sacred Heart Cathedral. One of the happiest days of my life.

The Month of June (1960)

I CELEBRATED MY FIRST SOLEMN MASS the next day, the feast of Pentecost. The music was superb and the liturgy very moving. Fr. Jack Hedges, a former assistant at the parish, preached the homily about the joy and challenges of the priesthood. As an aside, Jack and I continued to be great friends until he died about 44 years later, when I preached the homily at his funeral. I wanted to keep things simple and inexpensive so a dinner for invited guests, a small group of close family and special friends, followed. From 2:00 to 4:00 there was a reception in the parish hall for parishioners and friends from out of town. A women's group served punch and cookies. A proud mom and dad stood next to me as I blessed each person reminiscing about "How they knew me when." Fr. Paul Tuite, the priest who inspired me to consider priesthood when I was in the second grade, came to receive a blessing and congratulate me. I had not seen him while I was in the seminary, so I was most grateful that I saw him that afternoon. He died a few years later humble and serving faithfully until the end. I still see his smile and feel his warmth.

A few days later Peter Deckman (a friend of mine from the seminary who was ordained 4 years later) and I drove to New York City for some relaxation: movies and a few plays. The first night we were there, Peter reached into his pocket and gasped, "I forgot my wallet." I assured him that I had it covered: "no problem." In August Peter phoned me to invite me out to dinner and a movie. He wanted to express his gratitude for my generosity while in New York. We had a great Italian dinner before heading out to a movie. He reached into his pocket to pay the bill and gasped, "I forgot my wallet." During the fifty plus years we remained friends, we would laugh as we retold that story usually with some embellishments.

In the third year of my theological studies, the bishop became pastorally concerned about the number of Spanish speaking people arriving from

Puerto Rico. At the time we had no Spanish speaking priests to minister to them, so he asked the rector of the seminary to prepare some of our Rochester seminarians to learn Spanish. The rector selected about ten students to begin classes in Spanish. As always, people were chosen for special assignments at the seminary according to their grades. I was not chosen so volunteered for the classes. For the most part those who were "chosen" had no interest in the class nor working in that kind of special ministry. I did. This was my chance to be the missionary I had wanted to be when I started high school. Our teacher, a Redemptorist priest, had served as an assistant pastor in Puerto Rico for about 10 years. He had never taught a class (much less Spanish) before. Two years of classes with him were a delight. We did not have a book of grammar, so we repeated words and phrases after he explained their meaning. He encouraged us to speak, mispronouncing words, and laughing with us as we stumbled through our classes. "It is okay to make a mistake. That's the way we learn and laugh with each other." Another great lesson!

About a week before we would report for our first assignment, the newly ordained priests would report to the Chancery Office to receive our assignments from the bishop. We first met with the Chancellor who emphasized that when we applied for any dispensations for a marriage case, we should use "block letters" for submitting their names. The first bit of useless (but important in their eyes) information that continues to be part of the culture of institutions. My fellow classmates and I then walked into the meeting, greeted the bishop who was sitting behind a large desk, and sat down quickly. I was planning on a parish assignment that would use my new language skills and the hope to live out my dreams of being a missionary. Our assignments were given out alphabetically, so I was the third person to receive an envelope noting my assignment as the bishop announced it for us all to hear. Mike Murphy and I were the only ones to receive assignments in the city. Mine, however, was not to a Spanish Apostolate, but to a German national parish with a good number of Italian members. Years later I found out that my assignment was originally to a parish with an influx of families from Puerto Rico, but the personnel director thought it would not be a good idea for a newly-ordained priest to be assigned to a parish whose pastor was "unique in his policies." At the time I was disappointed, but my assignment to Holy Family parish was a blessing. I was in the neighborhood where I had spent my summers working at Charles Settlement House. Some of the youngsters I had as campers were part of the parish. In retrospect, "Not my will, but Yours" makes sense.

Then Came Ithaca (1965-1971)

SOMEONE ASKED ME WHEN I moved from Ithaca how I would describe my six years there. I remember saying very quickly, "They were war years." I would quote the opening lines Charles Dickens wrote introducing *A Tale of Two Cities*: "It was the best of times; it was the worst of times." For me leaving the Holy Family assignment was difficult. I was happy there and enjoyed going home every Sunday even if it were to nap on the couch while my mom would prepare dinner. My friends were nearby for occasional lunches or movies. I was about to move away from an area of the diocese which was homebase to a place where I knew only one person and to an assignment that I was reticent to embrace. Initially it seemed like it was "the worst of times." I settled in at the rectory where I was to live for a year. I knew how parishes functioned so adapted quite easily to the few tasks asked of me for that part of my assignment. Most of my time in the first few weeks was spent on the campus of Ithaca College where I arranged my office, met the other chaplain who had just returned from Scotland where he had been studying philosophy, enjoyed the company of a secretary whom we would both share, and toured the campus so I would know my way around once classes started. I found out very quickly that there was one perk given to the college's staff and faculty: we got free coffee at the cafeteria located in the center of the campus. It was there, over the years, I could meet other staff members, enjoy the company of the faculty, and get to know the students between classes.

Just when I had settled in, I had a minor setback. I had returned home for a visit and invited a small group of high school seminarians studying for the Congregation of the Most Precious Blood to my parents' home. My parents just had a swimming pool installed, so this would be a chance for them to swim and enjoy a hot dog luncheon. I was getting the fire started for roasting the hot dogs using a small amount of kerosene to help the charcoal along. One of these young men told me I should put more kerosene on the lackadaisical fire. I told him "no" three times. I had no sooner said my last "no" when he poured some onto the fire which, in turn, blew up into my face and hands. Fortunately, I was wearing a swimming suit and sweatshirt, or my legs and torso would have caught fire and severely burned me. I was able to cover my eyes, nose, and mouth with my hands quick enough so only my hands and the top of my head were badly burned. My dad rushed me to the hospital blowing the car horn to make room though the traffic. The emergency room was empty, so I received immediate care. Then I was put into a room where I would spend the next few days healing. I remember the nurse pulling off some of the burned skin on my hands between bandage-changings. She admired the fact that I did not yell out in pain. I asked her, "Would it make a difference if I did yell?" "No," she said, "but it is nice to have a patient not screaming at me." Two memories pop into my head from the week in the hospital: my dad sitting outside of my room talking through the window because it was after visiting hours; the other was my classmate who loved to talk visiting me for more than an hour. I was in pain physically at the time. I just wanted him to leave so I could deal with my pain in silence. After leaving the hospital five days later, I returned to Ithaca with bandages on my hands and a few more on my head. It was a great way to begin my new assignment.

During my time at Ithaca College, I had a variety of experiences that could consume a good amount of ink. I lived in three different places: I spent one year living at the rectory and served part-time at the parish while spending most of my time on campus. I was made full time chaplain at the college the following year so I moved to the residence for the priests (staff and student-priests) at Cornell University both for companionship and to allow me to focus full-time on my work at Ithaca College. The following year the president at Ithaca College, Howard Dillingham, offered me room and board on the campus in one of the residence halls. This became a truly memorable experience. I was not only able to minister from my office, but now in one of the residence halls. What a wonderful and fulfilling experience that was!

Life at Cornell was enjoyable. I met a variety of people like Father Dan Berrigan of the famous Berrigan Brothers who lived with us in-between his protests and speeches against the war in Vietnam that took him across the country. Another priest, a Jesuit, was working on a doctoral degree in sociology but did not finish. What I remember most about him was his very large girth. His physical size was so enormous that he could not sit at a desk but needed a table to do his writing. When he ate, he used both hands to get food to his mouth. He later moved into administration at one of the

Jesuit colleges. Another priest, a Sulpician, was learning Old Icelandic to do research for his doctoral studies. He ended up leaving ministry with the woman who typed his dissertation. There were a few hockey players living on the top floor to earn their keep by doing some chores around the house. It was also a time for all sorts of experimental liturgies which challenged the liturgical practices of the day. On occasion, I did use a copy of the Eucharistic prayer written by Phil Berrigan who had previously taught college English courses. It was beautifully written, theologically correct, but not an approved prayer for public use. Two diocesan priests, representing two theological extremes, served as chaplains. One of the campus ministers died suddenly during that year. The other remained as the sole chaplain. One weekend when many of the alumni/ae returned to campus for a special event, he conducted Sunday Mass dressed in jeans and a torn t-shirt wearing a stole. His sermon discussed the possibility that Jesus was not divine but only human. When I asked him what books had he used as a source, he smiled with a smattering condescension in reply, "It is my opinion and what I believe." So much for intelligent discussion of a key church teaching and appropriate garb for any formal occasion. You can imagine the reaction of the visitors that weekend. A few years later he left the ministry to marry.

My year there was very special for many reasons, mostly from being exposed to a variety of current opinions that floated around about the "possibilities" of what the Church might look like in the years ahead. There were points of view to define the role of the priest when dealing with the problems like war, poverty, racism. There were mixed ideas about celibacy, a married clergy, the possibility of women priests, and the suggestion that maybe the Church should ordain priests to serve a limited number of years before choosing to move onto another vocation. In France, for example, there was the priest-worker movement: priests would work in factories or some other blue-collar job during the day (maybe discussing religious issues over lunch or a beer in the local tavern) and "minister as priests" on weekends celebrating Mass, hearing confessions, or preaching the Gospel in a more formal setting. Some questions were about what constitutes a valid marriage, artificial birth control, and even the remote idea (at the time) of same sex relationships and civil unions were discussed. The list could go on, but there was always some topic to discuss over dinner or a late-night snack. The mixed bag of residents and visitors from other parts of the world and the United States fueled some heated discussions. It seemed that everyone was infallible except for the Pope.

But I am getting ahead of my story. My first drive to Ithaca was a difficult one. Five years of great memories of some fantastic people and special times kept me entertained for the eighty-mile journey. I had driven to the rectory earlier because I was assigned as resident part-time assistant priest along with my assignment to Ithaca College. The pastor had been quite welcoming. He noticed the number of books I was bringing so he had a large bookshelf made for my small office connected to my smaller bedroom. Two other assistant priests also lived there: one older than I, the other younger. The companionship between the four of us was delightful. The three assistants divided up the Mass schedule each night before we went to bed, usually when we were having a nightcap of milk and cookies. One of us would celebrate Mass at the convent each day at 6:30 for the ten Sisters who taught in the parish grade school; the other two would celebrate Mass at the other scheduled times. The pastor almost always offered Mass at 8:00. I did not help at the parish on weekends because of my scheduled Mass at the College and later as the chaplain at Camp McCormick, a prison camp for about one hundred teenage boys aged from 14-18. During my time at Ithaca College, I continued with working at the camp, mostly confessions and Mass each Sunday. Occasionally a staff member would ask me to speak with one of the young men about his behavior or some special need. About half of the prisoners were from New York City; the other half was from Upstate. The official thought that the Upstate prisoners would have a calming effect on the "City" prisoners. ("City" meant something different from my experience. It referred to New York City.) Another interesting fact I discovered in my six years at the Camp was rather startling: the average IQ was well over one hundred, but the reading level was at a third-grade level. Occasionally, around Christmas, some well-behaved boys would be furloughed for a week. I remember one of them telling me that he was looking forward to returning to the "City." I asked him what he was planning to do while home. With a smile on his face (which I will never forget), the young man said that the judge sent him to prison camp for stealing cars. "Over sixteen years I stole 198 cars. I plan to steal two more to make it an even two hundred."

In one of my conversations with a staff member I asked if there was a follow-up once the boys were released. The Upstate boys would go home to their parents having learned a lesson the hard way and would fit in with their peers. Many of the City boys would be released but to a single parent, a grandparents' home, or to a dysfunctional family. They would have to fend for themselves. After I had been there a few years, I had earned the trust of the staff and the prisoners. I proposed letting some of them come to Ithaca for a party on a Sunday evening for two hours. With the pastor's permission we could use the school hall.

To make this happen I asked some of the College's fraternities and sororities to help me with expenses: food, music, decorations, and entertainment. What an overwhelming response! A small band of artistic college students did a marvelous job with the decorations. A women's group from the parish prepared a spaghetti dinner with all the trimmings. We had the guys and gals interspersed with the boys for some casual conversation. Our disc jockey for the music was a music major who had a sense of the kind of music the boys would enjoy. I think my most memorable memory scene that night was watching the sorority members dancing with the young prisoners. One of the young women came to the dance wearing her usual fur coat. From a wealthy family, she enjoyed displaying her sophisticated background. I watched her as she engaged her dance partner with some conversation encouraging him about the proper dance steps, leaving him smiling as he left the dance floor. She would choose another partner and "danced all night." As we were leaving that night, I heard her say to her friends, "This was the best dance party I ever attended. I had such fun. We should do this more often."

As I was driving some of the youngsters back to camp that night, they were regaling each other with stories (some embellished) about conversations and dance moves that made the night so special. One sat next to me and in a quiet voice he teared up as he reflected on what he had done and where he was in life. His bottom line was, "I think that will be my whole life. I am afraid I will be back in prison again." I wanted to cry as I assured him that would be his choice, but I know he will make good if he puts his mind to it. Then I wondered to myself, "Who will be there to encourage him to make better choices?"

A few years later I once again called on the fraternities and sororities to assist with another project. In the countryside around Ithaca there were a few camps for migrant workers. I was concerned for the youngsters the parents had brought with them. To expose them to possible educational opportunities for their future, I arranged for a few busloads to visit the campus. Some went to the various athletic fields to watch different sporting events (lacrosse, soccer, and baseball); others went to the music building to watch some of the students practice their various instruments. They had an opportunity to watch and listen to one of the group rehearsals. We had a special luncheon with a variety of conversations mostly in English, but some in Spanish with a few of our language majors. After that day a few more of our students volunteered to go to the camps to tutor the youngsters in their studies. There are many ways to serve one another if we use the natural gifts we have. The youngsters learned a great deal, but so did the college students.

Let me switch gears for a few pages. Another reason I often refer to my Ithaca College years as the "war years" are the reactions to the conflict in Vietnam and racial inequality that easily led to academic and political divisions. One of the student-led groups that surfaced as a "problem" was the national SDS (Students for a Democratic Society). Founded in 1960 with roots in Ann Arbor, Michigan, its members challenged the rhetoric of the status quo and sought solutions to the war and social injustice. For any organization to function on most college campuses, then and now, there is the requirement for a faculty/staff moderator. No one of the Ithacan faculty/staff wanted to attempt to moderate such a radically leftist group (viewed as anti-American and possible Communists). This young and idealistic priest thought such a group should at least be allowed to meet and discuss issues like the conflict (the word "war" came later) in Vietnam or evident racial injustices. So, I became their moderator for about a year. My naive idea of resolving social justice issues was in the spirit of Gandhi and Martin Luther King Jr, through study, prayerful reflection, and peaceful action. I admired the core group's ideals and dreams, but it was impatient with my suggestion, "Let's study the pressing issue." Rather quickly the SDS members on the Ithaca College campus found reasons for not being able to attend our "study group." They organized, along with other like-minded students from Cornell University, to protest by marches, attempted classroom takeovers, sit-ins, and the occasional reckless damage to property. If nothing else, the discussions opened my mind to differing pressing views to the war, racism, and other social justice issues that our educational system (at that time) seemed to ignore.

I joined in some of the anti-war marches and so was accused of being a radical leftist. I did not participate in the more radical actions such as sit-ins with one exception that had nothing to do with war or social injustice. I assisted the local parish with evening religious education classes. The classes met the same night as the Knights of Columbus Bingo games in an adjacent hall. The sound system for Bingo would often break into the sound system for the classrooms where we conducted classes. This went on for a few weeks with promises that the problem would be resolved. I nicely tried to work with the Knights. Finally, one Monday night I warned them I would take more drastic action if the calling of numbers continued to interfere with classes. Sure enough, the next week the Bingo sound system kept breaking into the sound system in the school. I asked the students to join me as we marched into the Bingo Hall, sat down in the middle of the floor where I continued teaching my class. When the class time was up, I walked out as the faithful Bingo players continued with their games but between numbers found time to call me a "communist troublemaker." My one sit-in was against the Knights of Columbus Bingo. I laughed then and even now.

A few years later I was sitting in the college cafeteria (the managers still offered free coffee to faculty and staff) sipping my coffee while talking with two or three faculty members when two campus security guards came to our table and asked that I follow them immediately. As they led me out, I asked what was wrong. They told me that the president of the college was locked in his office; some leaders of the students had ransacked adjacent offices demanding that he make an appearance before a huge crowd of students gathered outside the Administration Building. He was to respond to their demands. The president said he would do so if I were to accompany him. I met the president at his office and walked with him to the gathering space. At his request I was to stand next to him during his talk. He stood remarkably close to me and when I edged over to give him more room, he moved with me, leaving very little space between us. At the conclusion of the president's remarks, the security guards quickly whisked him away to his car. I turned to the vice president and asked why the president stood so close to me. He told me that there was evidence that someone was going to shoot the president while he was speaking. The president thought that if I were present next to him no one would shoot out of fear that I might be hit. Now I know what it was like to be a member of the Secret Service who protects the American President.

Reflecting then and even now concerning the idealism of the students, I hoped that they would continue to be committed to a non-violent approach to address various social justice issues. I know some went into public service after graduation. It also helped me realize that there are issues that I can protest, but it is even more important that I be part of the solution. Maturity comes with study and reflection.

A Dream Come True (1966-1971)

EVEN WHEN I WAS in grade school, I dreamed of teaching someday. To be a college teacher was a consistent hope for many years. I finally had an opportunity at Ithaca College. I taught courses both at the graduate and undergraduate level. At the undergraduate level I taught the basic 101-102 American History courses. I was the instructor for two sections each semester. At Ithaca College students were most often assigned courses according to their major. I taught American History to Physical Education majors MWF at 8:00 in the morning; to Music majors TR 10:10. Talk about two different audiences. I adapted different strategies for each section. When I was teaching the music majors, I tried to make a connection between the times of historical events with music that might be composed and played at those years. With an 8:00 class of Physical Education majors I brought extra enthusiasm and stories much like an early morning TV program, *Howdy Doody*. One fall semester I noted that every Monday morning the sky was dark, snow, rain, or mist. You can imagine a class of thirty-five plus student athletes' enthusiasm for learning history on those Monday mornings after a weekend of games and parties. Yet, I enjoyed every moment of it except for grading tests and other written assignments. One of the students, forty-five years later, reminded me of the tests and my crazy questions: e.g., What woman used paper to set oil on fire? In case you have forgotten, it was Ida Tarbell, an investigative newspaper reporter (a muckraker), who exposed some of the unfair practices of Standard Oil Company.

    On a more serious side these were the "war years." I tried to make connections with our country's history with other wars to demonstrate the causes and consequences of any war. I spent a whole section of the course on the history of slavery and the consequent racism that was being played out during the civil rights protests of the Sixties. During subsequent years as a teacher, I remember those formative early classroom experiences. I think back to the classroom sit-ins and take-overs. There was the spring semester (1970) when the National Guard killed four students at Kent State that forced the early closing of many colleges across the country. I think back to the day when the national news reported that our Armed Forces had dropped some bombs on Cambodian territory. I was teaching American History that day. A group of students invaded my classroom and demanded that I stop teaching so they could take over the class. I asked them, "Do you know where Cambodia is?" Their answer was an indifferent, "No." I then told them that I did. I was talking about the issue during my class before I was so rudely interrupted. They muttered, "Okay then" and walked out with their tails between their legs.

My dreams of teaching were taking on flesh. I was having lunch with a few professors in the faculty dining room when the dean of the graduate school asked to join us. The discussion eventually turned to teaching sexuality and marriage in the classrooms. At the time New York State was considering mandating such courses, along with material about "recreational drugs," in elementary and high schools. I offered my opinion, but the dean countered that it did not count because I was a priest and so hardly knew anything about the topics because I was committed to celibacy. The conversation continued with a variety of arguments by the whole table of my dining mates. The next day he called me and asked if I might be interested in teaching a graduate course for future teachers about marriage and sexuality. I quickly responded in the affirmative and offered the course for the next two years before I left the college for another assignment in the diocese. What changed his mind? He told me that my openness, willingness to listen, ability to formulate a positive argument and my passion all impressed him.

As an aside, because the State was requiring some kind of sex education, teachers in the elementary schools needed some "how to…" education. I gave a series of talks in parts of the geographical area to teachers who were uncomfortable approaching the subject. I remember one teacher objecting because she would be embarrassed to use the word 'penis" in a classroom. I asked her, "Then what word are you going to use?" I suggested a few words but she would have been even more embarrassed to use them.

One summer Nazareth College in Rochester invited me to teach a two-week course to some of the nuns who would be teaching sex education in the Catholic schools. At the time, the Sisters were still wearing their religious garb including the veil and a rosary hanging from their belt. I really found them much more open to the material than most of the other students I had been working with through those years. During one of the classes, I mentioned as an aside that many of the boys were learning about sex from a magazine called *Playboy*. Two of the Sisters thought it would be a good idea to stop by one of the magazine stores to pick up a copy. You can only imagine what the cashier was thinking. When they reported their purchase at the next class (and that they had put it under the mattress in their bed lest anyone saw it), there was much laughter. However, I did not suggest any outside reading for the rest of the course.

A year later the same dean became the president of a new two-year college, Tompkins-Cortland Community College (affectionately referred to as TC3). One morning, I received a call from Bishop Fulton Sheen, our bishop of the Diocese of Rochester at that time. He told me that he had received a call from the president of the new community college asking him if it would be okay if I were to join the founding faculty of the college. Bishop Sheen called me to see if I would be interested. A dream had come true: to be a full-time faculty member at a college. I replied, "I would really enjoy the opportunity, but who would replace me at Ithaca College?" His response, at which I still chuckle at when I remember it, was, "Ah, but Father, all of us great men are called to do two jobs at the same time." I replied, "Well then, Bishop, how about if I work at the new college part-time and remain here full-time?" He agreed and then continued talking about an unrelated topic for about fifteen minutes. I joined the faculty at TC3 and taught two different courses each semester for two years despite the idea that I was not "a great man doing two jobs at the same time."

One of the courses I taught at TC3 was Introduction to Personal Development. It was to be a required course for all incoming first-year students to acclimatize them to college life and give them an opportunity to explore their own journey past, present, and future. During one of the fall semesters I decided my class would spend Friday night and all-day Saturday camping out in a nearby park. This would give the students the opportunity to get to know each other in a less formal way than the decorum of a classroom, work together getting meals ready, and to spend some time alone exploring nature for a few hours. I asked the students to go into the woods by themselves to use their five senses to explore the environment: e.g., listen to the sounds, but also listen/attend to the silence. At the end of the exploration period and before we left, we sat in a circle when I encouraged each one to share what they learned from the experience-especially the "alone time" walking through the woods. Becoming aware of all their senses was a new experience for them. For the remainder of the semester the students behaved differently toward one another, especially during small group discussions: a mutual respect and an awareness of differences that allowed for a unity of purpose and care for one another. In the succeeding fifty years of teaching (graduate and undergraduate) I have used similar techniques in all my courses to bring a sense of student-bonding for mutual support and success.

Drugs and Alcohol

Over the years I have often used music as a way of teaching. In my American History courses, I played music that the people might be listening to as they went about their daily chores. An anthem of the Sixties, for example, praised drugs as one way of finding a happy life. I vividly remember Dr. Timothy Leary addressing our students at Ithaca College with "evidence" of how important the use of LSD could be to self-discovery as well as a possible tool to explore scientific problems that might elude professional scientists. He admitted that anyone who chose to use the drug should have someone to guide them through the experience. What I remember was the misuse of the drug or its faulty chemical ingredients that might indeed cause harm. One of the students I knew was found digging into a grave at a nearby cemetery with his bare hands. The purpose? He was hoping to find some peace for himself. Another student who lived with his parents in town had taken some "bad" LSD. A graduate student in another city was making his own recipe in one of the chemical labs at his college. One of my most poignant memories of LSD still haunts me fifty-five years later. I had a lively conversation with the student who lived in town with his parents. We debated about LSD's possible dangers and how it might affect him and possibly his family. His response was, "It's *my* life." A hysterical mother called me on a Sunday night to come to the house; their son was acting very strangely. He was in his upstairs bedroom when I arrived. Indeed, the poor guy was acting and talking in a bizarre way. I immediately recognized the issue. I sat with him and talked him down from the "LSD high." The scared college freshman started to cry and ask himself and me, "What have I done?" We talked a bit and once I knew that he was okay, I walked down the stairs into the gaze of a very worried mom and dad. I did not know for sure what to say except that he would be okay, not to worry, and call me anytime. As I got into my car, I muttered derisively, "Like hell. It's *my* life." To this day I reflect on how "*my* life" does affect the lives of those around me.

In a very few years the misuse of drugs was affecting college students across the United States. With the necessary permissions the school psychologist, Dr. Martin Rand, took a survey of the kinds of drugs students were using and why they chose to use the illegal ones. The entire medical staff agreed that it would be better to work with the students caught using drugs rather than to dismiss them from the college. The doctor in charge of the medical facility at the college, Dr. David Hammond, together with the school psychologist asked me to work with about a dozen students in a small group setting who had been caught using drugs illegally. The purpose was to explore why they were using them and how they might choose an alternate way of meeting their needs. The mix of the group was quite telling, male and female, families of wealth and power as well as students who came from less privileged backgrounds, different religious or no religious backgrounds, and different majors and levels of their studies. The weekly meetings were well attended along with some deep sharing. At one point the group became aware that we did not have enough time for the meetings. With their permission (and excitement), I made the necessary arrangements to spend a night and full day at a nearby monastery.

The Prior of the monastery was more than welcoming but asked if the novices could join in so they would be exposed to the drug issues they might encounter in their future ministries. The students agreed and so we left campus on Friday afternoon, enjoyed a meal with the monks, and then began our discussions that evening and continued all day Saturday. Towards the end of the day one of our group asked the novices, "What about you? What are your stories?" The students listened intently as each of the novices spoke about their journey with its "ups and downs." Saturday evening, we met for our last meeting for an evaluation, the discovery of new insights, and possible plans for further action(s). The conversation was really inspiring. At one point one of the students turned to the novices and said, "What I am looking for using drugs, you have found with your way of life." Then other students spoke up in agreement. I can't remember all that was said, but I do recall words like "acceptance, peace of mind, unity of purpose." The novices expressed their gratitude for being allowed to be part of a group who was so "open and honest" and assured them of their prayers in their journeys. As I drove home, I kept thinking how we are seeking similar goals, but our choices for attaining them, indeed, are different. Are sex, drugs, and rock and roll all we really need?

Because I was teaching some classes, attending the concerts and athletic events, visiting the infirmary every day, hanging out in the cafeteria with the free coffee, celebrating the various Masses and other religious events, and was a resident in one of the residence halls, I was seen as a safe person to talk with no matter what one's religious background (or none). One night a student knocked at my door with a large grocery bag in his hands. He needed some help. Earlier that day he had flown to NYC to pick up $10,000 worth of marijuana which he had intended to sell to make a profit. Now he was having second thoughts and wondered if he could leave the marijuana with me for safe keeping. Next day he would return the marijuana to his seller. I agreed with his plan along with some fatherly advice. His return flight brought the issue to a happy conclusion: one less drug-pusher!

One year rumor had it that security officers were going to search the residences for drugs and drug paraphernalia over Christmas vacation. Some of the frightened students asked me to store their drugs until they returned. I was a bit nervous about their request but put the cache into a cigar box. I took it home with me when I spent the holidays with my family. My mother asked me what was in the box. She berated me for my foolishness. My retort was, "But Mom you have been on my back to join the family on one of their trips. Here is our chance! We can take a trip now." She did not laugh.

In 1968 I hit a low point in my life (it was not the last). The changes in the Church, the turmoil in our country, the war in Vietnam, the changing culture, protests that divided family and friends, and the many new challenges of ministry on a college campus all came down heavy on me. "What should I do?" I kept asking myself. "Where do I go to find some peace and direction for my future?" "Confusion" was the word. At the time I was reading the many books written by a Greek author, Nikos Kazantzakis. *Report to Greco* was one of my favorites. The book is an autobiographical novel of a man (the author) who is searching for direction in his life. One of the places he visits is the land "where Jesus walked." I said to myself, "Hey, there is an idea!" It took me a few days to arrange for the flights to Israel/Palestine with return flights to Istanbul and Athens. Lodging was available at the Franciscan Hospice in Jerusalem. Off I went in early June with no definite plans except for the places. I wandered around Jerusalem for a few days with some side trips to Nazareth, Jericho, and the Dead Sea, always asking the same questions: "What do I do to find some direction in my life? What should I do?" One day when I was walking outside Jerusalem's city gates, I came into the Garden of Gethsemane where there is a church dedicated to the night where Jesus gathered with some of his disciples. He prayed that the cup of suffering that would be his should be taken away. He quickly added, "Not my will, but yours be done." When he found some of his best friends asleep, Jesus told them to "Pray, lest they enter into temptation." I entered the church. I found it very dark having come from a very bright sunshine. I sat down on an uncomfortable chair muttering what had become a mantra-like question: "What should I do?" I sat there for about an hour. As I stood up to leave, I asked my same question: "What should I do?" As I did, I looked up at the cupola and written in Latin I read "Pray, lest you enter temptation." The answer to my prayerful question. I enjoyed the rest of the trip, especially the ice cream in Athens and the pickled sheep-brains in Istanbul.

Because I decided to make the trip to the Holy Land so quickly, I did not make any reservations for lodgings except for Jerusalem. That allowed me freedom to explore new places and meet new people without specific plans except for the plane reservations. While in the city of Jerusalem I met a seminarian from the "little town of Bethlehem" who invited me to his parents' home for dinner. The table was set for three. I was wondering why only three before I noticed that there were four women in the kitchen. The women, as custom would have it, prepared the meal, and waited on table. The men sat by themselves. For dessert we walked into the garden and picked fresh fruit from the trees. A real experience of a way of life that I had only read about.

I took the bus to Nazareth the next day preparing to stay the night after a day of visiting the holy sites. A busload of tourists was returning to Jerusalem. The Jewish woman guide invited me to join them. No problem! She mentioned that the group was to have lunch in Jericho. While we were having lunch, I asked her if there would ever be peace in the Holy Land? She slammed the table so hard that my beer bottle flew up into the air (I caught it mid-air) loudly proclaiming, "No! We will continue to fight until all this land is ours. There is no room for any dirty aliens to live here." I quietly asked her about the Old Testament telling its readers to welcome the foreigners and to love our neighbor.

The next day, safely back in Jerusalem, a Muslim guide took me to the Dead Sea. I asked him the same question, "Will there be peace in this Land?" With a deep sigh he expressed similar doubts because of the recent violence (the Six-Day War in 1967) and its consequences because of the Israeli victory. For the most part the Palestinian territories came under Israeli control especially the entire city of Jerusalem. "We will not have peace until our land is returned to us," he muttered. Then I asked him about the Quran's suggestion for peace and mercy. The following day I had a Christian guide take me to a few places on the outskirts of Jerusalem. When I asked him the same question about peace in the Holy Land, his response was simply, "We can only pray for it." I quoted the New Testament about love of neighbor. The same question asked to the three: Jew, Muslim, and Christian. The same retort to my quoting the various scriptures was a quick "but it is not practical." Over the years I have gone back to those encounters with the response that love, the basis for peace, "is not practical." Narcissism, power, and violence seemingly would trump peace, compassion, mercy, and love. In hope I pray for peace.

My Last Year at Ithaca

I SPENT THE SUMMER OF 1970 in Rochester at the University of Rochester working on a degree in counseling and education. When I came home from class one day, I found a message. A vice president from Ithaca College called me to set up a time when he could come to Rochester for a conversation. He arrived a day later to ask me to take on a new role at the college. Would I consider working with the Dean of Students Office and Career Planning as an ombudsman? I would have to surrender my position as the Catholic chaplain but continue doing what he judged to be the reason for asking me to assume this new position: I knew faculty, staff, students, and could easily make some connection with them all. I was trusted. After some thought and with permission of the bishop, I accepted the position along with a new and bigger office with a great view of the campus. Another priest took on the role of campus Catholic chaplain. It was one of the more challenging years of my life up to that time. When I submitted my resignation at the end of the year, the vice president scolded me, "You always remained a pastor and never became an administrator."

The year was filled with meetings, student protests, and trying to keep everyone happy. I was not able to celebrate Sunday Mass (this was before concelebration was popular) with the college community or be involved with campus ministry. I did, however, form smaller communities with the students in my residence hall and a few of the fraternities for Mass. One of the fraternities, Delta Kappa, still invites me to their annual gathering. It has been fascinating to watch how many of them have become successful lawyers, judges, accountants, businessmen, entrepreneurs, and great family men. A few have remained very close friends for over fifty years as I witnessed their weddings and their children's weddings, phone calls, and now text- messaging on a regular basis.

I remember vividly receiving a two-page letter from one of the academic chairmen (not one of my favorite people) who outlined all the mistakes I was making, accusations about my deportment, and a general distaste for the work I was doing. In his last paragraph he wrote, "If I am mistaken about all of these, please forgive me." I read the letter, seethed for a few hours, took the letter, wrote at the bottom "You are forgiven" and sent it back through the campus mail. It was then that I thought I should move on. I called the bishop who was the personnel director at the time asking for another assignment; hopefully, one in which I could continue teaching. A month later I listened to my phone's voice messages to hear that I was assigned to Saint Thomas More parish in Rochester as an assistant pastor. I remember crying in sadness as I drove away from Ithaca College to my new assignment.

Reflecting on the past sixty plus years as a priest, I enthusiastically admit my years at Ithaca College were "the best of times; the worst of times." The challenges and the friendships I formed during those six years have sustained me. There is one that stands out: Dr. Marty Rand, an agnostic, and I became the best of friends. Faculty and staff commented often about our friendship: two entirely different characters and belief systems. How could it be? It was simple: we both cared about our family, friends, students, and the work that demanded continued growth. I list him very high on my list of most treasured friends who helped me seek answers to a recurring question: "What should I do?

A Different Kind of Life (1971-1972)

MOVING INTO A NEW assignment can be a challenge. I was bringing five years as an associate pastor (a title meant as a sign of some kind of equality) where the people were mostly blue-collar middle income to a parish where a few people were from middle income and a larger number of wealthier professional people. I had lived my life at Ithaca College as a leader and "Lone Ranger" when making decisions. The year I spent at St. Thomas More parish required a major challenge in adjustment. I lived in a beautiful rectory with other priests, celebrated liturgical events under the watchful eye of the founding pastor of the parish, and tried to fit in with a welcoming community of differing economic backgrounds. I remember taking Holy Communion to people living in trailers on the same day I did the same for those living in expensive houses. I adapted but felt out of place.

I yearned for the classroom and coffee with faculty members trying to make sense out of political and scientific disciplines. The resolution to the intellectual urgings was soon eased. St. Bernard's Seminary, my alma mater, was offering a master's degree in theology (MTh). I worked out an independent study course in the Old Testament with one of my former professors, Fr. Joe Brennan, to keep me busy that summer. The pastor, Fr. Frank Pegnam, was willing to pay for golf lessons for me and sponsor a membership in a nearby country club. I chose the library over the country club and the book over the nine-iron. That led to some rather interesting dinner conversations. The pastor was an avid golfer; I was an equally avid reader. I learned a golfer's language of "mulligans," "birdies," and "putters." He was not interested in the "big books" I was reading, but I was learning about golf and the pastoral problems that his "foursome" encountered on all eighteen holes as they tried to adjust to a changing church.

A Different Kind of Life (1971-1972)

Later in the summer I scheduled an oral examination with my mentor to test my understanding and appreciation of the Old Testament. I had done all the assigned reading along with some supplemental articles and reread a significant part of the Hebrew Scriptures. It was a beautiful warm day, so he suggested that we take a walk as he examined me. His first question was a simple, "Now that you have done all the reading this summer, what is the one thing that sticks out in your mind?" "All that reading, and I am supposed to pick out 'one' thing. Wow, now that is a challenge!" However, my immediate response flowed from my own frequent reflection all during the summer months. "The Israelites were a people of hope." It struck me that given the extended written history of travels and travail, wars and exiles, good and bad leadership, successes and failures, the people lived in hope that someday things would work out. These Chosen People would witness a Messiah who would bring them the kind of peace that satisfied humans' basic hunger to be loved and accepted. I have forgotten the other questions and answers, but my answer to that first question has haunted me and guided me since. Hope is a belief in the future. However, the future does not necessarily mean "in *my* lifetime." I only co-create a fulfillment of the future. Abraham, a model of faith, could only hope that his children would evolve into a community of faith. From among those descendants, their hopes and dreams would take on flesh and dwell among them as the "Anointed One, the Messiah, the Christ." Even now I think of hope as a powerful quality that keeps me moving ahead.

One mutual topic the pastor and I did discuss was the life and behavior of Schultzie, the pastor's dog. The day I moved into the rectory, I was busy unpacking when I heard the pastor and the other priest in residence walking upstairs. The pastor was telling him, "I hope that Schultzie likes Bill, otherwise Bill will have to go." At least I knew where I stood in the rectory's pecking order, so I decided to make friends with the dog to survive. Growing up our family always lived with a dog and at least one cat who became notable members of our home, so I was very aware of Schultzie's needs and demands. We got along famously so the pastor allowed me to stay. In late winter, however, tragedy struck. As she was driving out of the parking lot after the 5:00 Mass, one of our parishioners accidently struck and killed Schultzie. The grieving woman came to the door to tell the pastor of the accident. He assured her, "Nothing to worry about; it was just a dog." During dinner I watched him glance over to Schultzie's empty food bowl. He excused himself from the table saying he "was not hungry." I heard him go to his room and shut the door. I volunteered to make the funeral arrangements: picking up the dead body, wrapping it in a blanket, and then burying Schultzie near a tree outside the church the next day. Quiet reigned over the rectory the next two days. Meanwhile, unbeknownst to the pastor, the parish maintenance man started a collection from a few parishioners to replace Schultzie with a similar breed of dog. He presented "Schultzie Junior" to the grieving pastor three days before he and three of his golf friends headed out for a two-week golfing jaunt in Puerto Rico. I became the surrogate "father" until he returned. As if that were not enough, the housekeeper/cook suffered a heart attack and ended up in the hospital. The bishop suddenly assigned Fr. Bill Charbonneau, the other priest in the house, to another parish as its pastor. I remained alone to babysit my recent charge. I had a glimpse of a young parent's life when the first baby arrived into their home: loss of sleep, toilet training, and the need to be attentive.

Life in the parish was a homecoming for me. There were the usual expectations of daily Mass, weekly confessions, and preaching every other Sunday. One of the big differences was that, unlike my stay at Ithaca College, I did not have to set up and take down the altar every time and place I celebrated Mass. It was a little thing, but having a fixed altar properly decorated made things much easier. I visited the hospitals, but given the size and demographics of the parish, there were fewer patients in the hospital to visit. I pulled together some of the youth to form soccer and basketball teams. The parish gym was state of the art but seldom used for sports. The pastor was not all that excited about the basketball team and the possible cost of uniforms. I gathered a group of fathers together one night while the pastor was out to figure out ways to fund the team. The group was excited about the possibility of a parish team and quickly suggested that they would fund it themselves. It was an easy decision. Then, they thought, getting together to talk about other ideas for parish life would be exciting. At the time parish councils with their various committees were still rather new. The enthusiasm in the gathering sparked all sorts of ideas. As we were ending our meeting, the pastor unexpectedly walked in and greeted the group. He was quickly inundated with ideas they had, especially about raising money for the basketball team. He told them that they were too busy to have meetings and had enough bills of their own to fund a team. The parish would gladly take care of any of their concerns. It was like a bucket of cold water poured over the group's spark of excitement. They left. He turned on the television set. I went to my room muttering some unkind words.

The new assignment to parish life challenged me to accept where I was making lemonade out of lemons. I found three college students who enjoyed racquet ball, so we were able to schedule some regular court time. The humor, banter, and exercise were great ways to relax and put life into perspective. Over the years I met all three in different venues: one at a parish where I was occasionally assisting; another in a restaurant I frequented; the third at a college baseball game where we were both supporting the same team. We rehashed the racquet ball games and the usual visit to Friendly's to celebrate our wins/losses. I have found that playing a sport like tennis or racquet ball or viewing an occasional movie, followed by a hot fudge sundae with pistachio ice cream, is an easy way to form a bond of trust.

I have already mentioned Pete Deckman (the friend who twice forgot his wallet). He and I would often play racquet ball years later when we were in different assignments. After the games we would usually talk about what was going on in our lives ("the good, the bad, the ugly"). One Friday afternoon, after our game, he looked at me in bewilderment. "Why do you have to take the game so seriously? You really hit the ball with a vengeance." It did not take me long to admit, "I do play with vengeance. I do take the game seriously. It is my safe way to take out my frustrations. I thought it was better to hit the ball as hard as I could rather than hit any person who was frustrating me."

I did not, however, spend all my time on the racquetball court, or going to the movies, or reading books of theology and Scripture. During my year at the parish the hospital calls and home visits with parishioners opened my eyes to a different awareness of issues within family life and the workplace. Running big companies and the pressure of being an entrepreneur in a very competitive work environment was a daily challenge for so many of the parishioners. The issues were similar but the ways each dealt with them varied. Positive or negative, the ways did affect family life, especially the children. Sometimes parents are physically absent; sometimes they are emotionally absent. I admire the family that can balance both along with a dash of laughter.

All in all, it became a year of learning to be patient, listen more, and gently offering ideas. Spending time in the up-to-date school's classrooms to work with the committed Sisters who lived in the nearby convent (an old, converted mansion) opened me to many ideas for teaching and responding to the unspoken needs of the students much like the school children from my first parish assignment and later at Ithaca College: a need to be patiently accepted as they were and with compassionate love. I might add very quickly: that young people should do the same with their parents and each other.

Working on my master's degree at Saint Bernard's kept me connected with my fellow graduate students, all of whom were still in the seminary preparing for ordination. One of our projects was outlining and preparing a presentation of material that we would use for our master's thesis. I chose to deal with the sacrament of penance. It allowed me the opportunity to study its history and the different ways it was celebrated over the centuries. The presentation went well but I also realized that the seminary was preparing some very gifted men for service of the diocese. In different ways many of that core group, my classmates, did make a difference in subsequent years. I will write more about my own presentation later because the development of the thesis changed in subsequent years.

During the first semester of graduate work, the rector of the seminary approached me to ask if I would be open to teach Homiletics during the second semester. I jumped at the opportunity with the hope that it might eventually allow for a future full-time position on the faculty. I found the experience of teaching in the seminary exhilarating, especially the excitement of helping students develop the skills of bringing life to the Scriptures and the liturgy of the Mass. I often reminded the students that as preachers with eight to ten minutes for a homily, we had the challenge of inspiring many people, tired from a week filled with joys and challenges. to find hope and a sense of being loved by a caring God. Every Sunday we gave a living voice to writings thousands of years old. As preachers our task was to encourage people by letting them experience a sense of peace and hope, not further condemnation and judgment. Unfortunately, they too often experienced the latter all week in their workplace.

At the end of the second semester the rector approached the personnel director for priests to request that I be on the faculty full time to teach not only Homiletics but also Pastoral Theology (how to administer various tasks required of a priest: celebrating the sacraments, preparing couples for marriage, visit the sick, lead meetings, and live daily what we preached on Sunday).

Looking back over the one year at Saint Thomas More parish I believe that it helped round out my experiences of ministry, challenging me to meet new people in a positive way. My five years at Holy Family parish, one year part-time at Immaculate Conception parish, then Ithaca College for five years as Campus Minister, and lastly a year as Coordinator of Student Services became valuable textbooks for my classes at Saint Bernard's and later various teaching assignments. As I reflect on those eleven years, I became more convinced than ever: all people have the same needs: to be heard and to be loved as they are. Somewhere along the line I also became convinced that "saints are sinners who keep on trying."

Student to Professor (1972-1978)

I HAD SPENT SIX YEARS at Saint Bernard's as a student: two years studying philosophy and four years learning theology so I would be prepared to be ordained a priest. I joked about my new assignment as "a kind of divine retribution." One morning towards the end of my first year on the faculty I was having breakfast with one of the retired profs who still lived in the same room he occupied for about fifty years. Fr. "Frankie" Burns taught me and generations of priests. One of his most quoted statements after a test had been, "Sorry, Sir, you got a 64!" We became great friends once I was on the faculty, but we were not friends during my student days. In any case, at breakfast one morning I told him of one of my "insightful" comments I had made as a student: "The State is saving millions of dollars keeping the faculty here rather than in a mental institution." He laughed, looked at me, and said, "What do you think NOW that you are on the faculty?" It explained God's retribution in spades.

In late June I moved my books and belongings to the seminary. I write "moved" because my new quarters were being painted and so they were piled up in the hallway near my rooms…they were in the same spot three weeks later. In the meantime, the rector, Joe Brennan, a mutual friend, Dan Brent, and I headed to the Soviet Union on a "Peace Trip." The organizer was a former YMCA leader who had been in Russia at the time of the Revolution in 1917. His considered thesis was "If we can get to talk and know each other, we will have a path to peace between our two countries." The Cold War was still very cold. We were to visit East Berlin, Russia, Hungary, Czechoslovakia, and Yugoslavia to speak with various representatives from church and state about life under Communist leadership. It was a very exhausting experience filled with formal and informal talks, tours of historical sites, and great food and drink. The busy schedule is why the last part of the journey was spent on a small, quaint island off the coast near Dubrovnik for a relaxing and much deserved week.

The group included a wide variety of people: academics, tourists, religious folk, and a few very anti-Communist idealogues. We saw the tourist sites in the different cities we visited, but the conversations with their representatives were more telling. Each came prepared to defend their way of life and governing. At the end of each meeting, one of the more outspoken members of our group usually proposed the same question: "Will Communist rule survive?" The response was firm, quick, and loud: "YES! The people are happy with the way things are!" Time has answered that question differently.

A few things I remember about the time in Russia still linger with me. The streets and parks were immaculately clean. I saw a person drop some paper on the sidewalk only to be accosted by a few people yelling at him. The guide told us that the park belonged to everyone so the dropping of even a piece of paper was cluttering "our" park. This thoughtless act was an affront to the community.

One night we attended a circus. Two memories stick with me. In front of me was a mother with four small children trying to seat each of them in a way so they could see the various acts. She was having trouble with the smallest, so I offered to let him sit on my lap for the performance. You could see in her eyes a sense of relief. The little boy laughed and gasped at different times. At the conclusion of the show the mother smiled at me and said in Russian "Thank you!" My thought was maybe many years from that night the little boy would remember how an American held him on his lap for two hours so he could see the circus; I would often think about him and his story. He would be in his late sixties now and a witness to the changes in Russian life during those years. I wonder if he still goes to a circus and what might he remember. The other memory of that night was walking out of the venue, which must have held a few thousand people, noting how clean the floor was around the seats. The only paper I saw was a newspaper neatly folded and left on a chair near the entrance. No clutter! Since that night I am more attuned to the clutter after some of our public events and along some of our streets and roads.

One hot day we stood in line for two hours to visit Lenin's tomb. The guards with their rifles looked like they were eight feet tall. I laugh at the memory because a few years later I was visiting Rome. I stood in line for about twenty minutes to see the Pope. I thought of leaving the line because it was wasting my time. Fortunately, I did not and enjoyed a private audience, along with about two hundred others, with Pope Paul VI. Lenin versus the Pope! Where were my priorities?

I need to mention our last stop. It was a small island off the coast of the city of Dubrovnik in former Yugoslavia (now Croatia); a quaint pedestrian bridge connected it with the mainland. The island was made up of small huts (formerly houses of the local fishermen) and smooth paths surrounded by clear blue water. Each hut was furnished like an amazingly comfortable hotel room. The idea was to give us a rest after a very full and exciting journey. It was also a time to reflect and integrate the many conversations we had over the weeks together. Conversations with others, particularly with those who think differently, are necessary for a better life, a better world. Conversations mean *listening* as well as speaking. I welcomed those few days of rest in preparation for the flight back to the States. Then I was back home refreshed and excited about my new life as a professor of Homiletics and Pastoral Theology!

Arriving back at the seminary, unpacking my clothes, arranging my room with some old furniture, and putting my books on the built-in shelves kept me busy for a few days. Then I turned to writing my master's thesis I had been thinking about: *A History of the Sacrament of Penance.* That was a full-time project for the rest of the summer. On weekends I was assisting at Saint Christopher's parish located in North Chili, a Rochester suburb. While I was at Ithaca College, the bishop had asked me once to cover there for the pastor during the summer while he was on vacation. During that period, the parish community had rented a hall in a nearby medical building for Sunday services. Now the people had a new church building with an enthusiastic pastor leading a very committed community of worshippers. I served there for about two years (1972-3) before moving to another parish, Saint Charles Borromeo, closer to the seminary which also needed weekend assistance.

The summer passed quickly. I submitted my thesis in late August. The principal reader rejected the initial draft because the subject matter was not focused enough: "too broad of a subject and in need of a great deal of editing." Disappointed and a bit angry, I needed to find a new topic and needed a director. After two false starts and some angry exchanges with two directors I settled on an exploration of the concept of "*katallage*" (the Greek word for "reconciliation") in the Letters of Saint Paul. This choice of topic opened a whole new world for me. As I look back now it was one of the best experiences of my life and the most helpful to me personally. Studying the topic, not writing about it, became the basis for my better understanding of the theology of the Sacrament of Penance which the Church more accurately labels the Sacrament of Reconciliation. I now view the sacrament more as a healing experience. At the same time, I expanded my concept of the role of the church community now called to be more embracive in its preaching and the exercise of its many liturgical and social ministries.

The journey through the thesis project took me two years. I was able to review some of my Greek from years past. I also became acquainted more in depth with Saint Paul's letters because he was the one author in the whole Bible who used the word (noun and verb) most frequently to explain our relationship with God. Jesus, the Son, was the agent for reconciling the world with a merciful and compassionate Father most evidently through his willing death on the cross. I approached the topic by exegeting each time Saint Paul used the word to summarize the concept of reconciliation. This in turn could lead to a better understanding of the sacrament, but also as a basis for our interpersonal relations within the community as well as our embracing the world's challenges. I really enjoyed the research. Writing about it was the big challenge. I never saw myself as a writer in the first place, but I have learned that writing can be helpful to organize and re-organize my thoughts. Certainly, drafting the thesis challenged me to do just that.

The director of the thesis was not one of my favorite people in the first place. He tended to be a procrastinator and not one I could fully trust. The writing and rewriting over the two years lead me to despair on more than one occasion. At one point I told him that I wanted to quit the program. I could not get "reconciled" to what was going on with him and his inability to respond in a timely fashion. He countered with a simple "Write, you do not have to be reconciled." I countered that I was writing about a topic that I needed to practice. "It was theology!" We arranged a truce; I would finish the thesis. He would approve each chapter before I submitted the next.

And so, with his approval, I submitted the final draft. Then he stopped me in the hallway to tell me that I had to defend it in the presence of two other faculty members. I told him that I would not defend it, but I would be willing to discuss the thesis with them. We agreed to a date. I showed up with a stack of paper twelve inches high (the initial research, the first drafts, the rewrites, and the final written document). He, along with two other faculty members, sat on one side of the desk and I on the other. I knew the two others quite well and respected them for their knowledge as well as their very proper demeanor. We began with a prayer. My director asked the first question: "What did you learn from the experience of writing about this topic?" That was the wrong question.

It took me only a few moments to give my unexpected response. I began with "I grew up in the country and spent a great deal of time on a farm during the summer…" From there, I spoke about my experience with "sh*t." There was horse sh*t. The horses would empty themselves into "horse balls." As kids, when they dried out, we could pick them up to throw at each other or throw them into the air and hit them with a baseball bat. Horse sh*t was fun to play with and we could laugh. Then there was chicken sh*t. When we went into the hen house to collect the eggs in the morning, we needed to tip-toe around the chickens' droppings, or we could really cause a stink when we took the eggs into the house. There are some things in life we need to avoid so we learn to walk around them without getting upset. Then I proposed a third scene: cow sh*t piled up in the corner of the barnyard. Some of it could be taken out to the fields and used as fertilizer; other cow sh*t sat in the corner long enough so that small plants and bush-like trees could grow out of the pile. Some "sh*t" helps us grow. "That, in a nutshell, is what I learned from writing the thesis." My response to the director's question stunned the other two enough that the remaining questions were asked with more precision. I graduated with my master's in theology that May!

The curriculum for the fourth-year theologians changed during the summer I was in Russia. The Dean of Students and the Dean of School decided that the opportunity to integrate the students' theology and practice should become a course: Pastoral Integration Seminar (you can imagine the fun with the acronym). Some of the students were very unhappy with the decision. This was not in their planned fourth year. The course was developed to take practical parish issues (e.g., parish council meetings, dealing with a family upon the death of a loved one, marriage preparation for couples) and integrate the practical approach with the theology the students had studied in the more theoretical courses. I remember one mild-mannered student charging at me at the end of the first-class period. Now as an irate student he informed me that he had taken Clinical Pastoral Education that past summer. He learned how to confront people with whom he disagreed. "I am quite angry that I *must* take this course. I want you to know that." I never had a similar training for confrontation, so my reply was a simple, "Tough rocks! Suck it up!"

The other professor and I (it was to be a team-taught course) would gather the entire class together on Monday afternoons for two hours. Sometimes we brought in pastors, parish ministers, or experts on a particular subject for a two-hour period. Then we divided the class into two sections. Each of us was responsible for a one-hour period later in the week. I was assigned a challenging time slot: Thursday morning at 8:00 a.m. just after morning prayer and breakfast. Because I realized some of the students might occasionally miss breakfast, I provided coffee and donuts as we sat around my room for our discussion of the material covered on Monday. One of the students was absent for more than one class because he was sleeping. I warned him that the discussion was part of the course, but he continued to skip the class. One Thursday morning he was absent and I was upset because he had ignored my past warnings. I took the tray of coffee and donuts along with the other students to his room. I knocked on the door and the wayward student invited us in. He was in bed. He was surprised to see me, his classmates, the tray of coffee and donuts. His first words were, "You son of a *****!" I replied that those were the first honest words he had spoken to me all semester. We conducted our class discussion with him sitting up in his bed. He never missed another class.

Each year the Dean of Students assigned me about fifteen students as their advisor. I look back over the years I was at the seminary with my fondest memories of those times I spent advising students. We talked about their academic progress and the personal issues of each young man trying to make decisions about his call to priesthood. I remember one student claiming that he was "not worthy or ready to be ordained." My response was a simple, "None of us is worthy and it takes a lifetime to be fully prepared for any job." At the time, I had spent 34 years as a student in classrooms at the undergraduate and graduate levels with added seminars and workshops. By the time I retired I had spent 72 years taking courses for a variety of degrees with added workshops during the summers plus three sabbaticals. When I shared that tidbit with my students in later years at St. John Fisher College, they could not believe that I could bear so much learning. I never believed I was "fully prepared." There is always something new to learn.

Over the years I was on the faculty I had the opportunity to teach a variety of courses that had a pastoral element, not just the basic courses in Homiletics and Pastoral Theology, but also in special areas like spirituality of teenagers, the writings of Thomas Merton, elements for spiritual direction and the sacrament of reconciliation. Much of the material was from my "years in the field," but also the workshops, course work, and my own research with extensive reading. The students further allowed me to grow because of their questions and interests.

Saint Bernard's Seminary had a working relationship with Colgate Rochester Divinity School which had a long and rich history preparing ministers (male and female) for a variety of religious denominations. Some of our students would take elective courses there. Our faculties would have small gatherings to discuss theological issues as well as practical planning to work together in a variety of fieldwork experiences for our students. This allowed for a better worldview of theory and practice. Some of the faculty became good friends over the years. I remember giving one of my stoles to Ted Weeden, a Methodist minister and Scripture scholar, as a token of my respect and care that he be properly attired when preaching to his congregation. To this day I remember so many of these colleagues with great affection and appreciation for their wisdom and kindness. It was ecumenism at work!

Because of that ecumenical relationship I took advantage of their new program, a doctorate in ministry (DMin). My focus was pastoral counseling. Like myself, these professors brought experience as well as theory to the courses. I was assigned an internship in the mental health clinic at one of the local hospitals. Here I met medical school graduates who were doing their internships or rotations in mental health. It was helpful to be with others of a different background to focus on similar issues. Meeting with my director on a regular basis to review my assigned cases with helpful feedback was the highlight of the experience. One of the most often asked questions I remember was, "If you had to do it again, what would you do better?" It was a positive way to help me grow without being negatively critical. I made that question an important element in my own counseling and teaching from then on.

None of us in the program wore a white coat or any religious symbol that might raise unnecessary questions or problems. One of my favorite stories involved a married woman who was dealing with an exceedingly difficult husband. Both exhibited some serious issues that made their marriage quite volatile. During one of our meetings, I suggested that she might want to pursue some of her concerns with her minister or religious leader. She quickly responded that she was Roman Catholic and "I would be embarrassed to talk about these issues with a priest." I chuckled to myself, "If she only knew."

Before I joined the seminary faculty, I had been invited to join the Diocesan Marriage Tribunal. The personnel director, who was also a former member of the Tribunal, knew of my interest in marriage issues from my days at Ithaca College and my counselling background from my further studies. At that time, one did not have to be a canon lawyer to serve on the Tribunal as a judge. My faculty advisor at the hospital was aware of this. She asked if I would make a presentation at one of the Grand Rounds to the doctors and others who were interested in church annulments, the declaration of invalidity of a marriage. My first major talk as a counselor-intern was to over one hundred seasoned doctors and health care workers. Wow! The talk was well received, but their questions had me thinking more deeply about the fragility of some relationships, their causes, and church law and its procedures. It was still another learning experience that led me to dig deeper into the psychology of interpersonal relations.

My earlier theology degree gave me a new area of exploration for my doctoral research. I used the opportunity to organize and execute a five-day workshop for priests to share my research and readings to understand new insights about the sacrament of reconciliation. One of the newly published post-Vatican II Roman documents on the liturgy and the sacraments had addressed the sacrament of reconciliation. My thesis director approved the project once he spent time with me discussing an outline and content of the presentations. I enlisted a student to help me with the organization of room, board, mailings, typing of handouts, and as a general "go-to-it helper" during the workshop. Over five days about twenty-five priests gathered to learn more about the theology of the sacrament, scriptural basis for reconciliation and the concept of sin, with a practicum each day and an open discussion in the evening on the topics and concerns covered that day. What a fantastic experience for me. I learned as much as I shared. With the help of the student (he typed better and faster than I) I submitted the results of the workshop with an outline of the various talks, evaluations, and bibliography in a proper binding for the thesis project. The ensuing discussion was enjoyable because two of the three examiners were not Roman Catholic; the third was a priest-pastor with years of experience with the sacrament. I graduated that May happy to finish the work, but even more, because I found studying at the Divinity School the most supportive academic experience in my life. I received no word, not even a congratulation, from the faculty where I was teaching. The dissertation was done. What next?

A Month of Prayer (Summer 1975)

WHEN I WAS IN HIGH SCHOOL, I read the book *Seven Storey Mountain* by Thomas Merton, a Trappist monk at the Abbey of Gethsemane in Kentucky who authored the story of his journey to the monastery. His autobiography may well be the reason I am authoring my story now. For the next twenty-some years I read everything that he published. I also wanted to explore him even more via some kind of experience. One day I was reading a Catholic newspaper when I saw an advertisement to spend a month at the Thomas Merton Center located in Magog, Quebec. My decision to apply took me less than five minutes. That month changed my life significantly.

I arrived at the farm-like structure on a Sunday afternoon. I joined about twenty others who wanted a similar prayer experience. The Center was run by a Jewish husband (later baptized) and his wife who was born in Russia. Linda's life experience, education, and eagerness to share her journey as a way to experience Christian mysticism gave me the confidence I needed for the month. She introduced us to Zen meditation practices and to thirty days of silence. Each day I offered Mass for the group consisting of religious brothers, people exploring a vocation to some kind of ministry, and a few lay people who sought to live fuller lives as husbands or wives. We took turns preparing meals, enjoyed a vegetarian diet in silence, and meditated, formally and informally the rest of the time. We learned sitting meditation as well as walking meditation. We then recorded our experiences in a daily journal. Every other day we would have a meeting with Linda to share our journal entries and receive feedback and some advice if needed.

Two experiences were highlights of the month. Linda offered us the opportunity to spend some time away from the community in solitude living in a tent about a mile from the house. I asked, "When can I do that?" She quietly replied, "You will receive a sign; just follow it." I should mention that Linda and Peter had a dog whose name I have forgotten. About halfway through the month the dog came up to me and started to bark, then ran off a bit until I started to follow him. This continued for a few minutes. I told Linda what was going on. She said, "You were looking for a sign. Let the dog lead you." I put together some granola and some water for the adventure. When I asked Linda where and how long I should stay, she said the dog will tell you. Off I went following the dog.

Wagging its tail and occasionally barking as if to encourage me, the dog led me through the fields until I found myself in front of a small tent, my place for solitude. The dog sauntered off and I was alone. For the next few days, I sat and walked meditating. One day I was doing my walking meditation exercise and found myself on a small hill overlooking the farmhouse. I know that it was time for the group to be gathered for the afternoon sitting meditation. I extended my hands in prayer over the farmhouse asking God to bless them all. It was my way of being with them in spirit. On the third day the dog came to the tent, barking, and running off a bit until I packed up and followed him back to the Center. It was good to be back and enjoy a comfortable bed for a change. I had to sleep on the ground when I was living in the tent. The next day, when I was meeting with Linda to report on my time away, she asked me where I was during the group meditation a day ago. I asked "Why?" She smiled and said, "Joe reported in his journal that during the sitting mediation, he envisioned you standing on the hilltop with your hands extended praying for the group. Were you there?" Often during the sitting mediation, we were told, our thoughts might very well be shared with others without any effort on our part. Linda was right. I recall the many times I was thinking about someone only to hear from or see them that very day. Sometimes I show some initiative prompting me to call them to see how things were going. Often, I heard the same reply, "Funny you should call. I have been going through some tough times lately."

Another night I was doing my walking meditation. The nearest neighbors were a mile or two away from the Center. The night was dark, so it made the dirt road (a really "less travelled road") connecting the nearby farms a safe place to walk. I was pondering a question about my future and questioning what might be the right path and, of course, worried how I might know it to be right for me. As I walked along, I heard a loud voice shouting, "You stupid thing! How many times have I told you not to go there! You never listen to me. Stubborn! I suppose I will have to get you out of this mess again." My immediate reaction was fear. "Was that God talking to me?" The darkness along with the loud voice and the harsh words really scared me. I slowly looked around my shoulder. A farmer was waving his arms and yelling at a cow who had gone off by itself and got stuck in some mud. I wondered whether the farmer's words were meant for me. They did give me assurance that I should listen more and stop being stubborn about my way of thinking. Getting off any safe path can pose a new problem or offer a new point of view.

Leaving the Center was difficult because I had gotten used to the peace and extended periods of prayer. However, as I drove home, I felt a peace that I had never felt before. Even driving in traffic was much easier. I must admit one of the first places I headed for was an ice cream stand. I had missed my daily dish of ice cream.

A Five Month Change of Venue
(Spring 1976)

WITH THE NEW DEGREE, I ventured into some new territory. In early fall I read still another advertisement in a weekly Catholic journal. Notre Dame Seminary in New Orleans was looking for a professor to teach a course on marriage and sexuality for the spring semester. I sent off my resume immediately. A few weeks later the Academic Dean of the New Orleans' seminary called to tell me that I was just the right candidate they needed for the position. My first question was, "What are the dates?" He gave me one date in February. "Why that date?" I asked. He said that it is Mardi Gras day. That sealed the offer. For years I had hoped someday to attend Mardi Gras. Permission from the rector at Saint Bernard's came easily. Plans were arranged to cover my classes and the care for my advisees. I remember heading out on a cold January day driving through some snow. As I drove further south, I took off my coat, then my sweater, and by the time I arrived in New Orleans, I was wearing a light summer shirt.

My five months in New Orleans were a real learning experience. The seminary had a variety of students from all over the south, the faculty was diverse, the history and sites of the city exciting, the celebration of Mardi Gras fantastic. As always, the time in the classroom was my favorite experience. I taught a required course, Marriage and Sexuality, and a course on the sacrament of reconciliation and spiritual direction. The students and the president of the seminary were well-pleased with both courses. At Midterm the president of the seminary and the archbishop of the diocese asked me to stay on as rector of the seminary. I was excited about the possibility but told them I needed to talk with the bishop and the rector of the seminary in my own diocese. I have to admit that the conversation with the bishop, a former professor of mine, was rather unsettling. He listened attentively to the request. Then he said (and the words stick in my mind even today), "Bill you are talented, smart, and creative BUT there is no room for you in our diocese so you should consider their offer." I thanked him for his time and comment, but wondered to myself, "What the hell did that all mean?"

The return to Rochester to ask for the necessary permission was a challenge. Both the rector and bishop gave me permission (along with the bishop's suggestion), but I was feeling more uneasy about accepting the position mainly because I felt that the seminary would be better served by having a rector who was raised in the south with its unique history, character, and culture. As I flew back to New Orleans, I was still very uneasy about saying "yes" to the invitation. As I looked out of the plane's window, awed by the landscape, and with a prayer in my heart, I weighed the options: Saint Bernard's Seminary in the north or Notre Dame Seminary in the south. I took a deep breath and said to myself: "Saint Bernard's!" With that, I sat back and enjoyed the rest of the trip. Telling those in New Orleans was not easy, but I was at peace.

The semester at Notre Dame Seminary is a wonderful memory. As always, it is the people who made it so. The students were a real joy. It was the first time I had both Black and White students in a classroom. Their backgrounds, because of culture, age, and geographic differences, presented a challenge and a comfort: the beauty of future leaders in a variety of roles. One became an archbishop, another a president of a religious community. Still another, now a member of a religious order, became an auxiliary bishop for the diocese. I read about a few who took on leadership roles in their home dioceses. The faculty was a mixed group of religious and diocesan priests whose varied background and academic interests provided exciting faculty evening dinners. I had a variety of liturgical experiences: sometimes I offered Mass at Xavier University, one of the first colleges for Black men and women; other Sundays I attended a predominantly Black Catholic church with fantastic liturgies with music and processions as we all swayed to the altar to deposit our Sunday offerings into a basket held by the celebrant.

Another time I was invited to make a presentation to a group of about forty women. Their common bond was startling. Their husbands had left them suddenly without giving a reason: some just left without a word, others left a written "sorry it did not turn out" message, a few had the courage to call on the phone to announce they would not be coming home ever again. Spending that afternoon with some very brave women still sticks in my memory because of the cruelty of their husbands' departure. There was no real conversation on the part of the husbands to mend whatever was the possible reason for their sudden leaving. In later years I became an active leader in a variety of marriage programs that encouraged dialogue between spouses to help cement their relationship.

On a lighter note, Mardi Gras was everything it was famous for: the parades, the costumes, the floats, the music. It came to a startling climax at 11:30 in the evening when trucks revved up their motors at the foot of Bourbon Street in the French Quarter. At midnight they brushed off the confetti, beer bottles and any other refuse on the streets. It was the beginning of Lent and the season of fasting and abstaining. The party was over; now was the season to repent. The semester ended in early May. I rehashed the many special memories as I journeyed home to Rochester laughing and crying along the way.

Back to the "Rock"

As I mentioned earlier some alumni called Saint Bernard's Seminary the "Rock." Some others referred to it as the West Point of seminaries. As a student, I called it purgatory only because one could get out eventually unlike hell. After we left its halls, most of us were proud we were alumni. I know I was. By the time I returned as a professor, things had changed a great deal. There was much more humanity, and the food was much better. The faculty and students ate together in the same dining room except for evening meals when the faculty enjoyed each other's company in their own dining room. It offered an opportunity for withdrawal from the noise of the larger dining hall. Besides, it was a haven after faculty meetings when we had discussed student evaluations and possible changes in curriculum. Both such meetings could take a great deal of life out of me. The student evaluation meetings could be heated because each of the faculty members was trying to defend or oppose the recommendations of students for ordination. The recommendations were then sent to the bishops of their diocese. The curriculum meetings could be as difficult when each of us proposed our course(s) as important to the well-rounded education for future priests and yet stay within the number of credit hours required by the State of New York for granting degrees. Many a night I tossed and turned before the meetings and lost sleep after them. Our students' recommendations dealt with academic performance, but also emotional and spiritual growth over each school year. One of the faculty members would often surface the question: "Would you want this person to be your assistant in a parish or the pastor of your parish?" That question later haunted me on more than one occasion because some did end up as my associates or would be my associates. The probing question still unnerves me when I look back over these critical recommendations I made years ago considering what I know now, forty-five years later. Wow!

Because of some conversations I had while at Notre Dame Seminary and a need to pursue some other academic interests. I went to Saint Paul's University in Ottawa, Canada, during the summer to see if I could work out an option for a doctoral degree in theology (STD). I received a warm welcome because of my past work and my apparent eagerness to learn more. Much of the work could be done long-distance. This was at a time before it became popular. To pay the tuition, I was asked to teach a course in Homiletics. That would mean a trip to Ottawa each week. I would drive up for class one day, teach the course at night, and return the next day: a journey of 550 miles round trip. Over the next two years I made the trip which, during the winter, could be a challenge because of the heavy snowfalls on Route 104 along Lake Ontario and the Saint Lawrence River. Even now when I watch the evening news, I shiver as the weather announcer reports the conditions of that area of the State.

The culture at Saint Paul's University was different: the students were from different Canadian Provinces, spoke different languages (English and French) and some were members of different religious orders. Because it was a University, still others had entirely different backgrounds of interest. I really enjoyed it all. In some ways I saw myself as a missionary to another culture; in other ways I saw myself as a student of human nature. I listened to educational tapes during my weekly drive, had some great interactions with students and faculty, and most of all, I really enjoyed the classroom experiences. This was another set of advantages for enduring the long and boring drive.

My long-time interest in Thomas Merton, the Trappist monk and writer, became my focus for a dissertation, *The Concept of Freedom in Selected Writings of Thomas Merton*. I researched the scriptures, the church fathers, and the monastic traditions to understand more fully Merton's approach to freedom. One summer I took a course with a professor whose interest and excitement for Merton was the same as mine. The topic was the poetry of Merton who wrote over a thousand pages of poetry in his twenty-seven years as a monk. I passed the initial qualifying exam to continue with drafting the dissertation. Over the years of writing the dissertation chapters some were lost in the mail or arrived late. This was before the computer and internet. I would send them to my dissertation director; he would correct them and offer suggestions when we met in person. I would drive to Ottawa only to find that the chapter had not yet arrived. My director became ill and eventually died. In the meanwhile, I had also moved on to another pastoral assignment. The University had set a date for the dissertation's completion which I could not make. Saint Paul's University granted me a Licentiate degree in theology (STL) for the work I had done. I later discovered an alternative way to earn the desired degree: Columbia Pacific University which had, at the time, good ratings. The university was created for students who were working and could not dedicate full time to classes. Today we witness such universities of unequal quality and reputation advertised frequently. I transferred credits from my past degrees and courses to the university along with proper recommendations for my experiences. I took a qualifying exam, submitted the dissertation, and won my doctoral degree. It was a messy experience, but I did learn about Merton and freedom. That was my reason for the degree in the first place. It gave me a goal for bringing my interest to a focused conclusion. Much later in my life I spent time frequently with a Cistercian monk who was a novice under Merton and, eventually, a psychiatrist who came to know Merton quite intimately. I enjoyed some further insights into this "active mystic" who was a long-time hero.

When I arrived back in Rochester in mid-May from New Orleans, I attended the ordinations in the Diocese of Syracuse soon after. Three of my advisees were being ordained along with men from other seminaries. I had been invited to preach at the first Masses of all three. It was a busy Sunday going from one church to the other. Each had chosen a time for his first Mass so I could easily travel from one place to another. One of them was in Cortland for an afternoon celebration. I was a bit exhausted as I drove back to Rochester, but happy to be part of their celebrations. The summer went quite well as I went about plans for the following year as a teacher. I gave a retreat for the priests in the Fort Worth diocese in Texas. It was the first retreat that the bishop required that all the priests should attend as a group to have time together for prayer and conversation. I spent some time calming the feathers of some of the older priests who resented the request. "I am old enough to decide when and where I make my annual retreat" was the common objection. Noting their expressed and unexpressed anger, I listened with my ears and heart. "We all have rights but often we need to put our will aside for a while and work together for a few days to support each other." The retreat ended peacefully with many expressions of gratitude. Subsequently, I spent time during the summer months working in the same diocese with a wonderful lay group dedicated to spiritual renewal for themselves and their parishes. In one parish I met six couples I knew from Rochester who moved to Fort Worth to keep their jobs with the Rochester-based Xerox company.

In the fall I picked up my regular courses at Saint Bernard's using any spare time to work on my dissertation research plus my weekly journey to Ottawa. On weekends I assisted at a nearby parish; during the week I celebrated Mass at the Church of the Annunciation. Little did I know that someday I would be its pastor.

During the second semester of 1977 I continued with the same schedule but had a sense something was going on that I did not quite understand. In mid-March, the rector of the seminary and I enjoyed breakfast together one morning with lots of banter and conversation. After breakfast I picked up my mail and inter-house bulletins. When I arrived back in my room, I opened the letter with a Saint Bernard's return address with only my name on the envelope and no address. The letter was from the rector asking that I resign from the seminary faculty and move on. I was shocked. In retrospect my earlier uneasiness was making sense. After settling down for a few days, I had a conversation with the rector to discuss the whys and wherefores of the letter. He confessed that my big mistake was defending two of the students who other faculty members judged as unfit for ministry in the diocese. I had also suspected some jealousy from a few of my colleagues in positions of authority. It all made sense, but I was angry. I approached a member of the diocesan board of arbitration/ reconciliation to intervene. I had also asked the rector for a letter of recommendation for other possible teaching positions. The arbitrator reported back that "With a letter like the rector sent, I would want to keep you as a valuable member of the faculty, not ask you to resign."

I kept all of this to myself, discussing it with very few people, including students. At the end of the semester, I packed up my books and other belongings. My good friend, Fr. Jack Hedges, invited me to live at his rectory which was nearby. It would give me space to decide "what next." I left my keys in the rector's mailbox one morning and left without saying goodbye to anyone. Later in the summer as I was driving past the seminary, I saw the rector out for a walk. I parked my car and joined him. I apologized for my behavior and assured him of our friendship. I spoke of the five or six years I had been on the faculty when I met with him informally to speak about my work during the year acknowledging that at times I was stubborn or ornery about some things. I asked for any feedback, and I received none but was told that I was a valuable member of the faculty. He looked at me sadly, "I spoke positively because I cared for you and did not want to hurt you." My response was a simple, "That is not the way you care for someone." We talked for a few minutes more. I drove off. My time at the "Rock" was behind me. I was off to a new adventure. The rector and I stayed connected in subsequent years and I visited him when he was dying and assured him of my continued care and respect for him. He retired from the position the same year I left. The infighting to appoint his successor is a story unto itself.

My Year at Nazareth College (1978)

A S I TRIED TO DO every Sunday afternoon. I spent time with my mom and dad. This included a wonderful meal prepared by my mother who was a great cook. Occasionally my dad would prepare some sauces or salads. I could always tell because he would ask how I liked the sauce or salad mix. Naturally, I always praised it as I caught a glimpse of my mother's eyes rolling at my positive gushing about how delicious it was. How do I break the news I will be leaving my position at the seminary? I waited until the end of the meal. My father growled rather loudly, "Why do you stay a priest? Why not leave and do something for yourself?" My mother was speechless (and that was rare). Both offered suggestions and the meal ended quietly.

Growing up my dad never said "no" to any of my dreams or choices. I remember wanting to have a pony. He thought it would be a great idea but said "How are you going to earn the money to pay for it?" The same with a bike, a trip to the city, going to the movies; it was always the same, "Great, how are you going to pay for it?" When I was in fifth grade, I stole something from a store, a child's camouflage helmet like those soldiers wore in battle. The store owner told my father. That night, when dad came home, I was in bed asleep. He woke me up, sat on the bed, and gave his usual preamble: "Tell me the truth and we can deal with it; lie, and you will be punished." Then he asked me if I had taken the helmet without paying for it. I told him I did. With a look I will never forget, he uttered a phrase that has governed so much of my life, "Remember that the only things in life worth having are the things we work for." Years later when I entered the seminary, my dad told me, "Good! Work hard, and if you want to come home, you are always welcome." About five years after my ordination, my mom confided in me that my father was disappointed that I entered the seminary and chose to be a priest. He was hoping that I would become a lawyer or doctor, marry and have a family but he did not say "no."

For the first time that night when I broke the news about being forced out of a position that I really enjoyed did my father ever express his true feelings about my choice of a vocation. I learned a great deal about life from my dad not because he was book-learned, but because he was a man who could dream and then work hard for everything he had. I think his brief outburst that night encouraged me to keep pursuing my dream, but I had to work to make it come true. He would not say "no" but would always support me whatever I decided. With Saint Bernard's behind me, I took refuge at Saint Charles Borromeo parish. The pastor offered me space to store my books and other belongings plus two rooms and a bath on the third floor where I could do some reading and writing while I figured out my next move. Saint Paul's in Ottawa was my eventual choice. I could spend a year there working on my dissertation without any other responsibilities except to teach the course on Homiletics. It made sense; the personnel director okayed the move. Now all I needed to do was wait until September. "We propose; God laughs!"

On a beautiful early June day, I received a call from the Bishop's Office asking me to go to Nazareth College as the campus minister. The immediate full-time predecessor had moved to another assignment at Cornell University. Once he left, the "acting campus minister," who had previously held the position for over thirty-five years and taught at the same time, needed to cut back from the position because of health and age. "It would be only for a year," was the promise. "Asking" in our business is more like an order. I replied reluctantly. I had already signed up for a summer course in Ottawa and I would be able to work on the dissertation full-time in the fall. The new assignment would begin on the last Tuesday of June.

I drove to the college, met the president, and was promised a course to teach and nice place to live. It was a small cottage on the property with four small rooms and a bath but no furniture. The chaplain's office and worship place were just across the road from my new home. The large student center included offices for the staff working with student affairs, an athletic facility, auditorium, and dining hall. It took some haggling to get the necessary furniture so I could move in; all I requested were the basics (bed, chairs, desk). On reflection, the haggling and reluctant delivery of the basics was "strike one." The promised course did not materialize: "strike two."

From its inception Nazareth College was a women's college established and maintained by the Sisters of Saint Joseph. Times changed. About the time I arrived the president, the first male lay person, had seen a need for the college to become co-educational. To attract men to the college he believed that starting a men's basketball team would be a good start. The coach, the players, and I arrived the same year. In a conversation with the coach in the dining hall one day I mentioned that I had worked with the athletic trainer at Ithaca College occasionally. The coach asked me if I would serve that role with his new team. I taped some ankles, took care of some minor bruises, sat on the players' bench during the home games and was mostly an ear for their problems as they adjusted to college. It was one of the best experiences for the year I was at the college.

The worship space was a beautiful small chapel for daily Mass and the Saturday anticipated Mass to meet the Sunday obligation. On Sundays folding doors would open onto the auditorium for the larger numbers. That worked until I was notified at the last minute that the president and his wife would be using the auditorium for a Saturday dinner at the same time as Mass was being offered in the adjacent chapel. A compromise was worked out in theory but not in practice. Another priest was celebrating Mass while I was asking people on the other side of the folding doors to wait quietly until Mass was over. The two hosts for the dinner were not pleased to put it mildly. That was "strike three."

Working with the immediate staff, the coaches, and the students made the year a success in my eyes. That was why I took the job for the year: service. I spent time counselling students and supporting the faculty. I remember a male student (male students were in the minority) who was involved with a charismatic prayer group. He was trying to deal with failing grades and loneliness. Looking a bit frazzled, he stopped by my office one early spring day. He told me that he did not sleep very well that night, so he prayed for guidance. "God," he said, "told me to quit school and go home." I asked him to wait for a minute while I prayed for guidance. Then I said, God just told me that you should finish the semester and then decide what to do. He looked at me with a smile and gave a quick "Okay, that is what I will do." With a sigh of relief, the student thanked me and walked out happy as if his problem were solved. The now happy first-year student became involved in a few campus activities, passed his courses, and went home for the summer. I often wondered what happened to him.

Late one evening, near midnight, I received a call from one of the female students. She was desperate and had to talk to me right away because she was afraid of what her parents would say. She would be right over to my cottage. I began to ruminate about the immediate need for the cry for help. Did she have a fight with her boyfriend? Was she pregnant? Was she thinking of dropping out of school? A very tearful stressed-out young lady knocked at my door. I invited her into my sitting room. We sat down in silence for a few minutes while she tried to collect herself. After wiping her tears, she whispered that her parents were going to kill her when she told them the news. I assured her that they would not kill her whatever she did. "I know but they raised me as a Catholic and sent me to a Catholic college; they will be really upset and might want to disown me." I assured her again that they might be upset but would be there to support her no matter what. "Okay, then, I must tell them something that I just found out. One of guys I know told me the other day that he had been observing me and concluded: I am a Wicca witch." I did not expect that at all and had to admit that I knew extraordinarily little about Wicca witches. Neither did she. Apparently, her male friend was a warlock and had the gift of identifying women who were witches. She spoke of him as a close friend and as an authentic warlock. He offered to initiate her as a Wicca witch. They would sleep together and have intercourse. After she left, I checked out wicca witches and warlocks only to learn that "sleeping together and having intercourse" was not a part of the initiation ceremony. I thought, however, it was a new and creative pick-up line that I had not thought of before that night.

Each week I would drive to Ottawa to continue with my teaching on Tuesday evenings. I passed my qualifying oral exam for the doctorate before 7-8 examiners and continued to read books written by Thomas Merton. In the early spring I sent a proposal for a possible presentation to one of the first Thomas Merton celebrations, which later became a Society, to be held in Vancouver, British Columbia in early May. I discovered that Merton and Erich Fromm had corresponded with each other because of some mutual interests. I chose to speak about Merton and Fromm: two mystics in search of freedom. The proposal was accepted, and I delivered the address successfully. At the conclusion of the talk one of the attendees introduced himself. It was Gordon Zahn, a sociologist, pacifist, and author of a book about Franz Jagerstatter, an Austrian farmer and conscientious objector who resisted joining the German army during World War II. Imprisoned and later decapitated for his beliefs, Pope Benedict XVI beatified him years later. It was Zahn's book, *In Solitary Witness*, that brought attention to Jagerstatter's journey of faith. I had read the book, so we had an enjoyable conversation. He attended my talk because he was interested in the mysticism of Merton who was also a pacifist. Merton's writings had influenced his own writings. My new acquaintance appreciated my talk. I appreciated meeting him and was especially flattered that he attended my presentation.

The committee asked me to celebrate Mass for the attendees, some of whom attended my talk. Later a few asked me how was life as a monk living in a monastery. They thought I must be a monk because of my topic and the way I celebrated Mass. Little did they know! In a passing conversation with the retired campus minister, I mentioned that I was giving a talk at the Merton conference in Vancouver. We had a common interest in Merton, He thought he might make a proposal also and then we could travel together. This sounded like an ideal arrangement, but I would have to fly home alone because one of us needed to celebrate the baccalaureate Mass for the graduating seniors. Msgr. Bill Shannon, my colleague from Nazareth College, thanked me for encouraging him to attend the conference and pursue his interest in Thomas Merton. He later wrote books and articles about Merton, edited many of his letters, and became the Inaugural President of the International Thomas Merton Society. Years later I was invited back to Nazareth to give a talk about Thomas Merton and non-violence with special reference to Gandhi. I was especially nervous because I was giving the talk in the presence of three experts: Bill and two of his associates who assisted him editing the letters of Merton and writing books of their own.

As the semester continued, I began to explore other possible avenues for my next assignment. One of them was a position at Notre Dame University in Indiana. At the time the Holy Cross Fathers were looking for someone to support their priest-candidates pursuing their pastoral theology intern placements. The interview went well but I had a sense they needed a different kind of person much like my Notre Dame Seminary experience. A few weeks later I received a call that the position was filled but would I consider taking a position as a chaplain for one of the students' residence halls at the University. From the time I was in elementary school my dream was to go to Notre Dame in some capacity. I attended a few summer courses there when I was teaching at Saint Bernard's. I had walked around the campus dreaming of football games and praying at the Grotto to Our Lady. I felt that I belonged there. Now I have an offer! Again, "Wow!" A dream comes true! I tentatively said 'yes" but would need to clear it with my bishop. One of the members of the personnel board was a friend of mine who assured me that it looked like I could go to Notre Dame. No problem!

It was a Wednesday night. I was enjoying a quiet evening thinking about the meeting of the personnel board. The phone rang. I picked it up breathing with excitement ready to say "thank you" for letting me pursue my dream. My friend was at the meeting and the board was asking me to become the pastor of one of the city parishes. I listed all the reasons I did not want to accept the appointment. He understood my point and said he would get back to me. About ten minutes later the phone rang again. "The Board agreed with you. You made some good points. Would you be the pastor of this other parish?" My arguments were the same with a few added reasons why I did not see it working. "I will get back to you about your position at Notre Dame once I present your reasoning," my harried friend spoke with a tone of reassurance. Another few minutes passed. The phone rang. "Certainly this time I will get a positive response," I prayed. This call was no longer an invitation. I was being appointed to be the pastor of the Church of the Annunciation. The pastor was ill and needed to be replaced immediately. The director of the personnel board will check with me the next day to work out the details. I went to bed crying in anger, frustration, and a sense of failure because my dream job was a NO!!!

It was a restless night. When talking with the personnel director in mid-morning, I told him that I would accept the assignment. When should I start? "As soon as possible; hopefully by next Monday. Oh, and by the way, the present pastor does not want to retire officially until the first of September. You will be the associate pastor for canonical reasons but have all the responsibilities of the pastor. He is recuperating at his condominium not far from the parish boundaries so he can advise you." I hung up the phone and questioned my sanity for saying "Yes." Then I started to pack.

As I was packing my things, I found a cigar box with some gadgets and small articles I had accumulated over the years. I found a small silver ring that I had bought as a souvenir ten years prior. I had taken a student to visit Williamsburg, Virginia, to see the sites. Both of us were interested in history so it was a most wonderful adventure. I did want to bring something small and cheap back home to remind me of the trip. A one-dollar silver ring was my souvenir. I had forgotten about it until I opened and explored the contents of the cigar box. I picked it up and put it on my finger saying to myself, "I will wear this ring as a sign of my love and devotion for the people that I will be serving from now on. I made a pledge to be faithful just like a husband and father." I have worn the ring ever since. When questioned about the ring if "I was married" or, as I got older, "previously married", I would tell the story of its origin and its meaning. I like to think that I have lived up to that promise, at least most of the time. But the call from the bishop's office again reminded me, "We propose; God laughs."

Then Came the Church of the Annunciation (1979-1988)

I WAS NOT NEW TO the Church of the Annunciation. When I was on the faculty at Saint Bernard's, I assisted with daily Mass there for a few years. Even earlier, when I was a student, I went there weekly for a year assigned to teach religious education classes. I remember my student years vividly because the housekeeper had the best snacks for us after we taught our classes. After one of the class meetings, as I was walking to the rectory, one of the students started yelling some harsh curse words at my companions and me threatening with a "I am going to throw this rock at you." I whispered, "Keep walking and nothing will happen." We did and fortunately he did not throw the rock. When we were out of throwing distance, I turned around to see who my attackers were. I recognized the speaker. A few years before this encounter I helped two of my classmates who were summer counsellors at Saint Joseph's Villa, a resident home for orphans and boys/girls remanded there by the courts because of serious issues at home. This young man was horribly disfigured from burns suffered while rescuing his younger brother from the family's burning house. At the time he was so disfigured from the burns that his family did not want to deal with him, so he was placed at the Villa. By the time he wanted to throw the rock, the former Villa resident was healed with only a few visible scars. I am quite sure he had not recognized me although we spent good times together while he was a resident at the Villa. I never saw him again, but I remember the encounter and perhaps partially understood the reason for the angry threats.

Because I assisted with daily Masses at the parish, I knew the layout of the church, the rectory, and had coffee with the pastor occasionally. Msgr. Al Simonetti, the long-time pastor, told me often how lucky he was. He had inherited a blood disease that killed male members of his family before the age of sixty-five yet he was still alive and going strong. One of his often-repeated complaints was the length of time it took to get a church annulment. He blamed the local marriage tribunal. I never told him that I was one of its judges. Sometimes it's better to keep my thoughts to myself.

The founders of the parish were Italians, many of them immigrants, who did not feel comfortable in nearby parishes. They wanted their own. For many years, the original church was basically the basement of the building and so was nicknamed the "catacomb church." A group of male volunteers completed the building. It still stands after weathering many uses such as church services, parish social gatherings, classroom for religious education classes over many years. When I arrived one of the original women of the parish, one its key founders, was still alive. During the day she and some of her friends would visit other parishioners to collect small donations for construction materials. When the men came home from their day jobs, they would purchase the material with whatever money the women collected that day. Then they worked together for a few hours to build the church. When the foundation for the church and a rectory was ready, the bishop assigned a full-time pastor. I was the first non-Italian priest to assume the role. By the time of my arrival the parish had recently built a new church and supported a neighborhood school. The parish registered about 1500 families (many inactive). There were five Masses each weekend: one of them on Saturday evening at 7:00. Because of the late Mass on Saturday which meant weddings could be scheduled as late as 4:00 and the true beauty of the church, the former pastor witnessed as many as two or three weddings scheduled for every Saturday during the summer months. His chief maintenance man doubled as the marriage coordinator for the wedding rehearsals. On the day of the wedding, he appeared smartly dressed in a suitcoat that would match the color theme of the ceremony. At the Sunday Masses the ushers wore matching suit jackets with white pants during the summer months, otherwise black pants during the colder months. What struck me immediately was how neat and clean the entire parish property was. Two fulltime and extremely committed men for daily maintenance and two to three high school students on Saturdays saw to its upkeep with great pride and efficiency.

I began to move in, as requested, on the following Monday four days after the call from the personnel board. The pastor had moved out of his rooms so I would immediately have a place to sleep and be comfortable. He took up residence in a condominium not far from the parish boundaries. Two things happened on that first Monday that would govern the length of my ministry. A genuinely great and efficient secretary was my mainstay during those years. After I had made a few trips in and out of the rectory, I stopped to ask her what immediate issues I should address. Then I sat down across from her desk. She then reached over to hand me a shoebox. The box was filled with unpaid bills. "You can start with these," she said with a smile. Every Monday for my whole stay at the parish that was the same routine. The only difference was we were able to pay our bills on time and had a few dollars in a savings account. I remember some Mondays after the collection was counted, we would wait for the mail hoping we would receive a few checks from parishioners who were away or making up past Sunday offerings. With that extra money, we could pay our bills for the week hoping nothing would break and need repair. I cut down on rectory expenses, especially the cost of food. The other decision was to give myself a smaller salary than the diocese had decreed. I was to be paid a salary only if all our bills were paid by the end of the month. Sometimes I went without a salary.

The other Monday expectation was to be on hand for the weekly Bingo game. It became a whole new ministry for me. I would make it to the Bingo Hall, greet the players, and then help count the money that was brought to the rectory sporadically until 9:00. We did not want to keep too much cash in the Bingo Hall for safety's sake. After the players left, I had arranged for some refreshments to serve the dedicated volunteers in the basement of the original church now serving as the Bingo Hall. That would give me a chance to express my gratitude and carry on some great conversations while sometimes listening to complaints about some of the things I was doing (e.g., establishing a parish council, or committees for liturgy, social justice, family life). The complaints bothered me at first but then I realized I needed to learn to be more patient and understand "why" the complaints. Bingo was essential to paying our bills and supporting the school. Teams of the school parents volunteered to work the games on a rotating basis. However, there was one key group of regulars who worked every Monday night. I admired them greatly. The members would return early from their vacations, miss a family party, show up after a long day of work or find a substitute if necessary. Their dedication taught me a great deal. Even as I write these memories, I can see their faces, hear their voices and laughter. They inspired me, then and now, to remain faithful to my commitment of care and service even if it requires a change of my personal plans.

I must admit that the first year I was at the parish I was angry and frustrated because my dream job at the University of Notre Dame was denied. During the summer, the pastor made an almost daily visit to the rectory. His housekeeper was splitting her time watching every move I made and arranging/cleaning the retired pastor's new condominium. The three of us had a delicious dinner each evening with an unwanted guest (on my part): the

TV blaring in the dining room. One of the first things I did when I officially became the pastor on September 1st was to unplug the TV and relegate it to a nearby living room. The housekeeper told me that she was thinking of retiring on the same date as "Monsignor." In a very quick response I accepted the fact and told her I was grateful for her service and probably would not be replacing her because of finances. I must admit to a devilish plot on my part. I knew she was reporting my every move to the pastor and was checking my mail. So, I had my mother, using her family name, send me a postcard telling me that she enjoyed the interview. She would gladly start her housekeeping duties at the parish in September. Then I waited for the mail to arrive and enjoyed the subsequent conversation at dinner that night. I was not disappointed. I went to bed that night not just smiling but laughing loudly.

I decided to conduct a series of listening sessions during the fall. They would give me a sense of what the people were thinking about the future of the parish and elicit their ideas about possible needs with programming to meet those needs. I divided the parish into small groups, met at the rectory, served some refreshments, and listened. It was time well spent. People were satisfied with the parish as it was but also suggested ideas that could meet other needs present and future. For example, one of the first committees, we decided on, would be one to deal with social justice issues. I contacted the diocesan Office for Human Development that was offering parish-based workshops to inform participants concerning social justice in general using theology and scripture as a foundation. Then the leaders of the discussions would offer a possible methodology for integrating the theory and practice as a follow-up. What were the needs of the parish and how could we address them? We gathered some interested parties to become educated in the theology of social justice, explore ways to discover the justice issues, and finally consider how we might address them.

On my Communion calls to the sick and shut-ins I discovered a pattern. One day a woman I visited showed me her kitchen cupboard. All it had in it was a box of Lipton tea and a box of Lipton soup mix. That had become her diet because she ran out of her Social Security money for the month and needed to pay the rent. She was in her seventies and had worked her whole life. Another of my visits found me with another elderly woman who could not get out of the house to shop or even get to a doctor because her one remaining daughter worked and had limited use of a car. Still a third visit found me visiting a home where the woman was wrapped in a blanket because the house was without much heat. She told me that she only had enough money to heat the house once or twice a week, alternating between heat and having enough money to buy her groceries. An Italian-speaking husband and wife on the committee followed up on these visits. They were able to take them (and others) to the county social service departments to serve as interpreters for some. For them and others, they were qualified to receive some additional aid that these shut-ins had no idea existed. The committee did not change the world, but it did serve a need for a few. That is what it is all about!

Later, Tom Petronio, an ambitious college student from the parish, was looking for a project for his course on business advertising. He and I co-authored an article that was published in a religious magazine, *The Priest*, describing the process and its results from our listening sessions. He received a good grade and, I hope, some readers used the idea for their people.

Another member of the parish, Norm, joined the sessions on social justice. He stopped by the rectory one day "for a recommendation." A married man and now on disability, he asked if I would recommend him for the diocesan diaconate program. I had no problem with the recommendation, but I was curious why he was thinking of becoming a deacon. The three-year program would require occasional weekends away from home, course work (classes, meetings, assignments) and involve a supportive commitment from his wife. He knew all that, but he felt called to be of service to the parish in a very tangible way. I asked if he had any ideas what he could do for the parish. "I would like to visit the hospitals, the shut-ins and maybe do something for the widows and widowers." That would be the focus of his commitment to service. Not that I would stop him from entering the diaconate program, but I asked, "Is that the reason you want to be a deacon?" When he responded with a quick "yes," I offered to pay for two summer courses that were being offered at Saint Bernard's Institute that summer: both courses dealing with visiting the sick and the elderly. By this time, the seminary was closed for lack of students and financial issues. It formed an Institute housed on the campus of Colgate Divinity School. Norm was ecstatic about the possibility. This possibility was more realistic and he could more quickly follow his dream to serve a special group in need. And so he did. One of the many other memorable projects of his was to gather widows and widowers together monthly over a shared meal with an occasional speaker or some entertainment. The men and women were a real support to each other as they shared their loneliness due to the death of their partner and some dealt with new issues for which they had not been prepared (e.g. banking. lawn care, budgets for food and repairs, cooking). Given the age of many of the parishioners, Norm had quite a gathering of members. His interest and projects continued until his death a few years after I left the parish.

Now I want to share my first major financial project. When I first arrived, I asked the pastor if there were any major issues I might have to address. His reply was a quick "Yes! The roof of the church needs repair." I laugh now, as I would find that all three parishes where I was pastor needed roof repair. I knew nothing about roofs, but parishioners told me that when the church was being built, many of them saw future problems with its basic design. I called the company who constructed the roof. The owner came to the rectory. I told him about the issues with the roof. He told me that he liked Monsignor who hired him to build the church. I seemed to be a nice guy so he would give me a deal. "I can do the repairs for $110,000." I replied very quickly, "I will pay someone $10 an hour to put their fingers in the holes of the roof before I would pay that amount." He was not happy and left. We contacted two other contractors who made offers from $20,000 to $60,000 and a third who would do it for $40,000. I went with that one and was very satisfied with the work. No more leaking roof!

A few years later, after becoming the pastor, I hired a finance officer to take care of repairs, bills, and other financial matters. I realized that finance was not my gift. He had retired from Xerox and so did not need a large salary. The furnace that heated the school and church was malfunctioning. Our new hire asked me what I usually do when we have trouble with the furnace. I referred him to the company with whom we had a contract for annual maintenance and inspection. The cost for the repair would be $10,000. When he told me the potential cost, he asked if he could get some other estimates. I quickly responded, "You are the boss now and I trust your judgment." He approached another company who estimated the cost would be $4-5 thousand. Now daunted by the extreme difference in the two estimates, the "boss'" called a third company who inspected the furnace to give an estimate. The third company solved the problem by charging us for the necessary parts for the furnace ($79) and labor ($100). In the first 2 months of his hire, our new staff member saved the parish enough money to pay his salary for the year.

My Sabbatical (Fall 1982)

AFTER A FEW YEARS at the parish, I had the opportunity to go on sabbatical if I could pay for it myself. Two things were prompting me to go. I had contacted the Basilian Fathers to explore the possibility of joining their order so that I could teach full time and be part of a community. I had talked to the Superior General who urged me to pursue the idea. He, in turn, would check with one of the Basilian Fathers in our diocese to get his input about my leaving the diocese and joining their religious community. The other reason was to finish my dissertation about Thomas Merton. I made the arrangements for the sabbatical. I would spend the first 40 days at Guelph in Canada making the Spiritual Exercises at the Jesuit Prayer Center: 3 days of preparation, 30 days making the Exercises, and another 7 days reflecting on them for their possible use in my own life as well as sharing them with others. The Superior General of the Basilian Fathers arranged for me to live at their House of Studies near the University of Toronto's campus. In return, I would work on a regular basis with the non-Basilian seminarians residing at their House of Studies conducting a weekly group meeting as well as individual counseling or spiritual direction. This arrangement would allow me to spend the rest of the time researching and writing at no financial cost. I would return to the parish in early December to prepare for the holy days. It was a well-thought-out plan for me and for the Basilian community. "We propose; God laughs."

Before I left on the sabbatical, I received a call from the Superior General. He told me that a Rochester-based Basilian priest thought it would not be politically a good idea for me to leave the diocese to join a religious community. His argument was that the bishop was new to the diocese; he might be offended that one of his priests was asking to leave the diocese to join the Basilian Fathers. They and the bishop were on good terms. The Rochester Basilian thought it might cause a rupture in the relationship if they accepted me into their community. The Superior General assured me that the invitation to reside at the Basilian House of Studies was still there if I chose to accept it. I did.

My new associate pastor, a former student, was more than capable of handling the parish while I was away. Things were running smoothly with schedules and committees. I had no reason to worry about the parish. With that in mind I drove off to Guelph with excitement and an openness to the adventure. I wanted to explore the concept of freedom that was the basis for my dissertation. I thought a personal experience of the search for freedom would enable me to write more freely about Thomas Merton and his concept of freedom. As I drove to Guelph, about a four-hour drive north into Canada, I sensed a lightness of heart and relief from the worries about the parish. It was the first step in the journey to discovering the fruits of freedom.

Our group of retreatants met on Sunday night for an orientation meeting. The next three days would be an opportunity to slow down during a mini-retreat to prepare us for the thirty-day experience of the *Spiritual Exercises*. The group was international with Canadians, Australians, Americans with a combination of lay and religious, all told men and women all over thirty and most near fifty years of age plus. We met our own spiritual director the next day who would guide us through the Exercises. Mine was a Jesuit priest, a missionary, who was spending the year directing various retreats and giving talks in parishes to support his mission (I think in Japan). Our rooms were simple but comfortable: air-conditioned, bed, desk, a chair for the desk and another for relaxation and reading, and a private bath and shower. I think the idea was if you are comfortable, you can pray better. It worked! I found the food for our daily three meals to be outstanding, better than most restaurants. On the feast of Saint Ignatius of Loyola (July 31st) we had a particularly grand meal. Ignatius, the author of the *Spiritual Exercises*, founded the Jesuits in 1540. We celebrated him and those who lived his spirit for over four hundred plus years. The retreat center was away from the crowded cities and towns with a huge acreage of woods, trails, swimming pool, and a nearby cemetery. So, we had plenty of room for quiet walks and for me a daily 30-minute jog. Each retreat day we lived the same schedule: three one-hour periods of meditation after which we recorded our thoughts (a fourth hour could be added with permission), daily Mass, an hour with our director, time to walk or swim, and all this in silence: no talking except with our director. For me, the whole experience was like heaven on earth.

I have many memories of this time at Guelph. One of the ways I needed to be free was "to learn to let go." I had been praying for that gift for a few weeks. But how? Almost from the first day I had decided to give up lunch and go swimming. The other retreatants would be eating so I could go jogging (ah, those were the days!), relax in the sun in a comfortable deck chair next to the pool, then go for a swim. We had the same schedule every day except when it rained which was seldom. One day when I was in the pool foolishly by myself, I began to sink. I could not move my legs or arms. I panicked. "Why was I so stupid to go swimming by myself? Okay, what do I do?" Then it hit me. "Okay relax, let go, and see what happens." I did just that: I relaxed and let go of any struggling. I then had a sense that something (or someone) was holding me up with its hands. I began to float slowly and gently towards the side of the pool where there were steps. As I walked back to my chair, I muttered to myself "now I know how 'to let go': relax and someone will hold me up until I am safe." I knew who that "Someone" would be for me.

Another memory that has stuck with me over the years was my walks in the cemetery. It was close to the retreat center so I would usually walk there after dinner. I could walk off the dessert I ate and think about the day's events. One night I noticed a man standing next to a gravesite. He was apparently talking to the person buried near the tombstone. He left and I walked over to where he had been standing. Sure enough, it was the grave of a recently deceased person. I said a prayer for the man and the person buried there. I continued my walk. The next few days as I was on my usual walk, I noticed the same man talking at the gravesite. Not to disturb him I continued walking at a safe distance. One night I found him sitting at the same site weeping uncontrollably. I decided to go over to him and ask if I could help. He poured out his heart about the death of his wife; their wonderful relationship; how much he missed her. I listened without interrupting, expressed my sympathy, and told him I would pray for his wife and him: "Nothing profound," I uttered to myself. I returned the next night for my usual walk. There he was again. This time he was just standing at the grave, but when he saw me, he called me over. "I want to thank you for last night. I just needed to talk to someone. I appreciate the prayers. Keep them coming." Over the time I was on retreat he and I would have an exchange of greetings and a few words. I talked about the meetings with my retreat director. The bottom line was "Learn to listen not just with your ears, but your heart." I cannot solve my own problems, much less others, but I can listen.

Listening became a key practice for my subsequent years in ministry. A few years later I was called to the hospital to anoint a seventeen-year-old. His older brother had stopped by the rectory a few days earlier to talk about the possibility of being confirmed. He had been away from the practice of his religion for a while but wanted to set a better example for his brother. His parents were Italian who spoke little English. He became the spokesperson on their behalf whenever there was an issue outside the family house. When I arrived at the hospital there was a small group already standing around the bedside weeping. None of them spoke much English except for the brother who had visited me earlier. His younger brother's illness was sudden. Luckily, I had a copy of the anointing service in Italian. I could read Italian easily but had not mastered sufficient vocabulary for extended conversations. After I finished the anointing, we joined hands to recite the Lord's prayer in Italian. Looking around at the family and their friends, all that came to my lips was the phrase, "Mi dispiace" ("I am sorry"). Walking back to my car I was so angry with myself that I could not say anything more because I lacked the vocabulary to express my thoughts. Then driving home I had a sense of peace come over me: at least I was present, listening to them "with my heart in silence."

The four weeks of the Exercises ended. We spent the last week rehashing our experiences and attending a series of lectures that would help us use our experiences when we arrived back home. We had time to laugh together, share our experiences, attend a Shakespearean play at nearby Stratford and continue with informal meetings with our director. As I drove away from Guelph and headed towards Toronto, I had a sense of deep peace. Maybe it was the freedom I had because I had learned in different ways to "let go" and "listen with my heart."

I arrived at the Basilian House of Studies midafternoon on a very warm August day. I quickly unpacked my bags. Then I walked around the complex to find the chapel and the dining hall. Both would be the main places I would need for the next four months. I met with the rector to let him know of my arrival and to discuss what he might expect of me. Basically, he asked me to meet with the non-Basilian students one night a week for a few hours to discuss priestly ministry and listen to their issues. I could also set up individual meetings for counseling and spiritual direction. Then we headed out to Mass and dinner. The next few days I was busy learning names and asking questions like "Where is the laundry room?" I walked around the neighborhood to get my bearings for trips to the nearest movie theatre, coffee shop, a place to buy the *New York Times*. I set up a personal schedule: write in the morning for 3 hours; type and edit for 3 hours in the afternoon; jog for two miles and shower before afternoon Mass; read Thomas Merton books in the evening for a few hours; and finally read a lighter fare for an hour before going to bed. I kept to that schedule with a few exceptions for the length of my stay. Sundays were days to relax. I usually picked up the *New York Times*, stopped by a French coffee shop for coffee and French pastries, and read the paper. In the afternoon I visited museums, went to a movie, or browsed around bookstores. Sundays were a reward for the work of the past week. They also relaxed me for the week ahead.

In early September I was walking toward the library when I met one of Saint Michael College's popular professors. Some had pointed him out to me suggesting that I talk to him about my dissertation. I introduced myself and asked if he had any ideas how I might work on the project. He thought my planned schedule was a good start. Practically speaking, I should stay connected with my dissertation director on a regular basis. He encouraged me to keep writing to avoid the proverbial "writer's block." And "yes" I could make a significant dent in the writing in the remaining months of my sabbatical. I walked away from the conversation with added direction and a sense of hope. I continued my writing schedule. After I had finished chapters one and two, I called my director in Ottawa. We arranged for a meeting in two weeks; I would send the chapters out immediately and he would have time to make corrections and suggestions. I sent them as promised. When I arrived at his office two weeks later, he told me that they had not arrived, blaming the postal service. This was all before computers, file copies, and e-mail. Fortunately for me I had kept a carbon copy of my typed chapters but had not brought it with me. We talked about what I had written and some ideas for the next chapters. I drove back to Toronto frustrated and discouraged by the turn of events. By the time I arrived home, I was determined not to give up and so started chapter three.

Living in a House of Studies while writing my dissertation was ideal; almost all the residents were taking classes, preparing for tests, or writing a paper. It provided a mix of conversations over dinner. My weekly meetings with the non-Basilian members proved to be enjoyable for many reasons. The mix of participants alone was fascinating. Our conversations revolved around their acclimation to the courses, problems within the House of Studies ("we against them"), preparing for ministry within a parish assignment, celibacy, one's prayer life, and whatever other topics arose. I tried to establish a core topic for each session that allowed for a focused discussion with room for other issues. Because of a range of ages, different dioceses/religious communities, and even a member of an Eastern Rite Catholic studying for the priesthood, issues and opinions varied. For example, there was a unique conversation with the Eastern Rite student. Unlike my other advisees over my years as a seminary professor, his Rite allows for a married clergy. If he were to marry before his ordination as a deacon, he had the option to seek ordination as a married priest. His immediate problem centered around the young woman he was dating: Could she be the right partner as a priest's wife? How would he support a family? As a start, I gently counseled him just as I would the average young man dating and seeking a life-long partner. How he would integrate his married life among clergy, some of whom decided not to marry, would also be an issue that he had to weigh if he chose to marry. I often wondered what final decision he made.

Residing in Toronto I had the opportunity to celebrate Canadian Thanksgiving on the second Monday of October. Compared to the United States it was a low-key celebration but because of the number of US students, we did have turkey with all the trimmings (minus the cranberry sauce to my dismay). I decided to return to the parish and also spend some time with my parents for a more traditional Thanksgiving in November to enjoy turkey with cranberry sauce. I also picked up my mail at the rectory and arranged my schedule with the staff so that I would be home to celebrate the various end-of-Advent and Christmas festivities.

Apparently my lost two chapters eventually arrived in Ottawa. I had another two chapters done and so phoned my advisor to arrange another meeting with him. After three attempted phone calls, he still did not answer. I called the University to see if they could help me contact him. I was told that he had become extremely sick and was unable to teach his classes. "That might be the reason for his not answering his phone." Frustrated again I tried to figure out my next step. I was still thinking about it when I had to pack and return to the States.

My time at the Basilian House of Studies introduced me to some wonderful young men, a staff of Basilian priests who taught at Saint Michael's, a time for study and reflection. I returned to parish life with a deeper commitment that reflected my time at the retreat center, reading the works of Thomas Merton, and writing about him almost every day for four months. Reading, praying, and writing proved to be a formula for future action. The extended time away from the parish allowed time for me to think about other possibilities for my pastoral ministry through a different lens. I needed to "let go to be free."

Extra Parish Opportunities

WHILE I WAS ON sabbatical a new opportunity arose. I was enjoying the peace of writing my dissertation in Toronto when one day I received a call from Rochester's Saint John Fisher College (now, University). The Chair of the Religious Studies Department invited me to teach a course that was over-subscribed: Marriage and Sexuality. It was a very quick "yes." It had been a required course for all students in their senior year. Now it was an elective, but the number of students who wanted to take the class had grown. The full-time professor needed another section to accommodate the volume of students enlisting in the course. For the next 20 years I taught the course with him until his retirement. It became a trusting personal relationship. We both had a similar philosophy of education. Our commitment to deal with social justice issues in some practical way was a further topic of many conversations over the years.

The first semester that I taught the course, I had about thirty students, a bit smaller than the other professor's section. Then he decided to offer the course in the fall semester only and I would pick up the spring semester. That semester I had about sixty students and for a few years about 115. The Chair eventually suggested that I teach both semesters to allow for a smaller class size. No problem! Class sizes were initially restricted to 40 students until the college put a limit on classes at 30-35. This allowed for more personal contact with students, which I had hoped for all along. Little did I know that the part-time position would become a full-time position years later.

I began teaching the course using a combined syllabus from courses I had taught earlier at Ithaca College, Tompkins-Cortland Community College and Saint Bernard's Seminary together with the years of working as a presenter for Marriage Encounter, Pre-Marriage Encounter, as well as a program for the diocesan Pre-Cana teams. I also had prepared many couples for their weddings. My time as a judge on the marriage tribunal provided ample stories and examples of failed marriages. I was confident that I had enough practical experience over the years to make the course interesting for the students. It became one of the more popular courses at Saint John Fisher. One year the class was filled for in-person registration in 12 minutes. Some adventurous students arrived at the registration center at 4:00 a.m. and stood in line to be assured a place in the class. That story made me really feel good about the course and challenged me to work harder to assure that the students received their money's worth.

After a few years, I introduced a course on Catholic social justice issues called "Alienation and Powerlessness." I justified the course with the Chair of the department arguing that such a course was lacking in the college's Religious Studies curriculum. I also wanted him to recognize that I knew something about real life aside from Marriage and Sexuality. He agreed. To avoid competition with other mainline courses, we offered the course on a very unpopular day and time so it would not interfere with the other regularly scheduled courses in other departments. The first time it was offered I had a full class of about thirty-five students. I had hoped for at least fifteen. The second time, eighty students registered for the course. One of our department members was quite angry that the course was being offered and the numbers were outrageous. I heard about his anger so I made an appointment to see what the issue was. His indignant objection was a simple, "They do not even know what the word 'alienation' means." My response was equally simple, "Maybe they will by the end of the semester."

Over the years that I was an adjunct professor at the college, I also taught other courses to cover for full-time professors on sabbatical such as "Introduction to Religion" and "The Sacraments." When two of the professors retired at the same time. I was easily hired as a full-time professor although that came about 19 years later.

Before I started my sabbatical experience in Toronto, the neighboring Catholic high school, Bishop Kearney, called mid-semester to ask me if I could cover a required course on Catholic Church history because one of their teachers became ill. They were looking for someone to cover the course for the rest of the semester. I took the opportunity as a favor for them and for myself. I had not taught a regular high school class before. This would be a challenge in many ways especially because I had only taught graduate and undergraduate college level courses. Later they approached me again to see if I would consider teaching AP History because of my background in American history. One fall semester I taught an introductory course in philosophy since the teacher who proposed the course had found another job a few days before the school year began. About twenty students had signed up for it. Another time I taught a one term elective course, Introduction to

Psychology. My reading, workshops, and educational pursuits were paying off.

My time teaching high school students helped me hone my teaching skills and introduced me to some wonderful young men and women. The students in the AP history course were above average as students and very eager to learn. It was a small group comparatively speaking of 15-20 students. I could use a discussion-based approach and assign written assignments to prepare them for the required AP examinations. I knew most of them would continue on to college so, because of my background in college teaching, I was aware of what college required and that the AP examinations involved writing well-crafted essays. After one of the assigned essay papers was returned, a male student said to me, "There is more red on this paper than in the whole Red Sea." I had used a red pen for correcting papers. Another student later suggested I use a green pen because, "It is less threatening." I did and it was less threatening! A male student in another course, to my surprise, was doing quite well on the weekly quizzes and much better than I had expected. One day I distributed the quiz sheets but gave him a different one from all the rest. When I corrected the papers, I discovered, as expected, that he was copying the answers from others around him. He did not even read the questions. When I confronted him about it in a private conversation, he admitted that he cheated. "What can I do to make up for the cheating?" I told him when he got home to ask his dad what he should do. He reported back that it was one of the best conversations he had ever had with his father. Years later his father died. I went to the wake, having forgotten the "cheating event." The young man ran over to me, told me to wait there a minute. He went to the other side of the room, pulling the hand of a beautiful young woman along with him. "This is my wife," he said, "and I want you to meet her. I told her about you and how you got me to talk with my dad. I am so grateful that you made me do it. That is the best thing that ever happened during my high school years. And it made a difference in my life."

Back to the Parish

In case some might think that I had abandoned the parish, I can assure you that I was busy there also. I found some extra energy with the teaching. The salary stipends I earned, insignificant even by today's standards, subsidized what I was not taking from the parish. Looking back over the years of ordination, money was never the reason for me to do anything. Of course, I had no family to support, food and board was free, and my only expense was my car and trips to Stratford in Canada every summer for a week of Shakespeare and a musical. I was lucky to have a good staff of laypeople and some talented associates to support me. I really believe in a shared ministry, allowing staff to use their unique talents, and in our responsibility to each other as well as the parish family.

We had a happy rectory. One of our staff, Mike LaLiberte, lived at the rectory for a few years providing great service as a youth minister and helping with religious education programs. He was also an excellent cook, so I had no worries about eating good meals with lots of humor around the dinner table. He baked delicious apple pies! Saint John Bosco had long been my hero and one of the main sources of inspiration leading me to become a priest. He founded a home for boys who were homeless or lacking sufficient education to get a good job. I wanted wherever I lived to be such a place. I took into consideration the other priests' thoughts and feelings who lived with me and with their permission aimed to provide a safe haven for some young men trying to find themselves. Over my time at Annunciation parish, I provided space for a few college graduates who were devoted to the work of Dorothy Day and the Catholic Worker movement. One of them, named Bill, was working at Saint Joseph's House of Hospitality. When Bill returned to the rectory one night, he was bemoaning the fact that one of the men had no place to stay; there was no room for him at the House of Hospitality. "Could he 'crash' at our place?" We had limited space, but we could find a spot for him. He arrived at the rectory looking rather unkempt and rough on the edges. We toured the rectory and provided a place to shower and sleep. A few days later he disappeared. That is when I was told the whole story. The reason there was no room for him at the House of Hospitality was his temper. He had knocked another man to the floor and stabbed him with a knife. So he was asked to leave. Shortly after I listened (in dismay, I might add) to the story, I received a call from the bank questioning my credit card. There were some unusual charges: a dinner at one of the more expensive restaurants in downtown Rochester, a plane flight to one of the cities in Ohio, and a purchase of some bizarre gifts at one of the airline terminal's shops. Our two-night guest had stolen it out of my wallet that I had left on my desk overnight. The case was solved; the bank did not charge me. I was not upset about the theft but was angry because he went to a restaurant that I could not afford.

Then there was the time a judge called me. A young high school dropout had been arrested for stealing something from a store; his parents refused to take him back to their house. Could I help? What would Saint John Bosco do? His parents gladly relinquished their son into my care. We provided him with a bed and board. The next day we found him a job at a nearby fast-food establishment. Room, board, job, and a "family-like" living condition because what more could Tex (guess in what state he was born) ask for? Our rectory community welcomed him with open arms. All was going well. One day the transitional deacon who also was living with us took me aside to tell me "We've got a problem. Tex was dealing drugs from the rectory's front porch." As if that alone were not enough, the "drugs" he was selling were really altered aspirin tablets he pretended were "drugs." I shut down his business immediately and arranged for him to return to his family who by then had calmed down and welcomed him back home.

To update the records and find out how we could better serve the parishioners, the newly elected parish council decided that we should conduct a census of the parish. The census would help us plan and give us a pulse on the needs of people in the neighborhood. We looked for volunteers and had an amazing response. With the help of the diocese, we put together our own census form. We had a few meetings for the volunteers, went through the form with them, and emphasized the question, "How can we be of further help to you?" The time and effort proved immensely helpful for updating our Communion calls, planning our school enrollment, and other social needs. From then on, we would ask newly arrived parishioners to fill out a form so that we could continue updating data on new parishioners and their specific needs. The staff tried to do this in person so we would be able to meet and get to know new members of the parish. One of the points of information that proved helpful was observing how the younger families in the parish tended to move to the suburbs about the time their oldest youngster was about at third-grade level. Urban flight was a reality. We also discovered a few homebound people who would enjoy a visit from a staff member or, in some cases, a member of our recently founded Social Justice Committee. Although it was not the initial intent, the census also gave us sufficient information when we decided to pilot an increased-giving drive to encourage greater financial commitment in our Sunday collections. We hired a professional organization with highly successful outcomes to assist us with possible announcements, a form letter, and the mailings. The drive raised our income significantly. A few people were upset that we were asking for more money. One of them came to the rectory to tell us in person that she did not appreciate receiving a letter asking for money. "I don't even belong to this parish." When I checked our census cards she was indeed listed. I told her I was sorry, but we were using the information on our census cards. Her quick response caused me to laugh to myself. "Well," she said, "I did fill out the card when my husband was in the hospital. I heard of your parish's reputation for visiting the sick so I did want a church person to visit him. He has since died so I don't belong to your parish any longer." Her husband was buried from a nearby church.

To support the school, the parish had a long tradition of an annual two-day parish festival which took place towards the end of July. It was around July 26th, the feast of Saint Ann so we prayed for her intersession that the weather would be favorable. I remember at one of the planning meetings someone suggested that we should order some tents just in case it rained. I vetoed the idea, suggesting that we should have faith that our prayers for good weather would be granted. A few years later it did rain but stopped about two hours before the festival opened. That was a year my own faith in prayer was tested. We had a great committee who did the planning and worked hard during the whole festival. Some of our high school students formed a band. They used our church hall to perform. This added attraction provided our young people (and some older) a reason to enjoy the festival with popular music.

To help you better understand my next story I will give you some background. When I was studying theology in the 1950's the works of Teilhard de Chardin, a Jesuit paleontologist, philosopher, and theologian were suspect because of his views about evolution and how it would influence our understanding of Jesus. Later a friend of mine gave me a copy of one of his books, *The Divine Milieu*. It really impressed me, so I read more about him. He died on an Easter Sunday in 1955. Because of his writings, which had been suppressed, Teilhard was living in New York City while in exile from the Roman authorities. I had since read some additional books of his and became impressed by his deep faith despite the accusations levelled against him. It prompted me to pray often that I would die on an Easter Sunday myself. During one of the parish's festivals, I was touring the grounds to check if any supplies or added volunteers were needed. As I approached one of the booths, I heard some arguing and shouting. A man was brandishing a small handgun yelling that in the next two weeks, the *Inferno*, a nearby bar and restaurant, was going to live up to its name and burn. The gun was the problem. I insisted that he put it away or give it to me. About this time the police arrived as he was handing me the gun. They shouted, "Put it down." The man ran away. One of the officers told me, in no uncertain terms, I could have been killed. I could see the shocked look on his face as I replied, "No, it is not Easter." Then, I finished my rounds.

To add to the story, the *Inferno* did suffer a major fire a few weeks later. Two weeks after the fire the young man who made the prediction was killed in a drive-by shooting. His dream of forming a new "family" of young mob members was literally "dead in the street." I got to know his biological family because of the tragedy. About a year later in the winter his brother was arrested for burglary. I visited him at the county jail. We talked for a while as he assured me the police had the wrong person. He was convinced that they could not trace his footsteps "even in the snow" and that he could not account for an unusual amount of money in his jacket pockets. As I was leaving, I asked if I could do anything for him. All he wanted was for the bail-bondsman to get him out of jail so he could go home. I did make a phone call and he was released. I often wondered what happened when he returned home and where he is today.

I am not one who enjoys big celebrations for myself, but while I was at the Church of the Annunciation I wanted to observe the 25th anniversary of my ordination on June 4th, 1960. The Family Life Committee pressed me to have a small reception after our Saturday night Mass. My parents along with my sister, her husband and their children were invited. My mom wore a beautiful corsage (thanks to the committee) and my dad was dressed in a sharp looking suitcoat, shirt, and tie. My dad was usually informal so to see him dressed in a shirt and tie was a surprise. I think I could count on one hand the number of times I saw my dad with a tie. Someone took a picture of them that night which I still treasure. The music for the Mass was more beautiful than ever; the reception had enough Italian cookies to feed an army. I really appreciated the work of the committee. A surprise that night was a slide show.

The Barge (Erie) Canal divides the village of Brockport with three bridges to unite it. The north side of the village sits on the lower side of the

Canal. Many of the oldsters referred to it as "muckland" because of its soil. At one time in its early history the poor, especially the Irish, lived there. My dad's family lived there too when he was growing up. My mom lived on King Street on the south side of the bridge where the more privileged lived along with the core business stores and, of course, the college. My mother would humorously remind my dad where he came from and what side of the village she came from. His retort was "Remember where I found you: lying on a park bench, just a bag-lady." This banter was part of our family's joke for as long as I could remember. I told this story many times in sermons, talks, or marriage preparation meetings. Lo and behold, the narrator for the slide show asked the question, "How did Father Bill's parents meet?" The first slide showed a woman lying on a park bench with a bag at her feet. It was the loudest laughter I ever heard from my parents, The other guests joined in laughing and clapping their hands. My father asked for the picture so he could prove his point in future years. I did not want to spend money on a big dinner after the reception. The money could be used for the House of Mercy which was in its first house not too far from the parish. Instead, the staff gathered at my sister and brother-in-law's house for a hot dog roast. The 25th anniversary is one of my fondest memories.

I knew Sister Grace Miller, a Sister of Mercy, and her twin brother Neil, a priest of the diocese, for many years before his untimely death. Neil and I were in the seminary together. Sister Grace had made a strong commitment to the service of the poor and was known for her advocacy for peace and justice. She was hoping to purchase a small house as a haven for some of the city's poor and alienated. Our parish made a small donation to help her dream come true. Our Social Justice Committee also became involved. A few of them helped with some upgrades for the house and worked with some of its clients to collect clothes and food for the ministry of this new House of Mercy. I received reports from them about the progress of the renovation and its open-door policy. To celebrate working together, the parish committee invited their own committee to our parish hall for a special dinner. Because of its Italian roots, you do not need much of a reason to gather for a meal. Our committee would provide the food while theirs would provide some musical entertainment. Our seating arrangement was such that our committee made sure that the hosts and guests would not be sitting at separate tables but would have an equal number of each at each table. The conversations were loud and punctuated with much laughter. The meal and the entertainment met the standards of a high-class banquet. It was indeed a night to remember.

An essential element for any parish is its staff. I was incredibly lucky to work with some dedicated priest-associates, secretaries, lay ministers for youth, religious education, visiting the sick and shut-ins, liturgy, finances, janitorial staff, bingo volunteers, musicians, money counters for the weekly collections, social events, marriage and baptism preparations, and, of course, the principals and teachers in our school. Each brought different gifts; all had a deep and unselfish commitment to the parish and to each other. I could spend a great number of pages talking about each of them. The janitorial staff, for example, kept the buildings and grounds in perfect shape. Santo, whose mom and dad helped build the original church, was its meticulous leader. During the winter he would be plowing the parking lots and sidewalks around the school, church, and rectory at 5:00 a.m. to assure safe parking and walking for the school children and early Mass attendees.

Mary, a self-taught organist, provided music for weddings, funerals, and Sunday Masses faithfully without questions or objections: she was there to serve the parish. Two of the Sisters who taught school during the week led a folk group for our Saturday evening Mass. Both made their final profession of vows at the parish while I was the pastor. Both have continued keeping those vows to this present day.

While I was at the parish, we had two dedicated school principals: one was a Sister of Mercy, her successor was a very competent lay woman. The combined staff of Sisters of Mercy and dedicated lay teachers made the school a very special place. The students were so lucky to have them as part of their lives.

A mother and daughter team counted the money every Sunday and Holy Day without missing a day. They also made sure the priests had a good breakfast between Masses. Millie, the daughter, and her husband, Don, have continued to be an important part of my life over the years. Two sisters, Mel and Doris, at their own expense, spent two weeks at Notre Dame one summer to learn about liturgy. We were able to use their knowledge for beautiful, well-planned liturgical celebrations while I remained pastor. Our church always had a well-decorated sanctuary throughout the year. One of my favorites was Rochester's annual Lilac Sunday and Festival. Parishioners were invited to bring lilacs to decorate the church. The number of vases of lilacs allowed for a wonderful smell of lilacs to permeate the whole church. The parish was not rich financially, but it was extraordinarily rich in talent and commitment. My years there prepared me for the next two parish assignments as a pastor. The people were gentle and inspiring teachers. I like to believe that I was a good student.

Looking around the diocese with the declining number of younger priests and the fewer number of seminarians, I began to wonder about the future of clerical leadership in our parishes. For example, who would lead the parish of the Annunciation? My immediate thought was "the people from the parish." I sent out letters inviting fifty possible lay leaders for the parish to participate in a two-year course of discussion about the teachings of the church: its theology, moral teachings, history, and liturgy. Bible study had already been an important part of parish life. All fifty replied. Twenty could not do it because of other commitments. The other thirty made a commitment to the course. At the time, the only text that was available was Richard McBrien's book, *Catholicism*. We started with page one, reading, and discussing its content for two years. I had a series of video tapes that presented the history of the Church that I used to break up the more difficult hours of the class which met each week for an hour and a half. Towards the conclusion of the theological sessions, I asked if there was anything else they might want to discuss. Someone suggested "Canon Law." That took me by surprise, but others chimed in remembering different questions about marriage, annulments, baptism of infants that they heard people ask during our coffee hours or parish visitations. I invited a former student of mine, Fr. Kevin McKenna, who had his degree in Canon Law as a resource to answer their questions. Between the two of us we hit some of the high points of the Church's laws and procedures. This satisfied them because it was so practical. The members of the group were not being asked about the Trinity or questions about the historical Jesus, but they were asked questions like "Why and where my baby should be baptized?" After I left the parish, one of the "graduates from the sessions" challenged my successor quoting one of the canons to remind him what church law said about his responsibilities and obligations. I would have enjoyed listening in on that conversation.

Forty years later some of us (Don and Millie Lewis together with Fr. Ed Palumbos, a former associate pastor) continue to get together for dinner on a regular basis. One of the families, the Wiktorski's, had invited me to an occasional dinner while I was pastor. I still spend many Sundays, holidays, and family celebrations with them even after their own mother and father died. I think they were the first family of many who invited me over for dinner. Watching their sons, grandsons, an exuberant granddaughter, and now a great-grandson grow in their chosen fields reminds me of my own aging, but also how lucky I am that I went to the parish "kicking and screaming" only to find the kind of friends that no money could buy. To this day I do not use the word "friend" lightly.

Surprise (1988)

AGAIN, I WILL GIVE you some background. At that time in our diocesan history the priests of the diocese elected six members to the Priests Personnel Board, each representing a different age group. They served as consultants to the full-time Personnel Director. Pastors, when appointed, served for a term of six years renewable once. When their term ended, the parish provided general information about its staff, sacramental life, finances, and possible goals for the next pastor. This was sent out to all the priests of the diocese. If a priest was interested, he could apply for the assignment. The board would look at the various applications, considering the needs and unique personality of the parish. When the board made their choice, the candidate's name would be submitted to the bishop who in turn, if agreeing, would contact the successful candidate to make the appointment official.

During that same period, our diocese conducted an annual Thanksgiving Appeal. The money would be used to support the various offices and programs of the diocese. To meet the goal each year, pastors and their finance committees needed a great deal of energy and creativity to sell the purpose to the parishioners. The diocese employed a professional development company to offer suggestions, print material, supervise the mailings, and conduct training sessions to assure that we were all on the same page. One year the diocese contracted with a new organization whose idea was "big givers" and pastors with their parish committee chairperson would meet with the bishop (uncomfortably dressed in a cassock which was not his style of dress) for a reception with drinks and light refreshments.

Shortly before the required reception, there was an article in the newspaper about a parish that was up in arms with the pastor, the parish council, other parishioners, and the diocese. Each seemed to blame the other for a variety of issues. Basically, it came down to the style of leadership that each demonstrated (or failed to demonstrate). I heard rumors about some of the activities to quell tempers. One thing was for certain the diocese was going to appoint a new pastor. A letter went out seeking applications. At the reception I happened to run into the Urban Vicar. We had served together in Ithaca years before and had a good relationship because of our mutual enjoyment of a good laugh. After a few words about what each of us was doing, I asked him "Who was crazy enough to write in for that parish?" He looked at me and with his usual laughter replied, "Funny you should ask. We thought that you would be the ideal candidate." Everything was going well at my parish assignment; I enjoyed teaching my class at Saint John Fisher College so my answer was a very quick "NO!" "Think about it and I will get back to you by Wednesday." My answer on Wednesday was still a "NO!" "We can sweeten the pie and give you an assistant." Still "NO!" "Okay, if we can't find someone else to go, I will get back to you on Friday." On Friday, no call so I thought I was off the hook and continued my plans for the next year. On Sunday night I was listening to some music and reading when the telephone rang. It was the bishop. "Hi. Bill, it's Matt Clark. I want to invite you to be the pastor of Most Precious Blood parish." "NO!" I listed all the reasons I did not want to go. It was quite a list. He listened patiently and said, "Well, think about it, pray about it, and get back to me tomorrow morning. I will be in the office." I took a deep breath and said, "Matt, if the board thinks I am the right guy for it and you agree, I will go. Sorry for the outburst." He laughed. Then we talked about his summer plans and said, "Good night!" Off I went to my next assignment a month later. Once again: "We propose; God laughs."

Most Precious Blood Parish (1988-1998)

SAYING GOODBYE TO THE people whom I came to love and who taught me so much about becoming a pastor was difficult. One of the parishioners from Most Precious Blood parish arranged for me to have a truck to take my belongings to my new home. Packing, as always, was a chore: what to take and what to throw away. Once I survived that hurdle, I drove to the new assignment with some tears in my eyes and fears in my heart. I was sad to leave, but nervously excited about whatever was before me. The drive was less than 20 minutes, but it took me the last nine years to make it. Memories of those special years flooded my mind: grateful for the successes and repentant for the failures. To this day I have flashbacks to some challenging encounters in my various assignments and whisper, "I am so sorry! I could have handled 'that' issue or person better."

I arrived at my new home in midmorning. I carried the few items to my new quarters in a genuinely nice rectory that matched the simple architecture of the church, the school, and the empty convent. The Sisters who had helped staff the school had all left for other assignments. I stopped by the office to meet and briefly talked with the secretary, Marge, who asked me if I would like lunch. "We usually eat around noon." With a quick "Yes" Marge told me that the cook/housekeeper, Angie, would have something ready. I spent the next hour arranging some books in a neat built-in bookcase. Angie called me to the dining room for lunch. The table was set for one person with a cup of hot soup skillfully placed on my plate. I looked out at the kitchen where both the secretary and the cook had their places set for lunch. I invited them to bring their dishes with them so we could eat together. I would enjoy their company. Angie, an older Italian grandmother, proved to be a great chef and the most welcoming person whenever we had guests for lunch. There was always enough food for everyone. From that first day until the day I left, the three of us always ate together even when there were other guests, including the bishop. My fondest memories of the assignment are the laughter around that table for the next 11 years.

That afternoon I spent a few hours with the secretary who took care of greeting people who would drop by to pick up a Mass card, schedule a Mass, or just telephone her office to talk. Because Marge was so efficient, the financial books and typing the weekly bulletin were neatly taken care of every week. Her delightful sense of humor cemented our relationship almost immediately. We were a team from the first day. I quickly found out that there were some financial issues that needed immediate attention. That whole summer was spent trying to figure out our bills; some were overdue including the IRS. I made the same arrangement as at Annunciation. I was to be paid only when we had enough money for all the other expenses. In one of my early years as their pastor, I told the Sunday Mass-goers that I would welcome any donations of canned food they might want to drop off in the vestibule of the Church. This would save some money from the rectory food budget. I ate very well thanks to their generosity.

The second day I was there I went to the school to spend some time with the new principal and check out the facility. The school was the parish's prize possession reflected in the herculean efforts to build and sustain its enrollment and programs. At one time the beloved founding pastor, "Fr. Sebastian," drove a parish-owned school bus to bring the students to and from the school. When Bishop Sheen was going to close the school about twenty years prior to my arrival, the parish protested and won the battle to remain open. The weekly Bingo games, managed and sustained by committed families, were a major source of income for the school. Like my previous parish assignment, I made sure to be a part of the volunteer group every week. The faculty and staff provided a great education and a warm environment for the children. Because we had pre and after school care centers, some of the staff was committed to longer days than at other schools. Unfortunately, about halfway through my tenure the Catholic Schools in the county were forced to merge because of financial and enrollment issues. Most Precious Blood School was one of the victims. The meetings and committees dealing with the issue occupied our time for a few years. They seemed to be never-ending and not very comfortable for any of us. There were many angry parents and administrators! I was on sabbatical in the Holy Land when the news of the closing finally broke. Because of serious violence at the Temple Mount in the city of Jerusalem, our group as well as the whole neighborhood was under quarantine, bullets were flying on the streets, the smell of tear gas permeated the air, and armed patrol cars with loudspeakers passed our living space reminding people not to leave their homes or they would be shot. A member of our group was terrified by the violence. My remark did not calm him. "You think this is bad? You ought to be part of parish school closings."

Early in my time at the parish a small group approached me to conduct a weekly service on Monday nights at 7:00 p.m. with the recitation of the rosary and Benediction of the Blessed Sacrament. I agreed to it with the warning that I might occasionally be away on Monday evenings. "Would your group commit to leading the service (without Benediction) if I were not here?" "No problem" was the response. Eventually this was extended to a full hour of prayer. Every Monday we had a small group of volunteers who led the service and covered for me if I were not present. I am convinced it was this Monday "hour of prayer" that helped the parish deal with the pressing issues we faced over the time I was pastor.

Much like the Church of the Annunciation, the generosity of time and talent was overwhelming. The strongly committed liturgy group met each month. The enthusiastic group would discuss and delegate the members for decorating the church for special feasts with amazing artistic creativity. The church itself was always neat and clean. The worshipping community was extremely fortunate to have a great organist with a beautiful voice. She also rehearsed with the mixed choir weekly to provide moving music for our main Mass every Sunday. During those years our parish hosted a variety of retreats ranging from the traditional devotion to the Blessed Mother with small group-sharing in parishioners' homes to a series of sessions in the spirit of the popular charismatic movement. Father Joseph Girzone, author of a widely read book, *Joshua,* and other books, spent a week with us preaching and teaching. He used our parish family as a model for some of his later writings, especially our openness to working with others who were not members of the parish community. When he returned to Rochester to speak at other parishes, he would do so only if he could stay at our parish rectory. Another long-time devotion made the month of July special. Each year the Saint Ann's Society met for their annual parade during which the police blocked traffic until the marching band and participants reached the church, Mass (with a few words in Italian), and concluding with a luncheon to honor Saint Ann and celebrate the parish's Italian roots. I always enjoyed parades growing up but marching in one was another unforeseen challenge. Looking pious with a marching band playing some seasonal songs brought a smile to my face.

One Advent our parish council decided to have a Giving Tree as part of the Christmas preparation. Families would take tags for some needed items from two trees located in the sanctuary area and return the tag with a gift sometime during the Advent season. There was a large collection of gifts under both trees. Better than halfway through Advent, I walked into the church on a Monday morning. Most of the gifts were gone. The tabernacle had been broken into, and the sanctuary was slightly upset. The people arrived for daily Mass only to find their church "violated." Someone must have called a local TV station that reported on such events in their evening news segment featuring "investigative reporting." They arrived with cameras and a reporter who interviewed me. My comment was "I hope those who broke in needed the things they had taken. Our parish would have gladly given them the gifts without all the damage." For the next few days, the parish rectory was flooded with boxes of canned food, gloves, hats, soap, toothpaste, and money. I received a call from a man who volunteered to install a security system in the church for free. We took him up on the offer. The parish was able to help more people because of the break-in than we could have otherwise by distributing just the gifts under the Giving Tree. The church became more secure, the sanctuary was put back together, the tabernacle repaired, more people received gifts of food and clothing, and our parish family enjoyed the special blessings of the season.

    I was extremely lucky to have an excellent associate working with me during my time as pastor of the parish. Sister Francis Mary, a Sister of Saint Joseph, had served as a pastoral associate in a nearby parish so the journey from her one assignment to Most Precious Blood parish was only about five minutes away. Because she spoke Italian, she was especially committed to working with the older members of the parish as well as visiting the sick and homebound. Her smile and sense of joy reflected a deep faith in her calling. Our lunches together with the cook and secretary were so relaxing that it made our time together a source of energy for the afternoon's work. Sometimes the principal of the school would join us to enjoy a few minutes from administering school business. The parish was later blessed with the presence of a married deacon who helped with preaching, baptisms, and however else he could help. John blended in with our motley staff.

    One year the parish was fortunate to have a deacon intern, Tim Niven, as part of our staff. It was his pastoral year in preparation for his ordination to the priesthood. The various committees (liturgy, social, choir, parish council, school) worked together with Tim for the celebration of his ordination and first Mass. For a few days, the rectory was filled with some of his seminary classmates who ventured to Rochester to honor him and enjoy our parish's great hospitality. Tim asked me to preach at his first Mass. It was scheduled for Trinity Sunday. I was relieved that I did not have to preach about the mystery of God and the Trinity for a change. The event was a huge success. Twenty-five years later we are still able to laugh and tell stories about that very happy year. The entire staff made a great team dependent on each other to cover all the needs of the parish family with a sense of joyful commitment to be of service to all who came to our doors.

Allow me to change gears in my story. Over the years at the parish, we had many people populating the rectory. There were the occasional overnight visits of priests who had roots in the parish or people from my past who were in town for a few days and needed a place to stay, but we also had more permanent residents. Jack Balinsky, a graduate of Notre Dame University and an extremely capable leader, was hired by the diocese as the chief executive of Catholic Charities. Jack was single and needed a residence near the Pastoral Center that could provide a home base for sleeping and eating. Our morning breakfasts together allowed time to get caught up with activities throughout the diocese. Jack had meetings in every section of our twelve- county diocese so I heard the news firsthand of projects and issues that parish leaders were pursuing. Jack had boundless energy and a fantastic memory for facts and figures from his many meetings.

Jack moved out of our rectory to take up residence at another parish when two brothers from Ghana took over his room. Now there is a story! I continued my teaching at Saint John Fisher College sharing an office with Bill Sullivan, one of the full-time faculty who was strongly committed to many justice issues. Two of our students were arrested for allegedly attempting to sell illegal drugs. They were in jail awaiting trial. Bill, my officemate, was in contact with the two young men. The judge was willing to let them out of jail if they could be housed in a safe and controlled environment. Bill asked me if I would let them live at our rectory. Jack's room had twin beds. Jack saw the need and was willing to move to another rectory. A few days later the two young men moved in. I will never forget our first meeting. I met them at the door, Bill introduced me to Eric and Mike. Each was over six foot tall and built like well-developed athletes. They kept thanking me as both hugged me. I felt like I was in a vice. After Bill left, I showed them their room. Then the two brothers asked if they could sit with me for a few minutes so I could know their story. Their father was attached to the United Nations delegation from Ghana; they came as youngsters to the United States; both arrived at Saint John Fisher because one was recruited for the football team. By the way, they learned English by watching TV programs, especially cartoons. Neither had planned to sell the drugs but acted as "mules"' to transport them to Rochester. A student informant turned them in as part of a plea deal she made because of her own drug arrest. Because my two new residents were not citizens, they were easy prey for the legal system which would eventually deport them. At least that first night both were happy to be out of jail and in a safe place.

To detail their entire stay at the rectory would take a whole chapter. Suffice it to write that the whole experience during their residence was filled with laughter, court appearances, visits from a court-appointed social worker to assure they were not selling or using drugs at the rectory, shopping trips to help carry grocery bags for Angie, and their exuberant contributions to cooking and cleaning. I realized that I could not expect the parish to pay for the food and utilities they would consume so I arranged for financial help from outside the parish as well as from the money I was making from teaching. When their mother came from New York City to visit, they would shake in fear because each knew that they would be in for individual and "group" scolding for their misbehavior.

On one occasion Bishop Clark, a bishop who embraced anyone in need, came for lunch to enjoy international cuisine along with a great deal of laughter and banter. I will explain "cuisine" later. Bishop Clark would later visit them in the jail in Geneseo after their sentencing and eventual deportation. The older brother told me that the chief warden had all the inmates cleaning and polishing the whole facility. When Eric asked the warden why they were doing all the housework, his simple reply was "Your bishop is coming to visit you and I want him to see how clean we keep the jail." Our Marge and Angie also went to visit them. When asked by the guard what their connection was to the prisoners, they replied that Eric and Mike were family. Even when they were imprisoned, they both kept their sense of humor. Most of the times that I visited them, we would laugh remembering the many good times we all had living and working together in the "group home" (their term, not mine). We lived together for the nine months at the rectory. It was supposed to be a few weeks. Eventually, after a few other jail experiences to process them out of the country, they returned to Ghana. I think of the choked voices and tears whenever our "family" gathered around the dinner table and spoke of them. When they arrived back in Ghana, we kept in contact for a few years. Now, they are precious memories. I have lost contact with them both.

To explain our "international cuisine" I need to go back a few years after my arrival at the parish. The Priests Council had been working on a rotating schedule for priests who wanted to go on a sabbatical. This time around funds were available to allow for a mandatory spiritual as well as an educational component for the sabbatical experience. I had to fund my first sabbatical ten years earlier without support from the diocese. In mid-winter, the diocese sent a letter inviting anyone interested in going on a sabbatical to submit his request. The next day I opened the mail to find a brochure from the Catholic Theological Union (CTU) located in Chicago. The Union was offering a six-month sabbatical program to the Holy Land including time in Greece and Turkey, a three-month residence in Israel/Palestine, and a two-week excursion in Egypt. Two scripture scholars would be our leaders: Sister Barbara Reid and Fr. Carroll Stuhlmueller. I had read some of the books and articles he had authored so was excited about the possibility of learning from this renowned Hebrew Testament scholar while living in the Holy Land. I applied to the diocese for the sabbatical and to the Catholic Theological Union on the same day. A few weeks later both accepted me. Coverage for the sacramental life of the parish was arranged; the staff would take care of its daily needs. I began with a retreat at the Jesuit Retreat Center in Eastern Point, Massachusetts; returned to Rochester to pack for the next phase of the sabbatical and flew into Athens a few days ahead of schedule to explore the city for myself before joining my sabbatical group. When our group arrived in Jerusalem a month later, I contacted a young Basilian priest I had met on my first sabbatical in Toronto. He was working on his doctor's degree in Sacred Scripture at the Ecole Biblique, a prestigious center of learning with a faculty of outstanding scholars. Our meeting led to a discussion of how he would like to send a few Palestinians to the United States to earn a college degree, They, in turn, would return home to be leaders in their faith communities. My job, he suggested, would be to watch over them during their stay in Rochester. He would tend to the expenses of their education and living situations. I met with some of the aspiring students and dined with one of their families one evening. I was impressed with the family's hospitality and their hopes for their son if only he could go to America for his education. After he both graduated and returned home, I would visit him. I was treated like a "Messiah" who provided their son with an opportunity to live a better life. His parents are since deceased, but Youssef keeps in contact with occasional emails and even a telephone call. He manages a five-star hotel in Jericho, has a family of his own, and continues to be grateful for his time at the "group home." One other Palestinian student, Fadi, who would join our rectory family, graduated, and now manages the youth programs for the Palestinian community in his home country.

The summer after I returned from my sabbatical, I greeted the three young men and the priest who had made all the arrangements at the airport. Two of them stayed with me until the fall semester began. One would attend Saint John Fisher; the other would attend Nazareth College. The third would live with a family so he could attend Aquinas Institute, a high school run by the Basilian Fathers. I remember a few days later taking them out to the countryside so one of them could practice his driving skills to prepare for a driver's license. The three were in awe of all the green trees, grass, fields of corn and wheat. Their homeland did not have that kind of landscape. Of the three one would graduate from Saint John Fisher College. A second (the

Aquinas student) would later attend and graduate from Nazareth College. The third had been a "student activist" at Bethlehem University, a Vatican sponsored interfaith school for Palestinian students. He was committed to the Intifada movement and felt guilty that he was living in comparative freedom and luxury. After a few months, he chose to return home to support the Palestinian cause. For a different reason, the need to make their parents proud, the other two remained until their graduation.

However, neither adapted well to residential life at the colleges so ended up living at our rectory. The original plan did not work out quite as promised so a parish group from Canada helped with the expenses. I was able to find money locally from some parishes who were tithing their Sunday collections to help the poor and needy. I joined the University of Rochester's study for a cure for HIV and received a nice stipend for being a subject. That is a story for another day. The two young men helped around the rectory and once they received their drivers' license found part-time jobs for pocket money. One of them had studied to be a cook in Jerusalem. This is a long background story to explain "international cuisine." The two from Palestine and the two from Ghana became immediate friends and worked together to prepare meals from their culture along with traditional American fare. The four, all with ferocious appetites, worked together to prepare the annual Thanksgiving meal with all the trimmings. The meal was consumed in less than twenty minutes with little left over . . . including the turkey. I kid you not. I took note of the short time to consume the meal when I saw the empty serving platters and the individual dishes now clean of any food: twenty minutes. This is one of the stories I enjoy telling for many reasons, among which is the mutual support they gave each other . . . laughing all the way.

On one occasion, as mentioned earlier, the motherly Angie and the "Fearsome Four" prepared the "international cuisine" (a mixture of Ghana, Palestine, Italy) meal for Bishop Clark who, in turn, praised the meal. He probably enjoyed the banter and exchange of stories even more as we sat around the table: the four young men, the cook, the secretary, the bishop, and me. I felt like a proud father as I looked around the table to observe Christian love in action. The bishop, as I mentioned, would repay the experience with a later visit to the jail in Geneseo to check in on the two from Ghana. He would often ask about them in succeeding years. The bishop remembered the meal and the banter. Now back to the parish.

The parish members contributed much of their time and talent to making the facilities and daily needs run smoothly. We also needed money to pay our bills, especially the unexpected ones from the past, e.g., the huge IRS bill for unpaid taxes. Again, we were lucky. One of our parishioners,

Lou, served on the Finance Committee and helped subsidize the balance of our quota for the diocesan campaign called the Thanksgiving Appeal. Louie also gave us a used trailer that helped with storage space; he later helped us build a huge barn-like storage facility that provided enough space for all our needs. He and another parishioner plowed our parking lot for free every winter. Both came up with another idea to raise money by reaching out to their influential friends for raffle tickets at $100 per ticket with a free banquet and entertainment. This event provided an annual $25,000 addition to pay our bills. The money and the banquet relieved some fears about the future of the parish. I found our generous sponsor was not only helpful to the parish but also watched him assist many other people with their financial problems. Occasionally just the two of us would have lunch together. While we were eating one day, he received a call on his cell phone. The caller was a friend who needed a loan for $70,000. Could he loan him the money? He said "yes" and after he hung up, he turned to me to tell me that is what we do for our friends. Another time, we had lunch with some other businessmen. When the bill came, my friend picked up the bill. One other member in the group offered to take care of the tip as he counted out five twenty-dollar bills. The others at the table complimented him about his generosity. "Aw, that's nothing," he bragged. As we were leaving, I looked back at the table and saw him quickly pick up two of the bills and tuck them away in his pocket. There is generosity and then there is "generosity."

The Finance Committee helped with the sale of the convent. After the Sisters left, we rented it for a year to a large family whose father worked for the diocese. Then Mount Carmel House, a hospice facility funded by a wonderful couple and staffed by several volunteers, rented the convent; a few years later they chose to buy it from the parish. The added money helped us with our bills and further upkeep of the parish. A financial advisor volunteered his service to see how we could invest the money for a steady income. When the school closed, the same group, along with a lawyer from the parish, helped with the contract to rent out the school to a day care center that was desperately needed in our area of the city. We were convinced that with the school forced to close, we could still provide a place for our younger neighborhood children to enjoy a safe place for care. The places of business and factories in the area also had a more convenient place for their employees' children to spend the day. The positive working relationship with the Hospice and the Day Care Center continued the mission of the parish.

And, Meanwhile

THINGS WERE GOING ALONG well within the parish. Meanwhile, I continued teaching a course at Saint John Fisher College. While I was on my sabbatical, Monroe County Community College tried to reach me. They needed an instructor to teach one of their required courses for those pursuing a degree in one of their "helping careers": The Psychology of Interpersonal Relations. As soon as I arrived home in early December, I called the Chairperson of the Psychology Department to express an interest. He had heard of my background earlier from another faculty member. The college needed someone to teach such a course in the spring semester and was anxious to hear if I was interested. I was. I met with him, filled out the necessary papers, took a tour of the college buildings, and began teaching the course in mid-January when the semester began. Because it was a State school, there was a union that represented the faculty e.g. only thirty students maximum in a class. I also did not wear clerical garb. I was not used to small classes and so welcomed the opportunity to attempt some new techniques for smaller group discussions. I continued to teach there for about five years. During those years I also continued to teach a course in another department: Introduction to Philosophy and Philosophy of Religion. One summer the head of the psychology department asked me to teach the Sexuality and Marriage course. He had never allowed anyone else to teach the course but "trusted me." The course, with its mix of students, made it one of the most open discussions about sexuality and marriage that I ever had. I walked out of the classroom after each session with a sense of exhilaration because of the students' challenging questions and differing insights.

I have many happy memories of my experience at MCC. One of the compliments I received involved student retention. My classes had one of the best retention rates. One of the requests I made of the students during our first class meeting was a simple "If you are thinking of dropping the course, talk with me or with another student. We can help each other and successfully finish the course together." The approach introduced a support system for those thinking about "dropping out." One semester I taught Psychology of Interpersonal Relationships in the evening. I introduced a period of meditation as part of the class whose members arrived tired from their day at the place of employment, a quick meal at home, or after a busy day of other classes. I was sympathetic because I was feeling the same way. The short period of meditation and mindfulness allowed us all to slow down and relax before we began discussing the course material. One night I forgot and was immediately reminded, "We need to slow down and meditate." The students discovered that this kind of practice could help them in their daily lives as well as their interpersonal relationships.

In another section of the same course another year I met an outstanding student, a young man of color. Joe was attentive during the classes, asked the best questions, and offered some thoughtful insights about the material we were discussing. He missed class for an entire week. Because I was concerned, I went to his counselor to see if he was sick or dropped out of school. "He is back in jail," she said. Later when I visited him in the County jail, he told me his story. He was arrested for stealing and served a short time in jail before being put on parole. Joe was then caught shoplifting and was now back in jail. My immediate thought was, "How could I help him finish the semester and get some college credits?" I talked with a few of his teachers who were equally impressed by him and arranged to tutor him every week in jail for the remainder of the semester so he could earn college credits in English and Sociology courses as well as mine. We provided the required books he needed to read. Joe wrote some papers, and I quizzed him on his weekly reading assignments. It was amazing how well he comprehended the material. Our discussions were a joy and, moreover, I learned so much from his pointed questions and insights myself. His ten-page handwritten paper was perfect with well-constructed sentences with *no* misspellings and was amazing to read. He discussed Michael Harrington's *The Other America*, a book required for his Sociology course, with keen insight, making a few suggestions that Harrington might further explore. He finished the courses and earned college credits.

Between the time Joe was in jail and his sentencing for violating his parole, I decided to go to Albany to talk with the gentleman who could make a recommendation about further prison time or its alternative. I went with the intention of exploring the idea of finding a way to block the young man's return to prison. There were a few sleepless nights and lots of prayer to make my decision. I offered to take his place. Rather than he be returned to prison, I asked the chief parole administrator for the State if he could arrange for my incarceration rather than this bright young man. As I drove to Albany that morning, I became more convinced that I wanted to make that kind of deal. When I presented the possibility to the administrator, he thanked me for the offer. There would, however, be no such possibility for it to happen. I drove home that afternoon. relieved in some ways but sorry in other ways. What a waste to send him back to prison! At least I tried.

Joe did not get released from jail but was transferred to Elmira Reformatory. I kept in touch with him so when he was released, we met for a meal and conversation. He found a job, eventually got married, and at the reception I had a chance to meet Joe's mother who had travelled from Florida for the wedding. What a happy event for us all. I often wondered what became of him. He inspired me and I hope his troubles inspired him to make a difference.

Monroe Community College still holds a special place in my heart for many reasons but mainly because the college had a wide diversity of students. In one of my courses, I asked the thirty students what language they spoke at home. Five languages were noted as well as one student who volunteered that his family used sign language to communicate with one of his parents. In another class there was a wide diversity not only of skin color, but also of age, economic background, and reasons for being at MCC. The latter included high school graduates who could not afford tuition at a four-year college; students who had failed out of a four-year college who needed to make up courses and/or raise their GPA; students laid off from work who needed to prepare for another job. I enjoyed the natural diversity as opposed to the forced diversity. In the course, Introduction to Philosophy, I spoke often that we are all "natural philosophers" seeking answers and formulating a way of life that sustains us in our daily lives. Because I used small groups for discussion, there was a chance to exchange ideas on a more intimate level.

There was a small group of four or five older women of color e.g., married, single parent, or just holding down a full-time job while going to school. They asked the best questions which, in turn, allowed for other groups to suggest a possible answer or ask for more information about the stories behind their questions or "philosophical" insights. The dynamics in the classroom were both spontaneous and challenging. Sometimes I felt I needed to blow a whistle to stop the "heated" discussions within the group and/or between the groups. The group of older women of color often shared their philosophies of life in such a way that they settled questions of some and/or gave comfort to some of the other younger students' questions or challenges. These women were "natural philosophers." They proved my point that we are all people seeking answers and developing answers in search of better questions and answers.

The faculties and administrators at the various schools and colleges I was part of over the years often spoke of the need for greater diversity in their classrooms. I was lucky enough to have enjoyed that gift. The experience of true diversity prompted me to listen better and discard biases that interfere with relationships. I received a salary for the time at MCC but learned more from the students. I could pay them back with a heart filled with gratitude for their honesty and support.

After teaching at the college, I returned one year to take a night course in German. It had been a long-sought desire because of my interest in German composers. For example, I wanted to translate the chorus from the third movement of Beethoven's Ninth. Yes, I could have found a translation, but I wanted to make my own translation. Our teacher was raised in Germany during Hitler's regime. She migrated to the United States, taught German in a few colleges, authored a textbook for introducing the German language, and became an adjunct at MCC. One of the things I remembered most was the cost of the course, roughly $150 per semester. She was also an adjunct at the University of Rochester where the tuition would have been at least $1500: same text, quizzes, and methodology. In one of our private conversations I discovered that she thought I was a farmer who used good English grammar and was committed to learning. This unique teacher shared that she enjoyed teaching at MCC because the students wanted to learn; at the University, the students just wanted an A. At the conclusion of the first semester, with the help of a German dictionary and my grammar text, I translated the Nativity story from the Gospel of Luke as a way of thanking her for a great learning experience. She was impressed.

As if teaching at MCC and Saint John Fisher College were not enough, Sister Edwardine Weaver, a Sister of Mercy and Chair of a certification program to prepare future Catholic school principals at the University of Rochester, contacted me to ask if I would be able to teach two graduate courses during the summer months: Catholic Philosophy of Education as well as a second course, Leadership for Catholic Educators. The invitation to return to my Alma Mater where I earned a master's in history and a master's in education was a surprise, but also an opportunity to teach at the graduate level after 30 years of undergraduate experience. She had encouraged me over the years to earn a doctorate in Educational Leadership. With her help and financial support, I started the degree part-time at the age of 62 and graduated at 66. I was committed to Catholic education so helping promising Catholic faculty become certified as principals and leaders in the Catholic school system was a way of putting my money where my mouth was. The courses I took for the degree offered me the opportunity to explore my own philosophy of education and practices that I had been using during my many years of teaching. I often think the degree became more of a time for reflection than of just trying to earn a degree for a promotion. The summers I spent with the adult students, already well-read, experienced, and eager, made the time with them more of a comfort than a challenge. By the way, I hired one of the graduates from the program to be the principal of Most Precious Blood School. The hiring committee was impressed by his knowledge and his enthusiasm for the job.

Allow me the opportunity to write about some of my experiences as a doctoral student in my mid-sixties. First, I was older than my teachers. Because of my years as a teacher, I tended to be more critical, in a positive sense, of the different professors. I did not identify myself as a priest because I wanted to be treated like any other student. The Dean of the School of Education taught a graduate seminar in the Sociology of Education and Religion. He had an extensive and impressive background in education and in religion. This engaging teacher spoke often of his Jewish roots and how his interest in education helped him strengthen his own religious beliefs. In one of our discussions, the dean spoke of the use of time and its influence on the learning process. I reminded him of the use of verbs, present and past, in the Hebrew language to support his thinking. I was not trying to show off the little knowledge I had from my one year of the study of Hebrew while in the seminary. I did, however, make the point he was making a bit clearer. With a shocked look, he smiled and promised to take it into consideration. When he later asked the Registrar to find a Catholic priest to offer a prayer at the graduation ceremony, she suggested that he ask me since "You have one in your class every week." My secret became public.

In another course I discovered the educational philosophy of Paulo Freire. He had written extensively about student-centered education and critical pedagogy. Freire was just the man to provide a theory to my own approach to educational methodology. I finally found someone who could give me the theory to support my practice in the classroom. Although his primary audience was another culture, his thinking became an important influence while drafting my dissertation. His insistence on listening to the needs of the students was key. Over the many years in the classroom, I recognized that those needs are not always intellectual. I often found that many of the students just needed a supportive word of encouragement to explore their inner beauty. Too often they focused on the negative because the educational system too often used final grades as a sign of success. Getting an A in a course did not necessarily mean the student truly learned the material. On the other hand, many who received a C or B at the end of the semester did in fact learn because they had also integrated the material into their daily lives. They often made a better connection between the material and their own journey towards maturity,

One of my more humorous memories stays with me twenty-five years later. I was enrolled in a required qualitative research course. The first night the professor mentioned that she seldom, if ever, gave an A in the course. At our coffee break three of the female students expressed their anger that the professor would say anything so negative and condescending when it came to grading. Over the semester I was impressed by the work ethic and insights these same three women brought to the discussions. When we were asked to rate our classmates for their contributions over the three months, I rated them as the top three. When the grades arrived for the semester, I had received an A-. I found out later that the three women had received a grade of B+ and were quite angry. I never mentioned my grade to anyone until my last meeting with my dissertation director. As we were summing up my experiences for earning the degree, I told her the story of my A- and the three women with a B+. My advisor laughed. I asked if she knew about any of this. She said that all three had all complained about the announcement about "no A's in the course" but were even more angry when they all received a B+. I told her that I had kept my grade secret. She laughingly agreed that it was a wise decision.

As I was finishing the dissertation, my advisor told me she was leaving for a new position on the West coast. She said we could continue to work together by mail. My response was a very quick "NO!" I had that kind of experience before. I rushed through the final draft before her departure so she and two other readers could approve it in anticipation of its defense. I was off to a two-week seminar on social justice and education at Oxford University in England. A great experience, by the way! I could defend the dissertation when I returned in July. The date was set. I arrived back home a few days before I was to defend the fruits of my reading and writing. When I walked towards the assigned room, the Registrar stopped me to inform me we would have to postpone the defense until another time. The chairman for the dissertation committee was tired because his wife had a baby the night before and he had no sleep. As I was mildly protesting because of the tight schedule my advisor and I were on, the Associate Dean walked by asking us what the problem was. The Registrar informed him. He smiled and said, "That's okay. I will serve as Chair. There is no need to delay the defense." We all gathered to discuss the dissertation. Some of the members were asking/debating questions of each other rather than of me. I was satisfied that some of my work brought new questions. At the conclusion of the conversation, I was asked to leave the room so the committee could decide "pass or fail." A few minutes later, the Associate Dean summoned me back to the examination room with the words "Doctor Graf, could we have a word with you?" I breathed a sigh of relief. My advisor later asked me to correct a few errors in grammar and spelling and get it back to her. She would gladly sign off within the week. We celebrated with lunch at Phillips European, a fancy restaurant noted for its exotic desserts. The experience of earning a degree at the age of 66 was the intellectual dessert that culminated in a still deeper appreciation of life-long learning.

Again, Surprise

I AM GETTING AHEAD OF my story. Teaching, studying, and active serving as the pastor of a well-organized parish was a dream come true. I was enjoying all that I was doing. It required a great deal of time management, but I slept well and felt positive about our various "ministries." The parish committee system was really working thanks to a dedicated staff and a very committed group of volunteers.

I already mentioned that I had been elected to the Personnel Board for the priests of the diocese. The added meetings with individual interviews of priests about their assignments allowed me to use some of the techniques e.g., interviewing, listening, being supportive that I was learning in the classes I taught or was taking. At that time priests were allowed to apply for consideration of parishes that became available because a pastor of a parish sought retirement or expressed a desire for another assignment.

The pastor of the Church of the Resurrection sought a new assignment. He had just finished a major campaign for money to build a new church, but things had not worked out as planned. The Board was looking for his replacement. A letter was sent out announcing the opening. Two people applied but after spending time checking out the parish decided to withdraw their application. A second letter was sent out but no one applied. A third letter was posted: one person was contacted personally to consider the position. He eventually agreed to take it. Each year the priests of the diocese gathered for a Convocation, a three-day experience with speakers, discussions, and camaraderie. It was a tradition that the Personnel Board would meet during the convocation to make the final suggestions for new appointments so the bishop could approve them and, if possible, talk with the candidates by the conclusion of the convocation. I was walking to the meeting when the personnel director called me aside to tell me that we had a problem. "Our candidate for the pastor of the Church of the Resurrection has withdrawn his name." The meeting started with the pressing question "What do we do now?" I had interviewed the pastor who was leaving so I knew the situation rather well. I finally blurted out, "If we can't find anyone, I will go if for no other reason than that we need to fill the position today." I was planning on another sabbatical, but I could rearrange some of the plans if the board decided to accept my reluctant offer. I left the room so they could decide if I would be a good choice or, hopefully, consider another candidate. My presence in the meeting room might be uncomfortable for them to have an honest conversation. I stepped out into the hallway hoping they might have a better idea so I could stay at Most Precious Blood parish where I was comfortably happy. Two minutes later I was called back. The board would recommend me to the bishop as the pastor of the Church of the Resurrection. I would be able to have the summer off to do a mini-sabbatical. So yet, again: "We propose; God laughs!"

Church of the Resurrection (1998-2008)

Leaving Most Precious Blood parish was no easier than when I left other past pastoral assignments. I counted the many blessings, especially of the people who treated me with such warmth and respect. How lucky I was to have been part of such a vibrant community. The parish remained open for a few more years but is now closed with parishioners moving on to other parish communities. The Day Care Center bought the school and the playground; a non-denominational church group purchased the church and rectory; the marble altar and sanctuary pedestals were harvested and brought to Saint John Fisher College's new chapel. The memories are still alive as is evident when I meet past members of the community at different churches or social events. I keep in regular contact with three people who were young men starting their careers. Mark, who is in banking, is one with whom I lunch about every six weeks. Gerry is a lawyer I meet occasionally for lunch. The third is Tom who is now a psychiatrist living in Seattle who phones me regularly and enjoys lunch when he is home visiting his family. We all find ways to survive after suffering and death. It is called "Resurrection." And that was where I was going.

I had already made plans for a minor sabbatical experience. The Personnel Board was aware of this. The Board informed the bishop of my willingness to take on the new assignment and agreed that taking the "summer sabbatical" was not a problem. Meanwhile Father John Mulligan, the Vicar General of the diocese, took on the added responsibility for Most Precious Blood parish; a younger priest would do the summer coverage for the Church of the Resurrection until mid-August when I would move into the rectory to begin my new and last assignment as a pastor. At that time, the diocesan policy for retirement was mandatory at 70 years of age and, for a good reason, e.g., health issues, one could retire at 67. I was already in my mid-sixties. The sabbatical experience was a combination of a retreat on the

Mount Tabor, the traditional location of the Transfiguration of Jesus, and more extensive travelling around Israel and Palestine mostly in Jerusalem and Jericho. My twenty-year hope to return to Mount Tabor in the Holy Land someday for an extended stay was finally coming true. The time at the retreat center there was very relaxing. A small group of men and women from Italy volunteered a week there each summer to help with upkeep: painting, cleaning, and gardening. Daily Mass was in Italian as was the afternoon rosary. That helped to revitalize my very rusty Italian. The night before I left I enjoyed my final meal with the community. I was able to say a few words of good wishes and gratitude in Italian before I headed off to spend some time in Jerusalem. My next brief experience was a week in Rome for a conference to discuss ecumenism before flying back to the States. It was a great, although truncated, sabbatical.

Reality struck quickly as soon as I arrived at the parish. I no sooner unpacked my travelling bags then the Finance Director invited me to supper at a nearby pancake restaurant. She caught me up on the finances. We had money in the bank because of the failed drive to build a church but the problem now was what to do with it. She listed a few other issues that we needed to deal with quickly, then came the zinger! The young priest who covered for me until my arrival had triggered a backlash because of his hurtful assessment of the parish community. His last words at each of the Masses on the Sunday before my arrival criticized the people for their attitude: "Like a drinking glass full of negativity . . . they needed to straighten up." I returned to a well-furnished and freshly clean rectory just the right size for my books and me. That night I wondered what to do about the various issues. The next morning. I celebrated my first Mass in a beautifully decorated small chapel with about a dozen people. Present was a father and his young daughter. As he was leaving, he told me that both came that morning to "check me out." Apparently, they approved because we became friends over my time as their parish leader. A bit later a small group of young people under the supervision of their dedicated leader arrived at my door to help me unpack and arrange my books. The whole first week was filled with small meetings with staff, committees, and "drop-ins." Then came the weekend of Masses and meeting the other hundreds of curious parishioners accused of being like "glasses of negativity." At the end of each Mass, just before the final blessing, I took time to thank publicly the youth who came to help me unpack my boxes of books as well as the staff and people who had so warmly greeted me during the week. I then added "as I was checking out the kitchen cupboards, I realized this parish needed a great deal of prayer for their conversion because of the drinking glass I found on the shelf." I sensed a fearful gasp as I said those words. "It was a Buffalo Bills glass and I know that God is a Dallas Cowboy fan. In fact, I have snapshots of Him wearing a Dallas Cowboy sweatshirt all during the football season." At each Mass, the gasp turned to hearty laughter. As people left the church where I was greeting them personally, many told me about their favorite football team, sympathized with my choice of "that" team, or jokingly challenged me to start praying for the Buffalo Bills. My comment at the end of Mass broke the ice. We drank from a large positive drinking glass from then on.

The founding pastor, Fr. Bob Kreckel, reminded the new post-Vatican II parish community that "they were the church who met weekly in a building to celebrate the Eucharist." It was a very young parish with very young members. I remember one year when we had no funerals until December 30th. Because the parish consisted mostly of younger families with young children, we had very few weddings. The parish had a vibrant youth group and catechetical program for all ages. We invited speakers, local and national, to help the older members continue their faith journey. Many of the men and women had made a Cursillo; a small group of men met on Saturdays for breakfast, prayer, and discussion; a small group of women and men staffed the Stephen Ministry to assist those in need of emotional and spiritual support. Additionally, there was a Caring and Sharing Outreach to help others with financial and physical needs especially during the holiday season. The staff was equally committed to being of service to the parish community. Our committees were outstanding in creativity when volunteering their time and expertise. Many of those on the committees were leaders and specialists in their workplace. The parish community was bursting with talent. Early on, a few had voiced the opinion that the parish "did not really need a priest except for the sacraments." Initially I was put off by the claim but came to realize they were right in many ways. I saw myself as a leader of a symphony of talent orchestrating the many gifts in service of others. I was also the liturgical presider to lead a Eucharistic community in prayer to support healing, service, and gratitude.

My favorite memory of the time, talent, and sense of what a collaborative faith community was all about was the work of Resurrection's Building and Grounds Committee, an all-male group of architects, engineers, and professionals from a variety of other trades and experience. The question was a challenging one: What should we do with the money pledged or already in a savings account? The existing building was used for staff offices, meetings, classroom, dinners, dances, committee meetings and, of course, Sunday Masses. A small chapel was already part of the structure. The chairs were moveable and were often stacked neatly along the walls after the final Sunday Mass to make room for a social event. When the structure was erected, the parish could not afford an air-conditioning unit. Unfortunately, there were no windows for this large area that would allow for fresh air or cross-ventilation during the summer months. A few noisy fans circulated the air except during the homily at Mass. If we fix the large space issue and make it more "church like," where will we have our socials? Some parishioners questioned whether we should even worry about a worship space wondering if we would continue to have a priest? Rumors had surfaced that the diocese was planning to close the parish anyways because of a shortage of priests. The parish recently celebrated the 50th anniversary of its founding.

Finding out what the people acknowledged when they used the expression "they are the church" proved to be an excellent idea as they planned for the uncertain future. We had a few formal open discussions with interested people, did some asking around privately and informally, met with the various other parish committees, and finally compared notes. We decided to build an addition to the present structure for social events with an attached large kitchen. We planned the space so that eventually we could install folding partitions to provide small classrooms/ meetings if needed. An architect submitted a set of blueprints for our new addition. The Building and Grounds Committee liked the plan but knew our major weakness: we were all male and, for the most part, we were not cooks. We invited a group of women to assist the male architect to make some key changes, for example, where the kitchen should be placed in the new structural addition; the most efficient outlay for the sink, stove, refrigerator, cupboards, and serving shelf. And, I might add: what color did they want for the wall paint? The new addition was our committee's unanimous decision thanks to its willingness to listen to each other and then surface new approaches to solve frequent challenges peacefully.

To assure the people that our parish worshipping community had a future we also decided to arrange a more fitting sanctuary area with a matching altar, pulpit, and chairs. This would anticipate a further later renovation of the larger space with rugs, pews, and whatever else needed to beautify a worship space, but I selfishly raised an "immediate need." Could we invest in an air conditioner for the existing plant? The heat and the noise from the fans during Sunday Masses were a distraction. Someone said, "Well, if people want to be comfortable, they could attend other churches during the summer." I countered, "But why not have them come here and be comfortable?" One reluctant member of the committee wondered if we had enough money to pull this off so early in the renovation. A vote was taken, and a decision made to install an air conditioner by the following summer. It was installed. The first weekend the following summer was particularly hot. We turned on the new air-conditioner. As the "reluctant" committee member was leaving Mass, he smiled and quietly mouthed "Thank you! Thank you!"

Parishioners submitted a name for the new hall. The committee chose "Emmaus Hall" because on the afternoon of his Resurrection Jesus had dined late with two people who invited him to eat dinner with them. He socialized and they came to recognize him in the Breaking of the Bread. The name fit the spirit of the parish beautifully. The following September Bishop Clark celebrated Mass, blessed the new addition, and shared a meal prepared in our new kitchen with us. The spirit and reality of all who made the event possible reflected honest collaboration and respectful discussions.

The following year we worked towards refurbishing the worship space. The contentious issue was "the pews." Since the foundation of the parish, the people were used to plastic chairs and standing during the Eucharistic prayer. Most wanted pews but no kneelers; a vocal few wanted pews with kneelers. I checked out possible options with our diocesan Liturgy Director. If we were installing rugs, he suggested we could go without the traditional kneelers. Those who wished to kneel could do so on a comfortable rug. To settle the variety of opinions we chose to install pews but arranged for a few of them in the rear of the worship space to have kneelers. A very few were still not satisfied. A year later I was in my office located off the worship space when I heard one of the most vocal parishioners who was against having any pews at all showing a friend how beautiful everything was "including the pews." I laughed and whispered to myself, "It takes time to change." By the way, once again we asked a small group of women to pick out the color of the wall-to-wall rug and the matching upholstering for the new pews. The people who were "the Church" now had a newly refurbished church to celebrate our liturgies. Bricks and mortar do not form a Church but provide a place to gather as such.

Any pastoral leader will tell you that the people are the focus of our ministry. The Administration of everything from paying the bills, contracting for the repair of a roof or heating system, conducting an annual money appeal, approving of the bulletin or scheduled ministers, is what can be draining. That is why I believe a capable parish secretary, a dedicated finance director, a solid parish council with at least two high school students, and other self-run committees can do the administration. The parish family was very lucky to have all of them as a committed and talented team to keep a very vibrant faith community alive and well. My role was simply to show up, listen, express an opinion, remind the group "we are part of a bigger community of faith," and then go with the flow. I admit that I did not bat 100% all the time but I did try.

The Liturgy Committee appropriately decorated the sanctuary for the different seasons and services. The well-rehearsed musicians beautifully led us in song and praise with the new hymnals (they chose) every weekend.

The Building and Grounds Committee kept the whole structure and lawn neat and tidy. The Stephen Ministry faithfully responded to calls for help; the Care and Sharing Committee helped feed the hungry both as a parish and ecumenically for the annual Thanksgiving Baskets and regular Sunday dinners. Some volunteered their time with Habitat for Humanity to build houses for the poor. All were committed to social justice issues with study groups followed by prayerful action.

I need to give a separate paragraph to talk about young people. The parish was very lucky to have a full-time Director of Religious Education and Youth Minister. The weekly religious education classes met with committed and well-trained teachers. Depending on their level of maturity and active support of their families, the students were well-prepared to receive the Eucharist, Reconciliation, and Confirmation. The Youth Group had an annual weekend retreat experience with the main talks given by their peers. The leaders, Cathy and Greg Reitz, worked with each presenter in their preparation and during the retreat sat proudly listening to the young people share their thoughts and give their personal testimonies. The young people's peers received the presenters' message with enthusiasm because of the delivery and with an openness because of the content. In later years many of the youth would conduct a fundraiser to support their week-long volunteer trip to a region nearby or in a faraway state plagued by poverty to repair and/or paint houses or play games with the youngsters. Each night the group set aside some time to reflect on what they were doing but also why they were doing it. Over the years the "now" alumnae/i volunteers would tell me how important that experience of caring meant to them as they went off to college, settled into a new job, or found a partner for life. One of the graduates from our youth programs died on the basketball court while still in his twenties shortly before his wedding. I want to share the homily I gave at his funeral. It reflects the positive spirit of many of the youth who grew up with Mark and heard him share his journey in faith. I gave him the nickname, Marco, at our first introduction. We spent many hours together talking about his faith and the usual teenage problems.

A HOMILY FOR MARCO'S MEMORIAL MASS

> Having read over the scripture readings and doing some research I did what I usually do when it comes to preparing a homily: I spent some time in prayer. I did not seem to get very far: God seemed too busy to respond.

Finally, I had this minor vision when God came to me apologizing for the delay. God spoke of this young man who appeared at the heavenly gates just a few weeks ago. At first God thought he was the character from the new movie, BFG (the "Big Friendly Giant"). This big, smiling young man merely pointed at his chest as he demanded entrance: The words were from Luke's gospel when the repentant sinner, nailed to the cross next to Jesus was promised "Today you will be with me in paradise."

Not wanting to deny a promise made by His Son, God told me that he let him in. However, for the last few weeks this "gentle giant" has argued logically and passionately, asked probing questions, and made strong suggestions how God might have done a better job moving the universe towards a more efficient approach to peace and harmony. God was exhausted from the heavy conversations and was considering relocating, even suggesting a warmer climate where there might have been a snowball's chance to win an argument with the new resident of what had been a peaceful place to spend eternity. God then asked me if I ever had a similar person in my life. And. if so, how did I handle him?

I then confessed I did . . . Mark Alexander Callanan. How did I handle him? I listened to him attentively because Mark spoke from his heart as well as his head. I smiled because of his passion, enthusiasm, and self-assurance. I did add, however, "God, hold on! Wait until his brother arrives . . . the pressure will be off you!"

When Mark was baptized, he was marked with the sign of the cross to remind him that he would be challenged to walk faithfully in the footsteps of Jesus. As he grew, the challenges were there at almost every stage of his life. I think that is the reason Mark chose to be signed by words of the tattoo on his chest. Realizing that he faltered, made mistakes, and yet continued to struggle, Mark was living his life assured of the mercy and gentle love that promised "you will be with me in paradise." The words on his chest reminded him daily of the promise as he served his country and as he prepared for married life with Kristi with whom he found glimpses of paradise.

In one of our conversations (usually I was exhausted after them: as you know Mark was an exuberant conversationalist whatever the topic), I suggested that he read his namesake's Gospel: the whole sixteen chapters. Scholars believe that it was the first written story of the good news of God's love as lived and preached by Jesus. The author might well have recorded the reflections of one of the early disciples of Jesus who heard the words and watched Jesus in action. Later he traveled with Paul for a while until they had an apparent falling out (later there would be a reconciliation) so Mark began to travel with Peter who usually objected to almost everything Jesus said or did, and tradition has it, wrote down the stories for others to read. Young Mark did read Mark's gospel account: the story of the apostles' flaws, probing questions, and faltering faith. He took the story of Jesus who is the promised good news of mercy and forgiveness to heart . . . the promise of a place for all those who admit to their struggle, mistakes, flaws, and sins will find peace and rest.

I was taken by the reading we heard from Mark's gospel today. We had heard earlier in the second reading that we are all God's children. The image of older Jesus sitting under a tree with kids swarming all over him; tired from his talks and interactions with adults . . . captivates me. Children ask questions no one else wants to ask; they want to be hugged, paid attention to, wrestled with. Jesus had only one lap, but so many kids wanted to sit on it at the same time . . . each one vying for attention. Children do things and say things that embarrass adults.

And like we heard from the reading from the book of Lamentations: where there is so much hurt and disastrous events there are the words of hope that mercy and love is available today and even more there is plenty left over for tomorrow.

Mark remained the little child with his questions; outlandish statements about politics and economics: his smile when he knew he was wrong . . . his tears of repentance . . . his boisterous presence . . . his openness to rebuke or a new way of thinking.

Yet because we are all children, I also looked at the gospel story we heard in a different way. Like the Jesus in the story, Mark made room for others in his life. He listened and spoke with those who were hurting: he protected comrades who were in danger; Mark hugged those who felt alone or unloved: tired, he still found time to be with those who had questions or doubts.

I remember the prayer and self-confrontation that Mark experienced as he prepared his talk for the Search Weekend in his senior year of High School. He wanted his peers to know there is always hope even in the moments of our failures.

At this Eucharist and the many times that we gather around the table of the Lord we give thanks that Mark will always be a part of our lives. We celebrate his intelligence, wit, enthusiasm, and friendship. We believe, in our growing faith, that God has welcomed him into paradise.

For us who remain behind? Amidst tears of sadness and happy memories, we can read, study, collect data, be open to new experiences, so when we die and enter paradise, we will be ready for an argument with Mark knowing that we can try, but will not win.

I reflect often on less tragic, even humorous memories like the funeral of a wonderful woman that took place in the middle of a heavy snowstorm. Everything was running late. The casket was carried from a stranded hearse. Some of the cars went off the long driveway to the church. The pallbearers had to push my car so I could return to the rectory and into the garage. Family, other mourners, liturgical ministers, and guests smiled our way through it all. Years later when we buried her son, all went well until the interment ceremony when a heavy rainstorm arrived. We all laughed remembering the humor of it all: first snow and now the rain.

More than once a little boy or girl would leave Mass and with a smile greet me with "Hello, God" and would often hug me around my knees with their little arms; I would hug them back. The parents would explain that on their way to Mass they would tell the youngsters that they were going to God's House to pray. Apparently, they saw me playing my role as the leader of worship and, as the parents would tell me, "They assume you must be God." Their innocent sign of love made me feel like God.

Of course, there were difficult memories. Shortly after the clergy sexual abuse scandal was reported in the papers and every TV news program, I was wrestling with how to deal with it: Could I preach about it? Ignore it? Or what? I thought about it, prayed about it, and then decided. I would talk about it at the end of our Sunday Masses when we usually made parish announcements. I was quite nervous and admitted how difficult I was finding it to do so. It was a simple admission that there were cases of abuse and, in the name of the bishop and priests of the diocese, "I am sorry for the harm that was done. We need to pray for forgiveness and healing." I went on to say I know I sometimes hug the little kids as they leave Sunday Mass or religious education class during the week. I wanted to assure them when I did so it was not with any intention to do sexual harm to any of them. They are too precious. There was applause and we sang our final hymn. As always, I stood at the door to greet the people as they left the service. One of the male high school students who had never displayed any emotion about anything came over to me, put his arms around me, hugged me, whispered, "Thank you" and added "I love you." Then he walked away. I had a sense of what the prodigal son experienced when his father embraced him and welcomed him home.

As you can imagine, I was extremely happy with all that was going on within the parish community. I was also aware I was approaching retirement age and recognized the shortage of priests to fill all the other faith communities and ministries within the diocese. At that time, our diocese promoted and sustained a wonderful program of Pastoral Administrators, lay people men and women with an advanced degree in theology or its equivalent who teamed with a Sacramental Minister, an ordained priest, who would lead in the celebration of the various sacraments. The team would act in concert with each other living out their title: a ministry of one for administration and the other a ministry of administering the sacraments.

I was looking for the right person to team with, and hopefully be allowed to stay on as Sacramental Minister, who would be an effective Pastoral Administrator. I found the right person and made the right choice. Nancy was talented, creative, organized, and theologically very well-prepared. The parish hired her initially as a Pastoral Associate to help with the many duties and meetings that occupy a parish community. When I retired, she moved into the Pastoral Administrator position. I continued to live in the nearby rectory and provide sacramental services. Because we were both used to leading, there were a few tense moments when some decisions had to be made.

One day we had a difficult conversation. Nancy mentioned her Myers-Briggs letters (ENFP); mine are INFJ. Then it hit me. Because I had used this psychological tool in my classes over the years, I recognized from the very beginning of our relationship the Extrovert (E) and Introvert (I) difference. We were both Intuitive (N) and Feeling (F). Both of us were caring and empathetic working in the service of individual people. We differed when we would make a final decision: Judging (J) people are quick and definite: Perceivers (P) tend to want more and more information and tend to delay their final decision. Two well-meaning people had an approach that was completely different. Nancy enjoyed talking, conducting lengthy meetings, and was open-ended when decisions were to be made. I like quick conversations, short meetings, and finalized decisions. When I am upset, I need to calm down for a day or two: Nancy wanted to discuss the issue immediately. Despite our differences, we served the people with open hearts. That's what ministry is: it is all about service. After five years in our two different ministries, both of us moved to different areas of service. Nancy went to another parish, I to retirement and ministry at an Independent Living community, the Legacy at the Fairways in Victor, New York.

Pastor for Priests

WHEN I WAS ASSIGNED to Ithaca College in the 1960's, I was deeply aware of our diocesan program to attract young men to the priesthood. With permission of the Vocation Director, I embarked on a different program for those in the southern part of the diocese. With the help of some seminarians from Saint Bernard's Seminary, I gathered 25-30 young men from the high schools within about a 40–50-mile area. About six or seven seminarians from Becket Hall volunteered to make some presentations about their own journey of discovery of a possible vocation to the priesthood. I shared my life as priest ordained 7 years and then helped each one follow-up with a spiritual mentor in their home parishes. One of that original group, Chris Linsler, is still a priest pastor in the same southern part of the diocese. I invited two deacons, Chuck Latus and Jim Schwartz, to return to the college during the following Holy Week to help plan and serve as ministers of the various liturgies. Both recently celebrated their 55th year as priests.

Reaching out to the seminarians for help brought me an invitation to lead the retreat for the seminarians studying at Saint John Fisher College. Subsequently I gave a few days of recollection at Becket Hall, a newly built student residence on Saint John Fisher University campus. This helped keep me in touch with some of the men who helped me with the retreats at Ithaca College. The two deacons who helped me with the Holy Week ceremony must have talked with their classmates at Saint Bernard's Seminary who, in turn, invited me to lead the retreat in preparation for their ordination to the priesthood. The retreat, a combination of talks and guided discussions, went very well. The class invited me to their ordination with a place in the sanctuary followed by breakfast with them and the bishop, a longtime diocesan tradition. Bishop Fulton Sheen was our bishop at the time. As I was standing quietly off to the side waiting for a way out, Bishop Sheen almost ran across the room with wide open arms asking. "Father, what did you say to these young men? They are raised to the heavens with excitement." What do you say to one of the most famous TV orators of the 20th century so as not to reveal my material? I looked at the bishop as he embraced me and quickly replied, "Bishop, I told them exactly what you would have told them." With that the bishop let go of me, took me by the hand, led me to the breakfast table, pulled over a chair next to him and asked me to tell him more. I kept saying to myself, "How can I get out of here safely and with grace?" Fifty years later that same class invited me to their anniversary celebration with Mass and dinner in the evening. The next morning, we had a round-table discussion for a few hours listening to each other's journey over the years. During the sharing session, I was impressed that each of them remembered something I said during their retreat referencing an excerpt from the book, *The Velveteen Rabbit,* a reference about love, service, and pain. That unique and moving session made my day!

Over the years I have tried to minister to priests in a variety of ways. In the 1970s I worked with a committee of priests to provide learning experiences both with workshops during the summer at Saint Bernard's Seminary and one-day meetings, usually with a guest speaker noted for his expertise during the school year. At the time, these one-day meetings were a diocesan requirement for the continuing education for priests. I also travelled to other dioceses to speak about social justice and/or preaching as well as training workshops for budding parish lay ministers.

I already wrote about year the bishop of Fort Worth, Texas, invited me to conduct the first required retreat for all diocesan priests at the same time in the same place. Conducting a "required" anything is a challenge and two of the retreatants underlined that fact. The time of prayer and celebration of the various liturgies moved me. I still enjoy the voices of a priests' chorus singing the hymns which are second nature to us because of our lengthy seminary training. Four of the younger priests had already produced a professional recording of traditional and folk hymns. Priests enjoy telling stories often repeated frequently so that their friends could finish them, ribbing each other about them, and then laughing. The memory of the laughter, the walks with the older priests, and the overall expressed hunger "to be better" remains with me even as I write.

I worked with the Ministry to Priests program developed in the Rochester Diocese in the late seventies. Its origins and its goals were based on the observations of a Trappist priest who saw a need for support groups and on-going spiritual relationships especially for diocesan priests who could easily have a sense of isolation and loneliness. As a team leader, I enjoyed the one-on-one relationships I developed during those times. As a member of my support group, the "happy hour" and the stories over a good dinner prepared us for sharing our ideas about preaching on the following Sunday's readings. This proved helpful because of the different insights and approaches to the scriptures. I remained active with this ministry and the support group until I went on one of my sabbaticals. When I returned, I was looking for something deeper.

I had read the life of Charles de Foucault when I was in the seminary wondering if I could ever try his way of life: a contemplative in the desert, welcoming others from a different culture and background, manual labor, hours at prayers, and committed to a lifestyle of poverty. He wrote a rule of life that was so strict that, in his lifetime, no one wanted to join him. However, Jesus Caritas Fraternities did arise long after his death with the purpose to live in the spirit of his rule. I was hungry for such a group. It took about ten years but eventually I found one that was willing to live in that spirit. Death, new assignments, ill health, and other splinter groups depleted the original group but two members, Bob Schrader and I, continued to get together after nearly twenty years along with newer members. We meet on the third Friday of the month for lunch, pray for at least a half-hour, then share our varied experiences of "encountering Jesus" in our ministries and encouraging each other to "keep going." I never go to bed that Friday night without a deep sense of gratitude.

I also served on the Diocesan Board of Reconciliation (and Arbitration) as its leader for a few years before it disappeared for some reason which I still don't know. This Board assisted the aggrieved parties to reconcile differences of opinions and decisions that affected the broader community (parishes or the diocese, e.g.). I used it myself when I left Saint Bernard's. Working with a Board member at the time was very healing although things did not work out the way I had hoped. As an elected member of the Priests' Personnel Board, we were allowed to serve two terms of 3 years each. During those six years I had the opportunity to conduct annual interviews, help decide new assignments, and do some interventions when priests had issues. I encouraged more than a few to seek out a "rehab center" for their addictions or other psychological issues often brought on by their isolation and lack of trusting intimacy. Shortly after my terms ended, the Priests' Personnel Director asked me to assume the position as Director of Priestly Life and Ministry. I agreed with the proviso that I be allowed to work with a team representative from the geography and age groupings of priests. As a team we worked together for about 15 years before I chose to retire and begin to enjoy a quieter lifestyle. The team chose the director for the annual priests' retreat, organized our days of prayer in Advent and Lent, visited priests who were ill, and worked to provide educational opportunities to prepare for retirement, financial planning, or health issues. Once again, the team's creativity and dedication in the service of our diocesan clergy was done quietly and willingly.

As a Priestly Life and Ministry team of only three we realized we still could not be in touch with all the priests nor meet all their needs so we planned smaller informal meetings to explore ideas how we might challenge and support each other when serious issues surface. I remember three or four mutual friends, reluctant to challenge a member of their group, approaching me concerning his misuse of alcohol. I suggested that they gently confront him about their sincere concern for him. To a person their reply was, "No, I don't want to lose his friendship." My reply to the concerned friends was "And what are real friends for?" I did have a good conversation with the priest who became quite angry and defensive, surfaced reasons why he did not need help, went to a "rehab center," came home, stayed sober, and thanked me every time we met until he died.

After the sexual abuse scandals broke in the early 2000's, I met with some of the accused abusers and, in some cases, accompanied them to the bishop's office as each was put on administrative leave. I remember the tears Bishop Clark shed as he listened to each one's story. As a team and with the financial help of the Clergy Relief Society for which I was acting leader for that group at the time, we brought a clinical psychologist to the diocese who interviewed each of the priests who were put on leave. It was to be a personal interview with no information to be shared with any authority figures. All we asked was a brief report: what could we have done to prevent the abuse and what should we do as we deal with the abuse as a diocese and as friends of the accused. At the same time, we invited priests to gather for a group conversation to discuss the effects of the scandal on them. We brought a priest-counsellor from another diocese to serve as a moderator to listen to the pain caused by the scandal and give us a few concrete pointers for personal healing as well as support for the victims and our parish communities. Some priests wept because they were attacked verbally at our local shopping malls or received hateful telephone calls/letters. Others stopped hearing confessions of youngsters making their First Penance. I know, until this day, I become very nervous when I use a public restroom and a youngster is there. What might he tell his parents? The storm still brews in our diocese. What could we have done better to prevent the abuse and deal with it once it was reported? I have no simple solutions even today. I still deal with its effects in my pastoral life and pray daily for healing for the victims and their abusers.

My Saint John Fisher College (now University) Days (2001-2020)

MY RELATIONSHIP WITH Saint John Fisher College has been a long and most wonderful experience. When I was teaching AP American History at Bishop Kearney High School in the 1980s, the college was offering three credits towards a bachelor's degree if the student attended St. John Fisher College. I submitted a syllabus. It was approved. A few years later the college suspended the program but I enjoyed teaching the American History course and students were challenged to have an opportunity to write at a college level. At about the same time, I was also teaching a course in Marriage and Sexuality at the college. Over the next 19 years I was a part-time adjunct professor with no meetings to attend or involvement in the department's intrigue. I have already written about this. In 2001 the Chair of the Religious Studies Department asked me if I would be interested in a full-time position. It would be a dream come true. All I needed to do was work out the logistics. I asked the pastoral associate if she would like to take over the administration of the parish. I would not take a salary because I would be full-time at the college. I would stay on the diocesan health and retirement plan, but everything else would be simple: I would continue as a sacramental minister; she would do the administration. This became official when I was 70 years old and submitted my retirement letter to the diocese. My part-time teaching became full-time. I had my own office and would be teaching at least three courses a semester, serving on committees, and doing academic advising. I enjoyed it all.

Towards the end of my first semester the Chair of the Religious Studies asked me to assume his responsibilities. He no longer cared about functioning as the department's leader. There were some programming issues with the Administration he chose to avoid. At the conclusion of the semester, the members of the department elected me as Chair. I remained in that position for the rest of my tenure. What I liked most about the position was that it was one less step I needed to take when dealing with an academic bureaucracy. It also gave me an opportunity to suggest a few innovative ideas. For example, our department had been all male for as long as I could remember. There was only one exception: a woman professor who was briefly part-time and left the college when her husband found a new position in Florida. I proposed hiring a qualified woman to join the department. We advertised the position. Two equally skilled women responded and enthusiastically went through the interviewing process. We liked both candidates. The first choice asked if she could continue in her other employment at another college until she finished with a grant that would end the following year. We could not wait another year lest we lose the line in the budget. The other qualified candidate was available immediately, so our second choice was hired. A year later we had another line open for full-time employment. That gave the department the opportunity to hire the other qualified woman who brought added passion and creativity to the department's mission. We already had two other well-educated priests, Fr. Michael Costanzo and Fr. John Colacino, who easily brought a sense of pastoral ministry to their students. The department flourished because of the talent and commitment of a caring team of professors. Over the years John retired and later Michael died from brain cancer. In both cases it was a loss to the department and our students. The first woman we hired later resigned; the latter, Linda MacCammon, became Chair of the department when I retired. Over the years, because we could not hire new tenure-track faculty, we found very capable adjuncts to cover some of our courses. Because I was an adjunct for many years, I realized they were underpaid and not always appreciated. I made it a point to support them as best as I could but not as successfully as I would have liked.

Much could be written about the workings of the department. Our relationship was quite informal. Because our offices were located very close to each other we had our carefully prepared cup of espresso almost daily in Fr. Mike's office. He remained proud of his Sicilian background and often retold the story of how his bishop had allowed him to come to the United States to care for his parents. He remained in the country until his untimely death. His great hospitality not only provided our department members with espresso and great conversations, but other faculty and his own students also enjoyed the same informal conversation and the ever-present freshly brewed cup of espresso. Mike was well-read, enjoyed music (especially opera), and wrote four volumes of poetry. His course about Religious Themes in Opera was well received and often enrolled twenty plus students. I remember my panic when he became ill late in the semester. Mike ended up in the intensive care unit at the hospital. Who would teach the course? Others in the department already had full loads. I found and began reading a book about opera just in case it would fall on me to finish the semester with budding opera fans. Luckily for the students, I found a music professor from Nazareth College to finish the semester with them. Mike recovered from his heart attack after four days in a coma to resume his work as an advisor for our Religious Studies minors; I advised the majors. With renewed energy, Mike continued to serve his cup of espresso to anyone who showed up at his door. A few years later he developed brain cancer, forcing him into the hospital again and then hospice care until he died. In Sicily he taught music, at Nazareth College he had taught Italian, and at Saint John Fisher he taught introductions both to the New and Old Testaments, the Problem of Evil, World Religion, and, of course, the Religious Themes in Opera. Because our department enjoyed working with other departments, Mike also co-taught a course on love and another on Job from a literary viewpoint in the English department. His death left a big hole in our department that could never be adequately filled even if espresso were served.

I need to repeat two of Mike's favorite stories. I can still see his infectious smile as he would repeat a favorite criticism he received from his students when he returned their "corrected" assignments: "How come you know better English than I do, and you were born in Italy?" Another of his stories that he would enjoy sharing dealt with a discussion about the search for the meaning of life. He asked the question, "How do you find the meaning of life?" Students offered their own ideas, but one disinterested student offered none, so Mike called on him, "Joe, how do you find the meaning of life?" Without hesitation, the student replied, "I would Google it." Some questions with their answers need to be re-told to prepare us for the future of education.

I already mentioned that our department worked well together as a team. A few years into my time as the Chair our team contemplated and executed a possible way to recruit potential majors into the department or, at least, to study at Saint John Fisher. We ran ads in the daily local paper, the *Democrat and Chronicle*, and in the diocesan paper announcing a prize for the best essay outlining possible ecumenical relationships to work towards peace. By this time Fr. John Colacino, a priest of the Congregation of the Most Precious Blood, had joined our department. One of the courses he and Fr. Mike taught was World Religions. Their expertise and some money from our department's budget allowed us to receive some great essays and celebrate the contestants and their parents at a dinner when the winner would be announced. The college enrolled a few students, and the department did get a few minors. We did this for a few years before we switched to another idea. What I found most exciting with this experiment was the number of essays from a variety of religious backgrounds from both males and females who approached the same basic issues from diverse points of view but came to similar conclusions.

I was serving on a committee to study and promote the College's Catholic/Basilian tradition. The Basilian Fathers, a community of priests committed to teaching "Goodness, Discipline, Knowledge" founded Saint John Fisher College (now University) as a Catholic college that welcomed males from a variety of backgrounds. Years later it welcomed women as well. The committee was charged with the task of exploring ways we should live up to its mission. The points of view to accomplish this charge provided for some widely diverse ideas, but always with openness and good humor. The Chair of the committee was Charlie Constantino who, along with his family, had already established scholarships for first generation students. During one of our private discussions, I mentioned that our department had some majors and minors, but the students often had problems with the overall cost of books for all their courses. He arranged to furnish some money for our department to pick up the cost of any of the texts the majors or minors needed for the required texts for their religious studies courses. This idea surfaced about the same time as I had a student complain about the cost of books. A few days before, as I usually did during the first class, I asked the students to discuss in small groups why they chose this course and what their expectations were. After a few minutes of group discussion, each group would give a report of their conversations. When one group gave their report, I probed a bit deeper, "Does anyone else in your group want to add anything?" One male student bravely announced that he had to take a Religious Studies course, looked over the cost of the books and since mine had the cheapest text that was why he was taking my course. I laughed and said to myself, "Well, there is nothing like honesty." That student and I became good friends during the semester. At its conclusion, he expressed his gratitude for buying the cheaper text that allowed him to learn some material that he had not given any thought to beforehand.

About twenty years ago one of my former students from my Saint Bernard's Seminary days died. He had left the seminary before his ordination. Years later, after he had married, he decided to become a permanent deacon for the diocese. Mike Krupiarz was always committed to social justice issues. He inspired me, along with a few of his seminary classmates, to examine my own commitment to those issues. I wanted to do something to honor Mike. I came up with the idea of establishing a scholarship in his honor. It was called the Dorothy Day Scholarship to be awarded to students

My Saint John Fisher College (now University) Days (2001-2020)

who wanted to use their education in the service of others. She was a hero to Mike. It started with a small donation, but this grew over the years to a sizable amount. In addition to my own annual donation, I asked others to donate to the scholarship on the occasion of my various celebrations (e.g., birthdays, anniversaries) or on their own to help with the education of "future Dorothy Days." The first scholarship was granted to a student who later taught a student who in turn, 10 years later, became a recipient of the same scholarship. The scholarships were granted to future doctors, nurses, teachers, ministers, priests, lawyers. Some were Roman Catholic, some Muslims, some were Evangelical Christians while still another belonged to the Baha'i faith community. All of them expressed an interest in serving the poor after they graduated. Hearing from some of them later, I would breathe a prayer of thanksgiving that our trust in them paid off in their service to others.

While still an adjunct professor, I became friends with Fr. John Cavanaugh. John was a Basilian priest who had strong ties to the city of Rochester where he grew up. After ordination he returned to Rochester and was assigned to Saint John Fisher College's English Department. Over the years he regularly taught a variety of English courses, served as Chair of the department, worked with members of the Irish Community to establish a memorial to honor the many victims of the Irish potato famine, and regularly practiced the bagpipes. Our conversations, especially after his retirement, revolved around the topic of the mission of the college considering its relationship to a Catholic tradition. During our lunches and visits when he was later in the hospital and then in an assisted living center, he expressed an interest in assuring the college would remain faithful to its mission while embracing an interfaith approach to education of the "whole person" including the arts and sciences through the lens of religious beliefs and/or basic human rights. Little did I know that he had something specific in mind: maintaining a Catholic philosophy of education that welcomes and embraces a variety of views, that is, "catholic" with a small "c."

The summer following his death the then president of the college, Katherine Keough, arranged to have a statue commemorating John's dedication to the college be erected near Founders Hall, a newly built student residence to honor the Basilian founders of the college. I have often wondered if students who pass by the statue every day ask themselves who this man was playing bagpipes. After the formal dedication service one of the officers in charge of development told me in passing that John left a sizeable gift to the college to support our Catholic heritage. A day later a person in charge of public relations warned me that a newspaper reporter was going to interview me about the endowment John had left the college. I knew nothing but was assured that "You will think of something." To prepare for the interview

I spoke with a few other administrators who were equally unsure of what the endowment was and how it might be used. The interview went well and ended with "But we are still working things out." A few months passed with nothing further being said. I began to wonder to myself about a possible decision.

In a conversation over coffee, I asked the vice-president in charge of development, "Anything new about Fr. Cavanaugh's bequest?" The endowment was there but no one knew what John had in mind. When I told the development officer about my conversations with John, he asked me to put some ideas together and suggest a plan of action. We met with John's sister and her husband, a well-known lawyer and judge, to get their input about the William and Helen Cavanaugh endowment named in honor of John's parents. After a few more meetings that included the president of the college, and a re-written proposal that all could agree to, the college announced the new designation William and Helen Cavanaugh Chair of Catholic Studies. I was asked to be its first endowed chair which was also the first ever endowed chair in the college's history. I accepted the position with a few provisions. When I retired, a Basilian priest, Dr. George Smith, assumed the role. A great choice!

Each year the endowment supported a variety of speakers and programs in other departments e.g., Irish studies, African American programs, philosophy, history, to name a few. The endowment also subsidized an annual interfaith publication with articles, research papers, poetry and an occasional photograph all submitted by students and faculty across the campus. John's dream, and mine, was to use Catholic Studies to share our heritage and invite people from different disciplines to gather for a conversation regarding topics that offered an ethical approach and were more embracive which meant "catholic".

Over eleven years we invited speakers that included doctors, nurses, businessmen, sociologists, educators, clergy, politicians to a March dinner. For example, the guests would be professors in the School of Business when we had a speaker from the business community, who, in turn, would invite a student whom they believed to be committed to an ethical approach to their future positions in their field. We also invited the President, Provost, and Deans to join us. We named the event the Saint Thomas More Lecture and Dinner. Saint Thomas More, patron of lawyers, was a friend of Saint John Fisher; both were beheaded within two weeks of each other for remaining true to their beliefs despite Henry VIII's threats. Our planning group believed that Thomas More, a layman, chancellor, lawyer, author, and devout family man was the right choice for a lecture and dinner to discuss ethics across the workplace. We kept the event deliberately small to permit informal table discussion and questions from the students. I believe John Cavanaugh would have been proud to be part of an evening like this. The dinner and lecture reflected his dream to sustain the Catholic mission of the college while offering a venue for open discussions across disciplines with a variety of participants. I walked away after each event whispering a word of thanks for John's generosity that made the night possible.

The team approach to any event in the department allowed for discussions at our formal meetings. We had very few because we spoke to each other every day during office visits or drinking espresso with Mike. Each of us had a different approach to pedagogy but were committed to students first and foremost. One of my own goals was to reach beyond the self-imposed boundaries of "department autonomy." I believed we needed to be a team not only within our department but also form a relationship with other departments. We successfully offered many cross-listed courses with other departments: Psychology, History, American Studies, and African American Studies. The Philosophy and Religious Studies departments jointly sponsored an ethics minor. Prior to the ethics minor, our department worked with a variety of departments to sponsor a Peace Studies minor and Social Justice minor. I wanted to assure students and faculty that the study of religions is important to a well-rounded education. When the college first initiated a required first year experience on a common theme with two components: a course in one of the Arts and Sciences and a writing course paired with the English Department, our department immediately joined together with the latter for courses in Peace Studies, Social Justice, and World Religions. We also worked with the other Schools such as Business, Nursing, and Education to provide courses that would support their programs.

I joined one of these College's Learning Communities as they were called while it was still in the experimental stage in preparation for the time they would be "required." I had developed a course, Alienation and Powerlessness, as a stand-alone course. It fit in beautifully with the mission of the college: to prepare people to serve others. I later taught a course on Peace and Justice focusing on the lives of people who dedicated their lives to peace like Dorothy Day, Ghandhi, Martin Luther King Jr. Because of my interest in Celtic Spirituality and a summer institute in Ireland, I also offered a Learning Community with the theme of Ireland: Land of Saints, Poets, and Revolutionaries. In my last years at the college, I was still teaching that course. It helped support an Irish Studies Program which Dr. Tim Madigan capably directed. It offered an opportunity to partner with Fionnuala Regan, a member of the English Department, who had rich Irish roots. I focused on Celtic spirituality and the history of Ireland; she focused on the literature. We worked together developing syllabi, supporting the student presentations at the annual Learning Community fest, hosting occasional speakers, and, most importantly, checking with each other about the students: their grades, attendance, work ethic, and personal issues that often surface with first year students. We made a great team! Watching some of the Learning Community students' progress over four years and then sitting during their graduation often brought a tear to my eyes. I was proud of them and. in some small way, I like to think I helped start them on their journey. A few students went to Ireland for a semester abroad while some travelled with their grandparents to visit relatives. Others learned about another culture and realized how much alike we all are despite differences in language, religious beliefs (or lack thereof), geography, or politics.

One year, in late September, a student approached me after class to ask if it would be okay if he missed a week and a half of class in November. My natural reaction was "NO!" However, I gently asked "Why?" "My uncle is going to be made a Cardinal in Rome and the whole family is going." How could I say "no" after that bit of information? There would be no problem and we could work out the assignments so he would not miss any class material. I did, however, add, "You can go but you need to ask your uncle to come to the college for a visit." The following year during the spring semester Cardinal Joseph Tobin visited the college where he delivered a public lecture discussing Pope Francis' vision for the Church. We had a small dinner with the Cardinal, the president and his wife, members of the department and our majors and minors, Bishop Clark, and two members of the local Redemptorists community. At one time Cardinal Tobin had been the superior general of the Redemptorists Fathers and Brothers. Both knew the Cardinal when they worked with him during his time in Rome. His public lecture brought many people, including many of the local clergy, to the college campus that night. They left with deeper insights into the mind of a Pope who lived up to one of his titles: Pontiff. The title implies a willingness to "build bridges" between other religions, cultures, and social-economic backgrounds. Pope Francis continues to remind the Church and others that we need to "accompany one another" with an openness of mind and heart. Would that other leaders adopt that mindset!

Another speaker we brought to campus was Chris Lowney, a prolific writer and fantastic speaker, who wrote a book *Pope Francis, Why He Leads the Way He Does*. His talk and the one given by Cardinal Tobin both underlined the Pope's own background as the basis for the Pontiff's actions: his immigrant family background, his religious training as a Jesuit (the *Spiritual Exercises*, examen of conscience, thoughtful discernment), as a human being (the joy of soccer, the tango, reading, opera), and the difficult assignments he weathered as a priest and as a bishop.

Before I begin to talk more about my experience with students in the classroom, I need to turn to another facet of being a teacher and administrator at any educational institution: meetings and membership on committees. Most of us who signed up to be teachers did not envision lengthy faculty meetings which might be interesting only for the dynamics and the ruminations of the same cast of characters. Some members of the faculty came to meetings only when one of their pet projects or gripes were on the agenda. At our luncheon meetings of Departments Chairs, I, as did many of my colleagues, could predict when one of our members would leave the meeting: shortly after he had finished the free meal. I often played an imaginary game of Bingo during some of the discussions as I checked off the same speakers' pros and cons toward whatever was up for discussion. Another example was how the committee for producing the academic calendar would present its suggested dates for the semesters. One of our more outspoken faculty members would challenge the calendar each year suggesting that the semesters should be one week longer so the students could read another book or finish an added assignment. She did not receive much support for her well-meaning annual appeal, but I did admire her persistence. My mental Bingo card filled up rather quickly at that meeting.

In the nearly forty years I was on the faculty the core requirements for the School of Arts and Science changed at least three times in the last 20 years. Each time we went through this tedious and painful process deans and committee members guaranteed how this "new core" would add to the excitement for learning that students were seeking during their college career. Some good things did happen (e.g., the Learning Community with a focused writing component), but the confusion and frustration working through some of the changes challenged my patience. I became a bit conservative about the goals of education. I basically believed "teach people to read and they can educate themselves." That would put many of us out of a job. I viewed the professor's job, however, as creating an atmosphere in which students became curious and free to explore new ideas. Students might even discover something new about themselves or that the new material encourages their further growth. I can plant the seed, but hopefully it will grow and blossom as the student continues a life-time commitment to further learning. At least once a semester in one of my courses I would ask students. "If you could write out a check for $100,000 and we would send you your bachelor's diploma OR pay $100,000 and spend four years taking courses, doing projects, and writing papers, which would you choose?" Each time I posed the question about 70% of the class would vote to send in a check. Much can be learned at college if one is open and curious even about the dynamics of living together with others of different beliefs and interests. At the same time, I hear from former students who tell me what they are still reading: a current novel or self-help book for their job. They are the same ones who truly came to college "to learn to learn." It becomes a lifetime journey.

I relate the following story often. Bryan was a graduate student who was taking a course from another professor. In one of our conversations, the beleaguered professor told me about a student who lacked the necessary writing skills. He flipped pages of the student's latest assignment that proved his point with some examples marked with red ink. About a year later the same student approached me to ask if I would be the second reader for his master's thesis. He handed it to me on a Wednesday night. Because of my schedule, I could not promise him immediate feedback. Then I remembered a conversation with an old friend who told me how his professor would stay up all night reading the chapters of his dissertation to give him immediate feedback so he could make the necessary changes for its successful defense to graduate on time. I decided to do just that. I called the student on Thursday asking to meet with him on Friday for feedback. He arrived on time expecting a brief meeting but three hours later we finished going through the thesis noting grammatical errors and questioning his sequence of thought. Although I encouraged him to make the changes and offered to meet again to review his re-write, he left a bit depressed to put it mildly. He returned a few days later with a corrected version of the thesis. It was much improved.

Bryan was much more at ease and positive that he could submit the thesis for a final presentation to the thesis committee. The encouraged student then invited me to the presentation. Articulate and enthusiastic about his topic, the presentation was outstanding. When the Chair of the committee asked him what he liked most about the program, my new friend responded, "Working with Fr. Bill!" Later he entered the college's doctoral program in leadership. I could not be an official member of his committee, but he asked me to meet with him on a regular basis to discuss what he was learning and to bounce off ideas for his doctoral dissertation. For the next few years, we met at the Olive Garden for many dinners and Papa Jack's, a nearby family restaurant, for Saturday breakfasts. I suggested books he might read and asked pointed questions about his dissertation project. My meal-time student earned his degree and has continued to read. I treasure his comment over breakfast a few years later "I cleaned out all my textbooks when I moved. The only books I kept were the ones you gave me or ones that I bought because you suggested I might want to read." A successful businessman, husband, and father, he still reads new books and re-reads some of the old ones. My point? READ!

One of my favorite committees reviewed the academic standing of students. At the end of the year, we would approve the various rankings for the graduating seniors. That was an easy task: the numbers were there: 4.0, 3.5, 3.0 (summa cum laude, magna cum laude, cum laude). The more challenging (and difficult) meetings were when we decided who should or should not return the following semester because of poor grades or those seeking re-admission after time off to deal with personal issues or after taking courses elsewhere to receive sufficiently good grades to return. We listened to those in the academic advising office, the Registrar, faculty, and to each other. What I remember most about those difficult meetings was the care and concern for each student. There were painful discussions as we read the student's appeal including the reasons and the plan of action to do better and were aware of the consequences of our decision. If I knew the student, I could offer a more personal addendum to the appeal. I would often volunteer to spend time with the students during their probation period if they were allowed to return. Others would do the same, teaming with the academic advising department to assure a positive outcome. A semester later we would reassess the student's progress or standing. Most often there were significant positive changes to the students' grades and work ethic.

Many other memories surface. During one of our meetings, I heard a particular student's name mentioned as a candidate for dismissal for reason of grades. I uttered "Good" louder than I meant. My colleagues looked at me with surprise because I usually gave reasons to keep students at the college. I went on to explain that I had this student in class. Despite a few firm but gentle warnings he failed to hand in assignments on time and was frequently absent. My attendance policy was strict, but I allowed for absences if students notified me. Additionally he had a poor attitude during our "father-son" talks about the course (e.g., "I am busy with other things" or "I am tired after team-practice and need to rest"). I was not the only teacher who had similar problems. His grades were far from stellar so he was dismissed. Two years later he stopped by my office to tell me "I was in the neighborhood, and I thought I would stop by to see how you were doing." "I am doing fine, and the classes are going well," I replied as I was thinking, "Yeah right, 'you were in the neighborhood.'" He finally asked how he might get back into school. I told him about the appeals process. "Would you help me?" he asked very sheepishly. After two or three discussions and proofreading his appeal letter, the reformed student submitted the letter to the committee which, in turn, welcomed him back. He had taken courses at a community college, had a full-time job, and realized that negative behavior had its consequences. The now more mature student would stop by my office to chat, give me an update about his courses, and express his gratitude for my help until he graduated. Sometimes "tough love" is effective.

Another student was in a similar academic sinking-boat. We had more than one heart-to-heart conversation about all his courses. The committee initially voted to dismiss him. but he made an extraordinarily strong and well-written appeal. The committee was impressed by his plan of action if he remained in school with regular meetings with both his academic advisor and me. The chastened student was put on probation and graduated with good grades. When he told me he was planning to take a course in philosophy, I almost choked. He was far from a philosopher type but I encouraged him to try it. Not only did he attend class but he would stop by the professor's office for discussion and further questions about material covered in the course, Metaphysics. It became one of his favorite courses. Six years later we stay connected. Recently I found his appeal letter by accident and received a text from him as well. He has a job but still looks for the right one before he settles down to raise his own family. His major challenge as a student was procrastination so I am not waiting for a wedding invitation anytime soon.

I found my membership in the group of first year advisors a real joy. Each of the members was responsible for meeting with their advisees during the summer orientation programs, helping them to deal with their assigned courses for the first semester. We would meet with them both semesters to follow up on their progress and to advise them as they made their course selection for the following semester. Once a week we would meet as a class to deal with issues that often challenge first year students such as time management, living with roommates, misuse of alcohol, manipulating social media, etc. Each faculty member worked with a "student co-advisor." After a faculty nomination and an interview, the co-advisors enrolled in a course outlining the material to be covered, issues that might surface with their "advisees", and helpful ways to work with the faculty advisor. One assignment was to develop a class presentation to stimulate a discussion for one of our class meetings. Their creativity was amazing. On more than one occasion, especially when discussing social media, my co-advisors saved me from embarrassing myself. I remember one semester when we were told to discuss the various kinds of social media and their proper use. As I sat listening to the presentation and watching the various PowerPoints, I had a sense of how someone from a non-English country might feel listening to the evening news. It was almost literally "Greek to me" especially when I could not translate any of the abbreviated words flashed on the screen. I thanked the presenter with a sigh of relief. I did not have to show how ignorant I am when it came to social media and the new language of abbreviations.

During the summer orientation meetings, we would meet with our new advisees in small groups. To start off these one-hour sessions, we were encouraged to begin with a "creative icebreaker" so we could learn names and the interests that brought students to college. Members of the group would also have an opportunity to meet other incoming classmates. Icebreakers are not my favorite thing as a participant, so I was aware the same might be true for some students especially introverts. Most often I would ask the question, "What was your favorite book you read during your four years of high school?" The responses were typically books assigned for an English course. In one of our sessions, an energetic young man said, "I never read a book in high school. I think I read a Harry Potter book in eighth grade." I tried not to show what I was thinking. My thoughts did come true at the end of the semester when his name appeared on the Academic Standing Committee's agenda: dismissal because of extremely poor grades and class attendance. Because he was a first-year student, the committee allowed him to return on probation. He transferred to another college at the end of the second semester.

That reminded me of another student whom I knew well. During her high school years, she had been assigned to read *To Kill a Mockingbird* in three different courses. She never read the book but successfully passed the courses. When I suggested she should at least watch the movie, the reluctant reader told me she started to "but it was in black and white . . . so it would be boring." For her graduation I gave her a copy of the book and the DVD of the movie. She laughed but I doubt she read the book or watched the movie. Ten years later the same young lady saw me at a friend's home for dinner. She proudly told me she had her dream job and just finished a book that was a real help to her, wondering if I had read the same book. I had not but I would check it out and we could talk about it at our next get-together. Meanwhile I offered her a set of magazines that were along the same theme as the book. She was excited and grateful that she was reading more than when she was in high school or college.

One semester during an initial meeting with an advisee, he embarrassedly told me he had not declared a major and was not sure what to do. I long thought it might be best if no student came with a major in mind but instead explored a variety of courses and then chose a possible major at the end of the year. I know this is not especially practical for many parents or for a student who is convinced that "I have always dreamed that I wanted to be . . . " I assured him that it was okay to be uncertain about his major and he had at least two years to declare one. He informed me that his father encouraged him to be a business major. I countered with a simple "take time to think about this." His speedy response was, "But my father thinks I should be a business major." My response was as quick, "Your father runs your life at home; I run your life here. Give yourself time!" He did find a major that fit his intellectual needs and writing talents. He graduated, went to law school, became a successful lawyer, and has an even brighter future.

I remember one young woman who was all excited about being a nurse. A month into her first semester she arrived at my office in tears to tell me that she did not know that nurses had to study biology and other science courses. "I hate science." She did not know that nurses had to know science and, besides, "I can't stand the sight of blood." A much happier student, she graduated with a double major: sociology and political science.

Each year administrators would remind the faculty that we need to work at our retention rate. This makes the college look better, especially if it were a 90% plus. The faculty did work hard to retain students by tutoring, allowing extra time for examinations or submitting papers, permitting re-writes of poor papers, and advising courses that might better serve the student's interest. These were some ways to retain students. To the chagrin of one administrator, I admitted I suggested to at least one uncertain student each year they go to a community college or take a gap year to "find themselves." Once they found a direction for themselves, they could return to finish a four-year degree. If for no other reason, it would save them and, especially, their parents, money.

I remember one student who was doing poorly. We had a conversation about his grades and his lack of enthusiasm for learning. "What do you want to do with your life?" His quick reply was "I want to study photography. I want to be a photographer." "We only offer one course in photography here. Is this the right college for you?" I will not forget his answer. "No, but I can't afford RIT (Rochester Institute of Technology)." Each year we lost a few first-year students to homesickness or who needed to be closer to home. Other students left because of problems at home or financial issues. And of course, other students realized college was not for them. One wanted to be a salesman and make money. College was slowing him down. He did leave, became a salesman, is making a good salary, and is happy. When we talk or text, this same former student tells me he is reading some good books now . . . including the Bible.

I am not sure where he is today, but there was another first semester student at the college whose fall semester was "rocky" for many reasons. At our first meeting the new first year student told me he was a commuter and usually went home after his last class each day. Because he was a business major, he inquired if I had any idea where he might find a job relating to business. His father was president of a bank in NYC so he thought working part time at a bank might be a natural. I tempered his eagerness to have a job as soon as possible suggesting that he might want to spend his first semester acclimating to college life. "That made sense," he responded without any hesitation. At our next meeting he looked a bit tired and distraught. He had not been sleeping well because of tension between him and his girlfriend. She also was from NYC. I initially assumed that it was a long-distance relationship moving towards a breakup as often was the case with some first-year students. When I asked if he wanted to talk about, it was a quick "YES!" Then he told me his story. His parents rented an apartment for him and his girlfriend off campus. That explained why he was a commuter who told me he was from NYC. First-year students, unless they lived at home, were required to live on campus. The student admitted he had deceived the admissions office about his residence. His parents arranged for them to live together while he attended college. His girlfriend was to find a job to stay busy while he studied. She had not found a job and he was not studying like he should. Over the next few months his attendance record plummeted; he neglected his assignments. Even with our frequent conversations things did not improve. The parental arrangement and knowledge of the relationship made me think of more than a few pointed questions I would have liked to ask his mother and father. Over Christmas vacation he called to tell me he had been put on academic probation, ended the relationship with his girlfriend, decided to leave the college, and live at home until things cooled down. Need I say more?

So many memories of working with first-year students in the classroom and as an academic advisor come to mind, some with joy, others with dismay. During our final class I would ask questions about their first semester experience. From over 25 years of teaching these young men and women, the response to one of my questions "What was one thing you wish you had done differently over the semester?" was almost always the unanimous response, "Manage my time better." We talked about it during one of our first-year seminar courses; it was "theory" to them. Struggling to attend classes, be a member of a club or sports team, read the texts, submit written assignments, maybe have a part-time job on campus, enjoy a social life, eat at least two meals, and sleep was "reality." These exhausted students would end the final class with a resounding, "I am looking forward to vacation so I can sleep . . . next semester I am going to pay attention to time management." I became angry when new administrators, without consulting the seasoned faculty, decided on another untested approach to the First Year Seminar. None of the administrators had ever taught the course or were first-year advisors. Wisdom does not always come from on high!

Me, as a Teacher

TEACHING HAS BEEN MY PASSION for as long as I can remember. It was, however, always connected with being a priest. As I went through my pre-teen years, I could predict for each Christmas an educational set for something or other like a Chemistry set, a dentist set, a set of dominos, a dictionary, a desk for writing, etc. Whatever I received, I would think wouldn't it be great to be a priest-dentist, a priest-chemist, a priest-lawyer, a priest-teacher who would travel to different countries like China, Japan, Germany, England, Mexico to teach or explore its sites. Books took me all over the world. I was able to live through different periods of history and learn different languages. To this day when I think about all the places I visited, I imagined myself as a priest-teacher who was (and is) eager to learn. My main hope, as a college professor, was to share my passion for learning, especially with young people.

To paraphrase Charles Dickens, "I had the best of teachers; the worst of teachers." I was very lucky to have had some great teachers throughout my life. I look back to the Sisters of Saint Joseph who taught me in grade school. We memorized our catechism lessons, were taught how to diagram sentences and write good English sentences, read good books, and listened to stories of great people. In a word, I learned that I needed discipline if I wanted to do well in life. Sister Emmanuel, our 7th and 8th grade teacher and principal of our school, would remind us: "Emmanuel means 'God with us' but for some of you it might mean 'God help us.'" Twenty years later, she retired and lived at the order's Motherhouse. I was invited to give a talk to the community of retired residents. She sat in the front row proud as could be that one of her students had made it. Her sense of commitment to help her students be the best at whatever they did underlined my approach to teaching. I remember her berating a student who had failed to pay attention. "Look, you might not be very smart, but you need to do your best at whatever you do. Stick with me and I will help you" (not quite today's pedagogical approach). He graduated, found a job collecting garbage, worked hard for many years, and eventually became a supervisor of many of the local public works projects. He did do his best because Sister Emmanuel did help him.

I was very lucky to have some dedicated teachers in Buffalo's high school seminary. The bishop assigned them to teach "something" just as long as they cared for their students. About ten years ago I visited Msgr. Paul Juenker, the last living teacher then in his nineties from my high school days. I wanted to visit him to thank him for his care, enthusiasm, and assure him that I fashioned my teaching methods on his and that of other faculty especially care for the students and enthusiasm for my course material. Msgr. Juenker taught me sophomore English. He eventually became the rector of the seminary. Our conversation during that visit revolved around the different faculty: how each was assigned and how each had to learn to teach his subject. In those days teaching certificates were not a requirement for teaching in a private school. Over seventy years later I still hear their voices, see their faces, watch their movements, and catch their love for teaching because that was what they were asked to do. They were models for loving their students and great pedagogy.

I reluctantly choose to write about the "worst teachers," but I remember them because I learned what not to do and how not to treat students. I too have failed on more than one occasion but do remember our professor of pedagogy in graduate school. The first day of class he walked into the classroom yawning. He sat down at the desk still yawning even though it was an afternoon class. His opening words, and I kid you not, were "When you are teaching (yawn), you need to show enthusiasm for the material (yawn)" and pointing to the blackboard continued, "and be sure to use the blackboard." The course went downhill from there. When I was in college our first-year English teacher gave us frequent quizzes that still haunt me: e.g., list the number of ways one would use a semicolon, what color was the suit the main character was wearing in chapter three, etc. The quizzes were as bizarre as the written assignments and the grades. No matter how I answered the quizzes or wrote the assigned two-page compositions, I almost always received a C. When I compared my answers to the quizzes with other students, they were usually the same except they received an A or B. Years later in a conversation with a classmate about the course, my grades, and the teacher, he informed me that the same professor told him that he was giving me grades of C to make sure I worked harder. I wish the teacher had said something to me but looking back he never spoke to me. I do remember that 30 years later he stopped by the rectory where I was pastor. The visit was unexpected. I offered him a cup of coffee and then had a pleasant hour-long conversation about issues of the day. He thanked me for the coffee, shook my hand, and told me how grateful he was that I was one of his students. When he was driving off, I asked myself, "Why couldn't we have had a conversation like that 30 years ago?"

What does all this have to do with my years as a teacher? I wanted my students to share in my passion for whatever I was teaching. They could make mistakes, but I was willing to help them. Early on a member of the department was upset that I did not fail more students. "I thought my job was to assure they would pass the course" was my retort. The Dean hinted at the same issue during one of our meetings. I told him I usually give the students a chance to rewrite their assignments until they receive the grade for which they were hoping. I remember one student doing a third rewrite of a paper until he earned the desired B.

My attendance policy was a bit strict: I allowed 2-3 unexcused absences. My classes involved a group discussion each class, a brief lecture and a sharing of their weekly journal entries, when appropriate, a video clip or a movie might take a few classes to watch and discuss. The lectures were meant to help them understand the text and were like building blocks for subsequent understanding of the course material. Miss one block and the student might not be able to understand the next block. The students could email/call me if they were to be absent. It would not be counted against them. Why did I do this? I explained that I care that they do well. My experience taught me too many absences lead to late assignments poorly written, a lack of understanding of the material they missed or failed to grasp, and a general lack of knowledge of the subject. I was also concerned that they might be sick, have a death in the family, or "just be having a bad day." Part of the class sessions might additionally be a group project worth five credits. Their presence was required to get the group grade. When I explained this policy on the first day of the course, I added "I require this because I care for you as a person and that you do well in the course."

I do have a story about grades and group work. At the end of the semester, just before exam week, I asked the students to fill out a form indicating their grades for the semester, add them up and note the rubric for assigning different grades. I checked them with my own entries to see if I had made any mistakes when I entered grades into the computer program. The students then checked their Blackboard account on their computer to learn their final grade for the semester. Throughout the semester I noted the grades for their assignments (journal entries, quizzes, major paper, and group discussion grades) on Blackboard as well as for any other assignments. Sometimes students did not add up their grades correctly even when they used a calculator to do so. Following this process they would know their final grade the week before the final exam week. If they saw where they missed an assignment or desired a higher grade, they could check with me to see what we could work out.

With that lengthy explanation, I can now relate my story about a young woman who came into the classroom to tell me that she was not happy with her grade. She wanted an A-; I had given her a B+. I told her I would check it out. Without a doubt, it was a solid B+. When I tried to explain that her assignments were good, but her group discussion questions were not, she went to her desk only to return a few minutes later, threw the syllabus at me, told me to read it, and climaxed her fury with "There is nowhere in the syllabus where it says that the answers have to be correct." With a smile, I gently responded "B+." When I told the story to the provost, he observed, "Maybe she should become a lawyer." Then he told me about a mother and father who wanted to sue the college because their daughter had not received an A in one of her courses. The reason they gave for suing the college, "We pay a great amount of money for her tuition so she should get an A."

Over the years I was called too conservative, too liberal, too progressive, favoring women over men, favoring men over women, racist because I gave good grades or because I gave bad grades, favored athletes, treated athletes unfavorably, not available, not supportive of administrative decisions, blindly supportive of administrative decisions, lectured too much, did not lecture enough, used group work too much, did not have enough group work . . . to name a few allegations.

One student told me I was not available. I gave him the syllabus. My office hours were from 8:00 in the morning until 5:00 in the afternoon. I could be reached by phone or at home 24/7 both in person or leaving a message I would return the call as soon as I was free. My e-mail account was also available. I added that I usually got up at 5:30 in the morning for breakfast and prayer so, unless it were an emergency, please wait until I am available at 8:00 a.m. The only time I was out of my office was for class, meetings, or an occasional cup of coffee. I would tape a note on my office door with information noting where I was and when I would return. So I asked him, "Do you have any ideas how else I could be available?"

My office was in a corridor with other faculty offices and a classroom. One day a neighboring professor jokingly said, "I see all those Catholic school students coming to your office. They were trained well in grade school and high school." I laughed. For the next few days, I noted those who came to my office. I had an open-door policy so students could stop by if they were in the neighborhood or taking a class in the classroom near me. It turned out that most of them were not Catholic at all or were Catholics who had drifted away from churchgoing. I prided myself on welcoming anyone, anytime, into my office or into my classroom.

One morning before I drove off to school, I received an anonymous telephone call from a male student at a nearby college. He berated me for a few minutes with a few expletives and threats "to beat the sh*t out of me" because I gave his girlfriend a poor grade on her paper. Basically, I was a sexist SOB. I asked him to tell his girlfriend to stop by so I could check over the paper to see what I might have missed. He thought that was ridiculous because I always gave males better grades than females. With that he slammed down the phone. It had me thinking, "Did I give better grades to men over women?" I went to my grade book, added up grades of men and women, noted the ranking according to grades only to discover that grades for the women were better than those of the men. Armed with the information and my tape recorder I went to class. I did not mention the phone call but told the students, "I am recording this just in case there are any questions about my remarks at a later date." I told them about my grading practices, how I weigh grades by content as well as good grammar, my availability to discuss grades with an appointment in my office to assure privacy and time to review their paper before making the appointment. I further pointed out my willingness to read over their draft before the paper is submitted and, of course, that they can rewrite the paper after we discuss it to make sure they know why the grade was given. I also added a detailed statistical analysis of the grades between male and female students. I asked if there were any questions. None. I turned off the recorder and began the lesson for the day.

I can hardly forget the young lady who came to the first class offered in the early afternoon. She stretched out her arms over the desk so she could rest her head. I was willing to give her the benefit of a doubt because of the weather, time of day. and it was a Monday. However, this became a habit. When she was in a group for discussion purposes, her relaxed posture would be the same with little participation. Her group was to make a presentation. They came to me beforehand complaining that the "relaxed student" did not come to any of the planning sessions even after several texts and emails. Their presentation date arrived. I caught a rather tense conversation going on within the group. The wayward student was asking what she should do or say. Playing dumb, I asked what seemed to be the problem. "All she had to do is present her part of the assigned topic." Her reply, "I did not do anything." I told her that she had better just sit with the class to let her group make the presentation. "I do not want to see you embarrassed." She sat down reluctantly. After class, she asked me if she could make up for her lack of participation "like write a paper." I said calmly, "No, the purpose of the assignment was not only to present material but also to work as a group-skills for the presentation. The group work and discussions were practical applications of the course's goals and material." She walked away angry. It did not stop there. She later submitted an assignment which was poorly written. When she complained about the grade, I suggested that she go to the Writing Center to get some additional help. That was the wrong suggestion! She became quite angry at the thought of doing that. More words were exchanged, and I admit mine were not softly spoken. The young lady walked away muttering a few threats. A few days later I was summoned to the Dean's Office to explain myself. I did not detail her behavior for the semester, but admitted I could have done things differently. She passed the course. I began to be very cautious when suggesting anyone go to the Writing Center.

Teaching religion to any group can be a challenge but there was also the human dimension. As I looked over the various allegations about me (unfair grading, biased, e.g.), I often wondered could they be true. Sometimes I would lose a night's sleep when someone made an accusation to my face or when an administrator challenged me. I took them seriously but over many years (about 55) I concluded I am certainly a bit of everything (a bit liberal versus a bit conservative). That would land me in the center. That is probably where a good teacher should be: to present the different sides of the material, that is, teach people how to make a mature decision once they have reviewed their own research realizing that as we continue to grow older our ideas will be challenged. We might change our mind or learn to be tolerant of other points of view. Teaching is more about learning to ask better questions more clearly.

I think one of the most treasured compliments was from a devout Muslim. One semester I taught a basic course titled Introduction to Religion. Hussain stopped by my office to tell me that the course had made him a better Muslim. It had him thinking that it might be an innovative idea to bring people of different religions together in a social event to discuss their beliefs, their questions, and their own religious journey. It took two years for his idea to materialize. By the time this talented pre-med student was a senior, he had pursued a dual major in Religious Study Studies along with Biology. As a final project, Hussain organized such an event. Because free food brings people (especially college students) together, the food service agreed to feed students in one of the conference rooms near the dining hall. Students and a member of the faculty or staff sat at round tables to allow for better cross-the-table conversations with others. The seating encouraged students of different faith traditions to sit around the same table. There were no speeches. Hussain thanked them for coming, welcomed them, distributed written questions for each table to discuss, we ate, and discussed. He later talked with someone from each table individually to get a sense of how the evening meal went. "We came from different backgrounds, but all seemed to recognize we are on a journey." The faculty and staff were equally in awe: we are all on a journey. In the New Testament there are references to "seekers." They came from different regions around the Mediterranean area seeking a way of life that leads to the Truth that frees them. A good student and a good teacher is always "seeking." Hussain, always the bright young "seeker," later travelled to Qatar to spend a year to sharpen his spoken Arabic and study the Quran before beginning his studies to become a doctor. While in medical school, he received a grant to spend a summer in Chicago to study Muslim ethics for the practice of medicine. I am quite sure as a doctor he is still searching.

I am a firm believer that students are also good teachers. I was teaching a first year Learning Community course about Celtic spirituality and culture. At the conclusion of the first class, Emily approached me. She had a beautiful smile and a gentle voice. "Would it be okay if I missed class or was late for an assignment now and then? I have a medical condition and every now and then I need to rest for a day or two." She would faithfully notify me when she was a bit ill. Emily was otherwise exceptionally good at her attendance, always submitting her papers on time all through the semester. It was only during the second semester that she missed class more frequently or asked for an extension. What struck me most during that entire first year was how Emily always walked into the classroom with a smile. During our conversations Emily exuded a gentle energy and peace. I can still visualize her years later walking into the classroom, smiling, mouthing "How are you?" with her lips, finding a place to sit, and turning to the people around her to say "Hello." Emily had a sense of caring. Once Covid hit I did not see her any longer. She told me early on that she had to be careful about catching any germs. During the Covid crisis, I found out she had died. The cancer she had lived with during high school and into college finally caught up with her, but it did not stop her from finishing her course work. The President, Dean, and other faculty members gathered with her family for a prayer service and graduation ceremony. Emily was fully aware she might die before finishing college, but it did not stop her from smiling and using her energy to care for those around her. What a lesson for me! Whatever pain and uncertainty in my life, I can still smile and care for others.

For some reason, we can often forget the good things. Mark Antony declared in Shakespeare's *Julius Caesar*, "The evil that men do lives after them; The good is oft interred with their bones." I remember one group that included five of the "Most Interesting" young men I had ever had in my classes. I usually try to make sure every group has at least one stable leader. Five males formed their own group before I could intervene. Looking back,

I understand why no female student would ever choose to be in the group because of the five playful, disorganized men. The five were not bad but they needed a great deal of tender loving care to encourage them to stay on task. I enjoyed their banter as I would move from group to group during the assigned discussions. There were three from one sports team and two from another. Their latest games and scores were the usual topic not the assigned questions.

Towards the end of the semester each group was to present the results of their common research about an issue that surfaced during the semester. I held my breath the day this "Band of Brothers" was to make their presentation. First, they all came dressed in a shirt, tie, and khaki pants with sports jackets. They were a bit earlier than usual. Quickly and with organizational precision they set up the computer for the presentation, checked with each other one last time for the order of the presentation, and once the class began introduced themselves and proceeded to give one of the best presentations that I had witnessed over many years of teaching. At its conclusion, the class applause was louder than usual: my jaw dropped a foot. I later congratulated them, mentioning how proud I was of them and their presentation. With a mischievous smile, one of them spoke up and smiled. "We did not want to let you down." They did not. Fifteen years later I still remember them fondly: their good was not "interred with their bones."

Because of my open-door policy from my arrival at 8:00 in the morning until I left at 5:00ish, I had many special conversations with a wide variety of topics and people. I never kept track, but I must guess that a sizable number of them were about a "break-up" with their significant other. I was in awe of their openness. When a 220-pound, 6-foot-3 athlete broke down in tears because his girlfriend had ended their relationship, I felt blessed by his trust in me. I dealt with betrayed young women whose boyfriends were sneaking around with their roommate or from another college. For about 35 years I offered each semester the Marriage and Sexuality course. I always dedicated one section of the course to the importance of honest communication within a relationship. I warned them that "honest communication" around a complicated subject means to avoid using e-mail or texting. It is best to do it in person so there would be less confusion and misinterpretation. I offered that bit of advice on a Thursday afternoon in my 1:45-2:55 class. The next morning about 9:00 a male student arrived at my office, asked me if he could close the door, sat down, and started to cry. "If I had only listened to you yesterday. You were right. I texted my girlfriend last night to tell her I had done something wrong, hoping it would not interfere with our relationship. She texted me back to tell me the relationship was over. I called her to explain. The conversation got worse. If I had only listened!" I do not remember the exact thing he "confessed to" but I do remember it was very insignificant. If he had only taken my advice. They did get back together later after extensive "in person" conversations. He did, however, meet another woman, married, founded his own business, and now has three children. I hope he instructs his children not to text their significant other if they need to deal with a thorny issue.

I must put into writing one of my "conservative" thoughts. I mentioned earlier that I am accused of being too liberal or too conservative or too progressive and also accused that I am not conservative or liberal or progressive enough. That makes me a little of everything. I tend to be more conservative however when it comes to education. On a visit to one of my doctors he mentioned that the health care system "is becoming a disaster." He went on to speak about the cost of medical school, the insurance for doctors and patients, forms to be filed with different agencies, and a few additional complaints I cannot remember. I do remember him taking a breath and ending the tirade with question, "What can we to do about it?" My response was a very quick, "Well, doctor, I feel the same way about education, and I have decided that the best thing we could do is blow up the system and start from scratch." He looked at me, smiled, and replied, "You have a point."

Elementary school teachers blame the parents; the high school teachers blame the elementary school teachers; the college teachers blame the high school teachers; the graduate department teachers blame the undergraduate teachers. Everyone blames the administrators and sometimes rightfully so. Many of the same administrators blame the parents and the School Board. I remember one of my graduate school mentors bemoaning that she had to add a course on remediation for the master's candidates and doctoral students to better their writing skills. I think back to a chance encounter with one of my colleagues from the English department on one of our "bad days." We were both grumbling about the lack of our students' basic writing skills. (As an aside, I usually asked such a student, "Did you ask someone to read the assignment before you submitted it?" I already knew the answer.) My colleague and I both agreed that a main factor for poor writing is the lack of proficient reading and critical thinking skills. Were they taught to read and enjoy it when they were younger? I have heard more than one graduating student laughing as s/he bragged that they went through college without a visit to the library or even reading the texts assigned in many of their courses. One told me that he only bought one book while in college. It was a workbook that had to be finished and submitted to earn their final grade. These encounters had me thinking over the past few years, "Should we go back to the basics in elementary school: Reading, Writing, and Arithmetic?" All this before eBooks and AI.

If we could find ways to make reading enjoyable rather than a task, I believe we could let students find ways to discover history, literature, poetry, geography, and even some self-help books to meet their personal needs. I am also convinced that the basics could allow students to express themselves in essays, journaling, poetry, and even short stories. I have never been much of a math or science person myself but that has not kept me from trying to work out math problems or exploring simple science, even trying an occasional experiment on my own. Perhaps teachers could take more the role of a "guide" when teaching reading, encouraging students to pursue their own kind of literature. I remember a house painter with a high school education who carried a book with him to work to read during his lunch break. During mealtime, each night he would tell his family what he was reading and how the latest book got him thinking differently. Fifty years later his son continued with his father's reading habit. Another adult friend, an immigrant with an elementary education, read the *New York Times* every day. In discussions with his friends, he could argue different points of view, quote data, and address events that were occurring in a distant country. His fellow-workers admired his thinking and his insights about a variety of topics always done humbly and gently. His son, Chris, went off to college, graduated, and spent most of his career as a college advisor. I always found Chris to be one of the best conversationalists, who, like his father, read and encouraged his advisees to do the same.

I spent time with these avid readers enjoying their company and views about current events. Now for a contrast! A few years later I read of a local professional basketball player, whose coach I knew, who was suing his coach for firing him from the team. The coach had recruited him as a high school student for the local high school team and later for a nearby college where he had become the coach. The player graduated and entered the ranks of the professionals. The basis for the lawsuit was that without a place on the team he would not be able to earn a living because he did not know how to read or write sufficiently to get another job. Where did the system fail? Not even the basics? Now you have some idea why I hold to my conservative view when it comes to the basics of education. I could continue with another set of questions. "Is higher education living up to its name?" "Is higher education becoming basic training for a job in the marketplace?" "Is its emphasis on what 'we can do' rather than on 'who we are'?" Recent commentators suggest that in less than a decade robots and Artificial Intelligence will replace as many as 40% of our present jobs. Will a "higher education" encourage its graduates to be creative as they imagine, prepare the way, and find meaning to a new approach for living one's life? So much for my conservative rambling!

Life's journey has its ups and downs. There are the "good days" and the "more challenging days." Over the 55 years of teaching high school, college undergraduate and graduate students I can quickly say there were way many more "ups" than "downs." Most often as I walked from the classroom to my office, driving home, or after a difficult conversation I would ask myself. "What went well? What could I have done/said better?" I still do this as I walk back to my apartment after I celebrate Mass or teach a course for the residents where I live. It allows me the time and opportunity to propose for myself new approaches to change for the better. I also found time to give thanks for the basic goodness of each student (sometimes mentioning their names).

The Covid crisis certainly has changed my life when it challenged me to find "new approaches to change for the better." It began when the college rightfully decided to close after the Spring Break mid-March 2020. The remainder of the semester would be done online. Fortunately for me I had planned to finish most of the class assignments and lectures about that time to allow students more time to work on any missed assignments but also to allow them more time on their major courses. I am not good at technology so correcting papers, dealing with group work for grading, and manipulating all this for over one hundred students online was a serious challenge. At the time I was not prepared to teach via Zoom classes. That would come later. I did manage to finish the semester successfully. No one failed and the grades were submitted on time. Now I was hoping to breathe for a few months with the hope that classes would be back to normal in September. We now know that was only a dream (which became a nightmare) as the summer moved on. Meanwhile the Administration asked those who would be teaching first-year students to sign up for a summer workshop to learn how to use iPads. All entering first-year students were to be issued an iPad in the fall that they would continue to use for all four years at the college. I reluctantly signed up for the course because I needed some healthy space after the technology waterfall of the final weeks of the semester. Philosophically I was not convinced that iPads would be the educational miracle some suggested. I was, however, willing to try.

Graduation was cancelled. The following Monday I became ill. This mysterious illness lasted the entire summer. I was twice checked out for Covid, saw two or three doctors, underwent tests for cancer or some other intestinal disease, slept in a chair thirty days straight, not caring to eat and lost about forty pounds. There was no clear diagnosis. I started the iPad classes amidst all this. The iPad provided mechanical challenges which stymied both the local instructors and the provider. I had my own issues with the iPad: frustration and a sense of failure to finish assignments. I decided to drop the course. That decision did help me physically since I had one less thing to deal with. I spent the summer, like most Americans, in isolation. I was too weak to walk or even read in preparation for the courses I would be teaching in the fall semester. The big question was: will we be teaching?

During the summer months a variety of proposals about the fall semester flowed from the Administration. One was finally adopted. Our classes would be offered in person with added conditions to be used for students who were under quarantine or reluctant to attend in-person. Taking a required Zoom training course is one thing but execution another. With my training and upset stomach I gingerly approached my first class. When I arrived for my 9:00 class, the professor who preceded me from her earlier course was shaking her head. Two students from the technology department were busy pressing buttons and checking the wires for the computer and the sound system. All were trying to figure out what was wrong. I was of little help, only wondering if I might encounter a similar issue during my class. The students were getting restless; the technicians were getting more frustrated. My thought was a simple "Is this going to happen all semester?" About ten minutes into the class, one of the technicians received a call on his cell phone. The whole Zoom system across the country was down. Apparently too many people were trying to get online at the same time. At least it was not I who caused the problem.

Because of the large number of registered students in my three courses, I was assigned to the chapel as my classroom for the semester. Desks were spaced six feet apart with a large screen and microphone system. Because I regularly have students working in groups, I also had to work out the dynamics of arranging space for each chair in the group to be six feet apart in a circle. I regularly had to set up added desks and chairs before each morning class. The chapel was like a sound chamber. If I used a microphone, the students would have problems with the echo. If I did not use one, the students on Zoom could not hear me. Even without a microphone, the students had difficulty in the classroom because of the echo. We were not allowed to distribute handouts for fear of contracting Covid. I used the computer and the large screen to project the outline of my lecture and questions for group discussion. The sunlight in the chapel made using the projected notes very difficult. I often show parts of movies for discussion to help students to understand the geography or historical site under discussion. More technical problems! At the conclusion of each class period, I needed to sit for a few minutes just to collect myself; then I would drag myself to my office because my physical illness was hindering me from my usual lively pace. The fact that the students were mandated to wear masks did not help the environment. I saw their eyes but missed their smiles.

As I was finalizing the courses for the second semester, I made a very difficult decision: to retire. I was physically sick every day and not sleeping any better. I was also concerned because I did not feel I was doing a good job in the classroom. As hard as I tried to be positive, I found myself on edge during the class periods distracted by technology and the misuse of iPads or laptop computers. Students finished the semester at home because of the number of students with symptoms of Covid. That painful experience of teaching each class on Zoom confirmed it was a wise decision for me to retire. One day I saw on screen a young lady in bed fluffing her pillows so she could be comfortable during the lecture. On another occasion one student was riding in a car during the lecture, turned off the camera while she went shopping, and then turned the camera on again as she and her driver returned home. One of my most discouraging experiences during the same period was to discover that a student regularly submitted the very same journal entries as his friend. Notes went off to both. The friend was angry because the shared entries were only to be used to fill in missed classes or reminders of what was covered during class. The guilty party apologized, rewrote the entries and submitted extra work. I had never ended a semester so depressed, frustrated, and angry. I had tears as I walked away from my last "in-person" class but I breathed a sigh of relief when I submitted the final grades. My life as a college teacher was over.

Since leaving my position at Saint John Fisher College, I have been invited back to give lectures in the Philosophy Department to speak about ethical issues like care of the world and care in relationships. To begin the 75th Year Anniversary of the founding of the college, I gave a presentation to the alumni/ae about the life of Saint John Fisher at their monthly lecture series. I enjoyed attending the annual Saint Thomas More lecture/dinner series funded by the grant from the William and Helen Cavanaugh Chair of Catholic Studies. The annual retirees' luncheon provided a relaxing opportunity to stay in touch with other retired colleagues from the past. The Dorothy Day Scholarships are still available, but I am not sure how or what is the basis for granting the scholarship. All in all, I left the college (now a university) on a positive note, and it continues to be a source of many happy memories.

My Life at the Legacy (2008-Present)

THE ORIGINAL PROPRIETORS OF the Legacy at the Fairways, Mark4 recruited me to join them as a member of the growing community to serve the religious/spiritual needs of the residents. The Legacy was built to provide a facility for senior citizens to enjoy independent living. On and off over the years, a Protestant minister has served a similar role. Both of us have conducted an interfaith Thanksgiving Service and a Good Friday prayer service every year since its official opening. We take turns preaching and presiding. These celebrations allow for a variety of religious believers to get together for prayer and reflection on a few key times each year. On other occasions we lead memorial services for veterans of the armed services and members of the community who have died during the year. Early on, when I was healthier, I visited residents who were in the hospital. I remember vividly the blessing of the buildings shortly after I arrived. There were about thirty residents along with the owners for the brief ceremony in the main entrance of the building. Other sections were still under construction as was the golf course and individual villas. Prayers, laughter, words from the owners/managers explaining their philosophy: "We are family." A small reception took about an hour and a half to cement the family relationship. The owners were second generation Italians who valued family and a comfortable homelike atmosphere. One member took me aside to assure me that "we" can work together to make it happen.

Initially I was still teaching at Saint John Fisher. The ride to and from the college took about 12 minutes. I timed my trip to beat the traffic both in the morning and evening commute. Going into work I prayed for openness and patience; returning home I prayed for forgiveness for my lack of patience and openness. The ride home also provided time to figure how I might do better the next day. Because of the small number of residents, the meals were more informal for times and seating arrangements. This gave me an opportunity to join in for dinner. I could have had breakfast in the dining room, but I liked my early morning to be a time for prayer, a small breakfast, and time to read the morning paper delivered to our apartments. At that time the paper and the convenience of its delivery was worth the price. As our numbers grew, dining in the evening became more regulated for time, seating arrangements, and menu choices. Because of my schedule, I made the decision to skip dinner at the Legacy. I had dinners out with friends, students, and other faculty. Other times I came home tired because of the day so I enjoyed a bowl of soup or cereal in the quiet of my apartment. That has continued even into retirement. I enjoy dinners with friends, often spontaneously arranged, or just a snack at home when I eat while watching the news. Close friends like Don and Millie Lewis drop off prepared home-cooked meals (like shells, meatballs, eggplant, and sauce) or Mark Wiktorski gives me doggie bags filled with plastic containers of chili or sloppy joes from a dinner at his home. They all know what I enjoy so I have not starved from lack of food.

My new furniture (I only owned a second-hand recliner and bookcases) plus some kitchen items (knives, forks, plates, e.g.,) arrived a few days before I moved in. The two-bedroom apartment had a living room, two baths, a kitchen space, and a washer and dryer for my laundry. It was the right amount of space and extremely comfortable. One of the bedrooms served as my office . . . usually cluttered. I would later move to a similar apartment at the other end of the complex because a potential renter liked my floor plan and wanted a patio and I did not use mine. That is where I have spent the last ten years. If I did not have so many books and files, I could probably live in a smaller apartment. Surrendering the books and files would really be very difficult for me because I would be surrendering my "children" to live in a sterile orphanage or unloving foster home.

The central structure has a small chapel as part of its building plan. Our Catholic community gathered for our first Mass on Saturday afternoon, June 28th, 2008, at 4:00. This would continue to be our scheduled time allowing me the opportunity to assist in nearby parishes on Sunday mornings if needed. Within a year we outgrew the chapel. Family and friends of the residents along with some local non-residents seeking an earlier Mass of anticipation on Saturdays joined us. So, we moved into a larger room where we gathered until Covid struck. Services were suspended for a while during the pandemic. When we were allowed back to regular services, I was asked to use the chapel again. We are now in the chapel at capacity level.

Over the past years our Catholic community was blessed with many volunteers. From our modest beginning until Covid, Lori organized volunteers to arrange the chairs, move the portable altar into its place, appoint lectors, musicians, Eucharistic ministers, and anything else we might need. Without asking, three or four men would take down the chairs and return them to the storage space. We had former church organists, very talented amateur organists and a resident who went by the name of "Harmonica Pete." "Harmonica Pete" was a World War II veteran who had a national reputation for using his music talents at a variety of civil and religious events until his death when he was in his mid-nineties. I have been lucky that a tradition of volunteering continues when Gloria and Cay organize the chapel each Saturday for services and another two or three people help to put things back in order. We share the chapel with the Protestant community which holds their service on Thursdays. We work together to keep the worship space neat and organized.

When we gathered for Mass on the fourth Saturday in 2008, one of the men approached me to inform me that the participants talked among themselves. They wanted us to take up a weekly collection. I told him that there was really no need to do so. He countered, "But we want to!" So the weekly collection began. Someone provided a small basket at the door for those who wanted to contribute. I proposed that we send our collection money to a variety of charities that they could choose. Over the years we have sent money with matching funds probably close to $75,000 to local food banks, safe places for the homeless like Covenant House and the House of Mercy and migrants like Ukraine Refugee Fund, international organizations like Food for the Poor, Catholic Medical Missions, Sisters of Saint Francis, Maryknoll Fathers/Sisters, Red Cross, and Habitat for Humanity to name a few. We do use some of the money to buy our annual missalettes and needed supplies for Mass. Our community is proud of its record of helping others with their generous contributions each week including one or two women who usually donate their Bingo winnings in nickels and quarters.

In addition to our weekly Mass, we have celebrated a few funerals at the Legacy chapel, memorials and interment services, anointing of the sick, availability for the sacrament of reconciliation, but no weddings. The residents are so appreciative of the different ways we have formed a community. I am in awe of their faith, care for each other, and genuine hospitality. I mentioned "no weddings." We almost had one. Bob, age 92, was seeing a woman from another residence about fifteen miles away. Mary, age 88, was very much involved with her community. She was part of a book club, played a variety of board games, attended daily Mass, and was very independent. Bob found the trip between the two residences a challenge because he had to take the expressway. "The traffic is too fast!" Many a dinner was spent discussing his dates, the traffic, and what his thoughts were about their special relationship. One night Bob was particularly silent at dinner. One of the more vocal women at our table finally asked him, "What is wrong? You are awfully quiet tonight." He took a deep breath and with tears in his eyes told us the bad news. Bob decided to ask Mary to marry him. They could live in one of the newly built villas on our property. He was sick of the round-trip visits at her place. They were too dangerous. They seemed to get along and had shown some care for each other, but Mary told him that she did care for him but "did not want to get tied down." She enjoyed her freedom. "Thanks for the offer and we can still be friends." At the end of Bob's story, he sighed and said, "I guess that is that." We never heard about Mary again.

The ten first years I was a resident at the Legacy I was still teaching at the college. Once I retired, I had more time at home. That allowed me the opportunity to continue teaching but more informally. I have conducted a series on the Bible, its history and formation, then focusing on different books in the Old Testament and writings in the New Testament. My aim is to give background to the various biblical writings so the "students" then can do some personal reflection and sharing on their own. We had another series called, "What Religion Teaches about…." It was a question-and-answer series to allow the participants an opportunity to answer some of the questions they have been asking themselves or seeking clarification. Sometimes it forced me to do some research on my own to make sure I was correct. I also led a very popular series about "Aging and Spirituality." All the talks and series were open to everyone. This last series brought the biggest audience. Every now and then I am asked how I like doing these talks and lecture series. My answer is a consistent one. I enjoy giving the various talks because the "students" come because they want to. They take notes with pen and paper. No computers or cell phones are in evidence. The older scholars ask great questions. There are no quizzes or papers to correct, no teacher's assessment, and I do not receive a telephone call from their parents wondering why their child did not receive an A for the course. It is a teacher's dream!

Life at the Legacy has been a source of joy and a sense of community. There is the Catholic community that worships together but there is also the wider community that I meet on their way to exercise class or waiting to enter the dining room. The Coffee Cafe is a great place for my daily cup of cappuccino and often a conversation with like-minded residents. Sometimes the conversation revolves around a book one of us is reading, a recent visit from their children and grandchildren, the latest excursion to a ballgame, a musical, or the trip to a casino.

The very first night I took up residence the fire alarm went off in the middle of the night. I was not sure of the protocol but got dressed and made my way to the main desk to wait for some directions. The only other person who showed up was a male resident who was as confused as I. We waited for a while before the night manager arrived to tell us it was a false alarm. The next day I found out most of the thirty-some residents did not even hear the alarm go off. Yet a male resident and I were the only ones to show up at the desk for instructions about possible evacuation. What was amusing was that he was very hard of hearing. We all enjoyed the humor of the event at dinner the next evening: the deaf heard the alarm; the others did not.

Our dining room has a great deal of natural lighting with plenty of light even without the electric lights. The topic of conversation at dinner for two or three nights was a particular electric light bulb that was out. "Why were they not replacing it?" The hard-of-hearing male resident (who I found out could hear if/when he turned on his hearing aids) complained the loudest because "he could not see to read the morning paper." "There are 164 lights in this place. You would think 'they' could replace that bulb so I could read the paper." When I asked him how he knew how many light bulbs there were, he answered, "I counted them." Tired of hearing about "the light bulb crisis" I stopped by the concierge desk to inform him about the on-going complaint. Grateful, he sighed, "No one had mentioned it. Thanks! I will take care of it." About 45 minutes later I passed the desk on my way to my car. The concierge told me the maintenance crew took care of the light bulb adding "You can handle it anyway you want." That evening as we were eating dinner, we went through the usual reports of what we had been doing all afternoon. When it got to me, I told them how tired I was. "I spent about a half an hour sitting in this dining room praying for the light bulb to turn on. It did." They all turned to see that the errant bulb was now working. "A miracle! From now on when I need something, I am going to ask you to pray. You must have a special 'in' with God," some of the residents exclaimed. I was as good as gold after that "miracle."

The problem with living in an independent living facility where the average age is about eighty is a slow movement toward the need for "assisted living" often in another facility. At the same time, many residents in their nineties are still very active. One resident who was over one hundred years of age spent his winters in Florida and his summers at our Legacy. This allowed him to play golf all year round. At 102 John had just won a golf tournament for seniors while in Florida. He returned the following summer to play more golf but suffered a stroke. This put him in an assisted living residence where he died a year later at 104. Mentally sharp right up to the end of his life, I found my occasional visits with him delightful and inspiring. He knew how to live, and he knew how to die.

A few years back there was a report in the daily paper and the evening news. For every hot dog we eat we would lose 34 minutes off our lifetime.

I was upset because hot dogs are part of my diet . . . at least once a month I usually hit Tom Wahl's or Bill Gray's for a hot dog with everything on it. One night a few of us were sitting on the patio enjoying an after-dinner conversation. I mentioned the news report. One of our residents aged 103 looked up from her wheelchair, smiled, and said, "I think I will order a dozen." "Lady Jane" as her friends called her later moved to Florida to be with her children (all retired) and keeps in touch with her friends here at the Legacy. At 106 she is still alive and mentally sharp; apparently the hot dogs are not affecting her.

I am writing this as I begin my 15th year as a resident-pastor to men and women who are like an "eighth sacrament." They are a source of life to me as I think of their varied experiences: the sickness and death of many of their loved ones, the moments of joy and the times of frustration, the many acts of kindness they have shown others. They keep moving along. Maybe they are walking a bit slower or pushing a walker, but their smile and laughter are a bright light to the community. When their children and grandchildren and even great-grandchildren visit, they really come alive. One resident has a sign outside her apartment: "Grandchildren are God's reward for not killing our own children." Every time I pass by that apartment, I laugh but it is so true. She and her husband are the source of life for their children just as they have life because of their own parents. They cooperated in God's continuous and loving work of creation when as a loving couple they expressed their love with each other. I see a sacrament as a visible sign of grace. I am very lucky to live with these venerable signs of love.

That got me thinking. I realize the staff here at the Legacy are also equally caring. The cleaning staff have time for a smile and a warm "Hello!" when they are cleaning apartments or the hallways. Many of the residents are technologically challenged. The concierge at the main desk or one of the staff fixes their cell phones, the remote controls for their TV sets, or answers questions about outings, meals, or the movie of the night. The maintenance staff arrive to fix the plumbing, arrange pictures on the wall, adjust the heating/air conditioning controls, or screw in a new bulb. Thanks to the entire staff the whole complex is neat, clean, and well-groomed both on the inside and outside. The creative activities director with her staff arranges for a variety of activities from Bingo to crafts, movies, concerts on the patio, "happy hour" with alcohol and ice cream socials. Scheduling talks and courses e.g., travelogues, sign language, better memory aids are supplemented with opportunities to support canned food drives, school supplies, and clothing drives; raffles and barbecues support a variety of charities (Cure Cancer, Alzheimer's, e.g.). A resolute auxiliary staff organizes and teaches Yoga, meditation, and relaxation techniques as well as regular physical exercise classes. With the beauty salon available men and women can have their hair tended to. In the same area there are rooms for a visiting medical doctor, a podiatrist, or to have blood drawn for differing medical issues. For those who cannot drive any longer, a bus is available for shopping trips, medical appointments, or recreational needs e.g., tours, musical concerts, special meals at nearby restaurants. In a nutshell, the Legacy has a staff that is available for every need. How could I forget the director of the dining room who assures the residents of a healthy meal served by pleasant adults and high school students as waiters. Watching the high school students grow into their job over two or three years, then graduate either to go off to college or take a full-time position in a similar industry is like watching our own children grow into mature young adults. Like the residents, the staff treats each of us with loving service.

If my thoughts about the people at the Legacy where I live might sound like a dream come true, in a sense, they have some key earmarks. I spent most of my life working with young people or in a busy parish where there were meetings, business calls, visiting homes or hospitals, worrying about the budget and the latest needed repairs on the roof or furnace. For the last three years I have not had to worry about any of these. My life now seems more focused on preserving my health, enjoying meals and telephone calls with friends, reading books for fun, and appearing at very few meetings unless I choose to attend. I do not set my alarm to get up unless I have a doctor's appointment or am going out for breakfast with a friend. My Sundays are very quiet. I read, walk, enjoy a movie, and look forward to dinner with the extended Wiktorski family that adopted me since my parents died. The last three years, for me, have been like an extended retreat or novitiate to prepare for the next phase of my life.

Perhaps the most challenging issue has been my health "A-fib," congestive heart failure, edema, trouble walking because of arthritis, to name a few. My health over the past 85 years of my life was fantastic, thank God. Getting sick, going to doctors, getting blood work done, plus ultra-sounds and x-rays have cramped my lifestyle, but they have been amazing teachers. In a profound sense, the health issues have been a great blessing. It slowed me down, so I was forced to sit by myself to think, read, listen to music, and pray. I also learned there is truth to a prescription for helping older people to sleep: give them a recliner.

These past few years have given me the opportunity to reflect on moments of encouragement and moments of discouragement. The discouragements often led me to a better understanding of myself, opportunities to make changes in my life's goals, and encouraged me to try new things. In the middle of these times, I ended up in a hospital emergency room three times in about two months. The first time I remained for eight days just to empty the extra fluid in my system. I found it extremely difficult to read; the TV had poor reception; sleeping was difficult because of blood draws and checking my vitals in the middle of the night or sleeping on my back. I was not allowed out of bed on my own. An alarm was attached to the bed so if I tried, it would go off in the nurses' station and lights would begin to blink in my room. I discovered the workings of the bed alarm because a few times the nurse forgot to turn off the system before getting me out of bed to walk. On one occasion (in the middle of the night) I pressed the button for assistance because I needed to relieve myself. The diuretic medicine was working overtime. The nurse and his aide came in, turned off the alarm system, but then were figuring the best way to get me out of bed. I told them the way I did this on multiple occasions during the day. The nurse did not think that it was the best way. He thought he might need to find a special mobile tool to help. By this time, I was panicking lest a more serious "accident" occur in my bed. He stood there thinking and so I said loudly, "I don't give a damn what you do but do it quickly." He rested his head on the doorpost praying, "Jesus, please give me the patience to deal with this difficult man." He left, wheeled in a mobile unit with side handles which allowed me to stand up; then helped me out of bed…just in time. I thanked him and went back to bed. The next night the same nurse's aide came into my room to check on me and to inform me "My father is a minister, and I am not used to the language you used last night." I was happy that she could not read my mind. I am sure that her father never used some of those words.

The second trip to the emergency room was during Holy Week. An ambulance took me to the emergency department; I had with me nothing except for my wallet and cell phone. This unplanned journey turned out to be a seven-day stay during which I wanted to scream. The nurse in the emergency department took a variety of tests and then solemnly asked me, "Do you know that you have Covid?" I did not recognize it probably because I was sick for so long. Apparently, I did not even recognize those telling Covid symptoms. I was tested for Covid two other times but received negative results. In any case, I was whisked off to a room in the same unit as before. The medicine for edema and heart issues was the same, but I was in my room with very few visits from the nurses. Hospitals, as would be expected, needed to preserve the good health of their staff for the control of Covid among the staff. I have been lucky over the years to have doctors who listened to my issues. My primary physician of over 35 years retired because of technology and pressure to see more patients per hour. We used to spend some time each visit talking about our mutual enjoyment of the latest book about American History. The doctor assigned to visit me during this stay was very similar. He listened although we did not talk about American History. He visited me daily and my confidence in him grew with each visit. "Listening" to the other is not only a sign of respect but is also very healing.

The days passed very slowly. Even the ambulance trip to the ER seemed never ending. Thank God, at least, I had my phone with me. No visitors were permitted because of my Covid and little interaction with staff except for the basics. At least this room's TV helped, but I was not allowed out of bed or to walk outside my room. A few calls each day helped alleviate my growing frustration. For the most part I was left by myself. I had some idea of what solitary confinement is like. Towards the end of my time, alone in the room, I thought I would begin to throw temper-tantrums or some food trays just to get some emotional relief. I know all this does not reflect a spirituality of holy suffering, but it helped me realize a few areas for growth in my own life: cultivate silence and support those who are afflicted. One of the more interesting moments, considering my desire to die on Easter, was the Holy Saturday evening visit from the nurses. They took my vitals. My machine registered my pulse at 32. This was not good; their faces showed it. I said to myself, "I might get my wish." I added a prayer of contrition just in case. The nurses furiously tapped the machine and checked the wires. My pulse went up to sixty-one. All breathed a sigh of relief. By the time I was dismissed from the hospital, if I had wings I could have flown back to my apartment at the Legacy.

The third visit to the emergency room was less frightening for me, but more so for the ambulance crew and the Legacy staff who had called 911. My heart doctors (yes, plural) said that I should weigh myself often during the week to watch my weight. If I should put on five pounds or more in one day, I needed to call them lest I end up in the hospital again. One morning as I backed off the bathroom scale, I fell and hit my head on the corner of the shower. I could not get up from the floor by myself so I called the main desk on my cell phone. The concierge, according to strict Legacy procedure, called 911 to dispatch an ambulance. I did not feel any pain. All I wanted to do was get off the floor. They insisted I should go to the hospital to check out the head wound. I was terrified that I would go back into the same room I had left a few weeks before only to endure more silence and hospital meals. Fortunately, the doctors in a very crowded emergency room, after a few tests, declared I had suffered no serious damage. I was free to go home. Did God ever get my thanks that night!!!

The hospital experiences and the swift change of lifestyle brought on by my Covid and the reality I was no longer teaching initially did not sit well with me. I had to face it, deal with it, accept it, and now enjoy it. If nothing else, I have had more time to read new books that had nothing to do with class preparations; reread others discovering new insights that I missed when I was younger mainly because I felt compelled to get it off my "to-do" list. It has been like working on a puzzle: putting all the pieces together allows one to see the whole picture. My life makes more sense today because I can fit the pieces, big and small, together. Now I understand why writers, artists, composers needed to walk in fields and forests, sit on the beach or alone in a comfortable chair, listen to the sounds or the silence around them, to see old things from a unique perspective with time "to smell the roses." I also listen to the life stories of other residents who are putting their puzzle together; sharing their stories with other residents as they relax comfortably sitting on the patio in the warm sun.

A local reporter was looking for a story to fill some empty space in the regional paper. She came upon one of our residents who was in his nineties. He quietly shared stories about his life in the Army during World War II. Until the interview he had not talked about his war experiences with anyone. It so happened he was the commissioned archivist of events and characters that later were the basis for the TV series, *Band of Brothers*. He was one of the first to visit and take pictures of Hitler's Eagle's Nest, a get-away chalet for meetings with his top aides and his girlfriend, Eva. The interview gave him the opportunity to put his life's pieces into perspective to paint a whole picture of his life. The residents also got to know him better. Some began to tell their "war stories" too.

Wisdom comes when we make sense of how we dealt with all the "little stuff." The place for me has been life at the Legacy at the Fairways in a small village in upstate New York surrounded by a band of brothers and sisters. There were some catastrophes which led to some major changes, but the daily stuff of life gave me the tools introducing me to a better life perspective. I often met new people who later became cherished friends and who were the most gentle healers giving me a fresh vision of service. Even now I laugh as I think back "If I only knew then what I know now."

BIRTHDAY #88

It Has Been a Wonderful Life (And Still Is)

I AM JUMPING AHEAD OF my narrative with this chapter's reflection. I quietly celebrated my 88th birthday yesterday. It was absolutely the happiest and best birthday I ever had. I had planned on a quiet morning and afternoon with a possible dinner later in the day. It did not happen. My birthday celebration with food and a cake, along with four other family celebrants, was scheduled for the following Sunday to accommodate the family's schedule. It would be Sunday without our usual weekly dinner at the Wiktorski home. My big meal consisted of a bowl of clam chowder and a few crackers. Why? I spent the day on the telephone or responding to texts beginning at 8:30 in the morning until 9:00 in the evening. Calls from Washington, Texas, Montana, four calls from Florida, Massachusetts, as well as local ones with twice as many texts from even more places along with a few cards kept me busy all day. I enjoyed every minute of it! One call from Florida took about 30 minutes; the call from Texas was 75 minutes. All were great conversations sharing memories from the past. Some filled me in with their latest interests or additions to their family. One of the callers was reading the Bible and finding direction for his life. The one from Texas was from a student who dropped out of college. I had tried unsuccessfully to get him to read a book (any book) when he was in college. During our extended phone conversation, he was quoting me based on our lengthy discussions we had in my office, over occasional dinners at a local Italian restaurant, and still other ideas we had spoken about during a class period. The call from Montana ran about 15 minutes from a student I taught 50 years ago; his son called later to wish me a happy birthday. A former parishioner, now a psychiatrist, from 30 years ago called me from Seattle. We spoke about his family, his work, and his faith journey for about 30 minutes. I could go on about the variety of greetings. They meant so much to me because, apparently. I meant much to the caller. That is why this year's birthday was so special. I went to bed with grateful and proud tears in my eyes. I have long thought tears are a gift from God.

The "birth" day prompted me to look back over the years to re-examine my own journey of faith and the friendships I have enjoyed. I reflected on my evolving faith beginning with my simple faith growing up. I remember the first time I received Holy Communion. I was six years of age. It was spontaneous: everyone else was going up to the altar rail to get "something" so I joined them. After Mass two nuns descended on me asking who I was and where did I come from? In those days children sat together in the small chapel near the altar apart from the adults. "I just followed the crowd." This was hardly a sufficient response for the two nuns.

The time I officially received Holy Communion for the first time I was dressed in short white pants, white shirt, and tie. I watched the priest at the altar and said to myself I would like to do "that" someday. I became an altar boy, learned Latin responses (but did not know what they meant nor cared), and served at the altar the rest of my school years as I developed a better understanding of the words and a theology that caused me to remember in gratitude the gift of a loving sacrifice commemorated each time I attended or celebrated Mass.

In those pre-Vatican II days we needed to fast from midnight to receive Holy Communion the next day. That rule did not change until I was ordained. Mother's Day was a special day in May when we also honored Mary, the mother of Jesus. Each year in our parish the second-grade class made its First Communions and made cards for our mothers promising to pray for them in special ways. We often built shrines in our home to honor Mary all through the month. I can still see the shrine in my room and the lilacs I picked from the tree outside our home to decorate it. Well, one year on Mother's Day I broke the fast before Holy Communion. I think it was swallowing some toothpaste while I was brushing my teeth. At that time in my life I took things more literally than I would today so I decided that I should not go to Communion. The next day our teacher asked us if we all remembered our mothers when we received Holy Communion yesterday. Then, she added, "Will all those who did not receive Holy Communion on Sunday please stand?" The biggest troublemaker in the class and I were the only ones who stood up. I was so embarrassed that day I vowed never to put myself into a situation like that again. In some ways that incident has had a major and sometimes negative effect on my life ever since. In recent years Pope Francis has influenced me and my devotion to Mary. He had a prayer experience of Mary under the title "Undoer of Knots" that asks, "Untie the knots in my own heart and in my own life, and free me to love as Christ loves." That daily devotion has encouraged me to "let go" so I could be free to be more loving.

I already mentioned how important "story time" on Friday afternoons during my years at Nativity School played in my life. I need to add that the stories plus the books I devoured about saints and heroes during those years were key to my spiritual growth. I wanted to imitate the North American missionaries and martyrs like Isaac Jogues; saints who made a difference like Francis of Assisi who found nature to be a way to know God; John Bosco who dedicated his priestly life to care for poor boys; and Aloysius Gonzaga, a young saint in his twenties preparing for the priesthood. I read, and have read all these years, many biographies about Abraham Lincoln. In recent years Doris Kearns Goodwin's *Team of Rivals* about Lincoln and her later book, *Leadership in Turbulent Times*, have profoundly inspired me and reaffirmed my thinking about the need to read, listen, forgive, and take calculated risks when trying to make changes that will serve others, especially the alienated. I preached to my students and still do over the years when we talk on the phone or lunch: READ! Reading was my lifeline during my years as a student in the classroom and continues to be so very important. A few years ago, I had cataract surgery with a follow-up procedure. I could not read for longer than ten minutes at a time and became mildly depressed. Reading again relieved the depression. Audio books did not resolve the issue. I need a hard copy so I can underline and make notes. When I reread books years later, it is amazing how the underlining and side notes bring back memories or, sometimes, I question why I underlined the sentence or passage in the first place. Heroes and heroines model the "good life" for me and give me ideas how to proceed in its pursuit.

Of course, prayer and new experiences of prayer have been rather consistent, but ever-changing. I still use the morning and night prayer I learned in grade school. The daily rosary and devotion to Mary have been important. As a student I asked her for help to pass my exams. When my mom died, I asked Mary to continue being a mother to me. At different times I prayed that Mary be my "secretary" to remind me of appointments. In the spirit of de Montfort's *True Devotion to Mary*. I consecrated myself to Mary on August 15, 1952. This devotion also moved me to a renewed devotion to the Sacred Heart of Jesus including the annual parish novena in June when I was in grade school serving at the altar. This devotion resurfaced after I was ordained. I continue to keep a picture on the wall reminding me as I pray to "make my heart like yours." While I was at Saint Bernard's Seminary, I read about the life of Peter Eymard, the founder of the Blessed Sacrament Fathers and Sisters, who made a daily Holy Hour before the Blessed Sacrament. I then adopted the routine. Once I was ordained, I unfortunately fell away from the practice for a few years. A new assistant priest moved into the rectory at Holy Family Church. In one of our conversations, he mentioned how the daily Holy Hour was important to him, encouraging me to do the same. Over the past 60 years I have not always been able to do so in a church because of travel, hospital stays, living conditions without a church or chapel but, at least, I still have remained faithful to the practice of the Holy Hour of prayer and reflection. All of this is not to brag. I just need to put my thoughts down on paper about how prayer has kept me from doing and, especially, saying some stupid things that would have harmed others. My short temper, biting sarcasm, and impulsive behavior are issues I have worked on all my life. Daily prayer and meditation are practices I suggest to the same people I preach to about the need to read. I don't tell them they have to do the same as I do, but to do something for a few minutes at the beginning and end of the day. I usually spend a few minutes in the evening when I first get into bed reflecting on the day to find three events that I am most grateful for and say, "Thank you." One night I was having trouble finding the third event (it was one of those "bad" days). I found a third thing to be grateful for: I didn't hit or kill anyone that day.

From my first days in the seminary we had an annual retreat. Some were for three days, others for six days. Church Law requires priests to make an annual retreat of usually about three days at least. I have been doing that at our local retreat center, the nearby Trappist monastery, and an occasional distant retreat center like Eastern Point in Massachusetts, or another time in Assisi in Italy and still another on the Mount of the Transfiguration in the Holy Land. As I wrote earlier, I made a thirty-day retreat utilizing eastern meditation and later made the Spiritual Exercises of St. Ignatius Loyola. I also studied the University of Dallas' thirty-day course in Western Spirituality located in Italy, and more recently a course in Celtic Spirituality for a month in Ireland. These and others I cannot remember have assisted in my daily struggle to be a better human being and to develop a priestly heart. For many years I was able to drive to the Abbey of the Genesee nearby for an afternoon of reflection ending with sung Vespers. Well, not quite the "ending." I would stop off to relish a quiet meal at a nearby restaurant. Then I enjoyed the ride back to my residence feeling very refreshed.

A more recent experience, however, pulls other aspects of my spiritual journey together. Let me share my reflection about the experience. When I was in high school (around 1949) I remember playing sick so that I could finish reading Thomas Merton's *Seven Storey Mountain*. A longtime dream to spend time in a Trappist monastery became a reality after I responded to an advertisement, "Be a monk for a month" at Mepkin Abbey. My ordination as a diocesan priest in 1960 and my earlier desire to experience the daily life of a monk was not squelched. I had often wondered what it would be like to work and pray within a community committed to welcoming others with the hospitality of Christ. The inaugural Monastic Institute at Mepkin Abbey in the summer of 2018 became a time of healing and recommitment as a priest and college teacher. In one of my weekly calls to my sister, she told me that it must be a special time because she said, "I can hear it in your voice."

The daily rhythm of prayer, work and meals in silence offered an opportunity to take some much-needed time to listen to the voices within me. My arthritis reminded me I should walk more to keep my knee joints more active. It is amazing how much better I was feeling by the end of the 30 days at Mepkin Abbey. The meatless diet of delicious meals including ice cream on Sundays helped me as well. How many times I had been encouraged to exercise and watch what I ate. The Institute offered me the time and leisure to do just that.

I was drained emotionally because of the challenges that come with teaching college students and listening to the evening news. Negative voices were swirling around in my head as I drove the 925 miles to the monastery, but the silence and positive discussions following the first-rate lectures on prayer, the rule of Saint Benedict, friendship, and the charisms modeled in the lives of the fathers and mothers of the Cistercian tradition were all sources for healing. As I was driving back home, I reflected on all this and realized the positive conversations during our small group discussions after the daily lectures had brought a much-needed sense of calm and peace.

Singing the psalms seven times a day touched me spiritually. The measured sung tone of each psalm allowed for a deeper attention to the words of praise and thanksgiving. The occasional thought that these were the same hymns that Jesus sang in a Sabbath synagogue service in rural Galilee or on his way to Jerusalem became a happy distraction. Some of psalms reminded me of the hymn of nature written by Saint Francis and quoted by Pope Francis in his letter, *"Laudato si . . . "* All reminded me of the many ways all creation sings in gratitude as it blends into a powerful hymn of the universe. I studied the psalms as a seminary student, attended lectures and workshops about them over the 58 years as a priest. As a deacon and priest, I prayed them daily in Latin (prior to the Vatican II Council) and in English since the early seventies. As we sang the psalms at seven different times of the day, I experienced a deeper connection to the words as I sang them in unison with the bigger community of "fellow monks."

The Rule of Saint Benedict expressed in the Cistercian tradition requires the monks to do some manual labor each day to support the community, but also as a way to share "in the divine work of creation and restoration." I also viewed manual labor as a way of living in solidarity with others who do manual labor: an awareness of their struggles as they go to work each day. We worked, for the most part, in silence each day. Those three hours were the most helpful and healing for me. I thought of those who worked to support their families: some with rewarding positions, others with less rewarding jobs. I thought more about those in less rewarding daily grinds: What motivated them each day? What were they thinking? Did they even have the luxury of reflecting on their life within a supportive place of work that shared similar values?

The hours of working in silence offered me the opportunity to give thanks for my own religious and educational background that provided me so many opportunities for being creative in pastoral ministry and a college classroom. Those same times in silence challenged me about choices in my life when I carried on a conversation. Did I really listen to others before I spoke? Did I talk too much? Did I know when to stop talking? Did I leave the encounter on a positive note? Did I use my God-given gifts to give life? Am I willing to let go so the other person might explore his/her unique set of gifts? Cutting the stems off mushrooms and bagging the dried ones for sale at the monastery store in silence afforded me plenty of time to reflect on these and still other challenging questions. The experience also allowed me the time to count my many blessings and be grateful. If I were to choose the most sacred time for me during the month of the Monastic Institute, it would have to be the hours spent in silence doing manual labor.

The sixteen of us who made up the inaugural Monastic Institute came from various backgrounds and religious experiences. I had an overwhelming sense we were all searching for our answers to our own unique questions but were also deeply committed to walking together on the journey. At challenging times during the month that mutual care for each other is what kept me praying and working with joy. As often happens in my daily life at home, it is the selfless people I spend time with who fill my life with joy and laughter. I was very lucky to find such a community for the month of July 2018 singing psalms and harvesting mushrooms.

This present series of written reflections was made possible mainly because of the Covid epidemic. In the early seventies, moreover, I worked with the Marriage Encounter movement ("to make good marriages better"). The couples that invited me to be a priest-presenter told me it would make me "a better priest." That kind of invitation put me off for a few years. "Who were they to tell me how to be better?" I eventually made a Marriage Encounter weekend which prompted me to write a daily journal entry. I had also attended an Ira Progroff workshop on intensive journalling which I did irregularly for a few years earlier before the Marriage Encounter weekend.

Since 1976 I have written a daily journal entry every day except for three days before Covid and during the Covid years about 15 days because of my hospital experiences. I left Marriage Encounter in 1985 to help establish in our diocese, and then be part of (for over 25 years) a program called Retrouvaille. This program deals with marriages that are "in trouble." These two programs, journalling workshops, and my daily commitment to write a journal reflection has made me a better person and priest. Writing has never been my strongest suit but the discipline of writing something daily has allowed me to vent, rethink, challenge, and appreciate what is going on in my life.

I hesitate to put into writing another helpful practice that has been an important part of my life. I am very cognizant of the scriptural admonitions (basically, do not make a public display of religious practices to attract attention) about praying, fasting, and giving alms so pardon this reflection. About 30 years ago one of my former students was in graduate school and was suffering a nervous breakdown. I assured him of my prayers and continued support. Then I added, "I will fast for you every Monday to help you through these tough times." I still fast on Mondays not eating between meals and eating lighter at the basic three meals. Over the years, I have added a few other people to that list in support of dealing with their trials and tribulations. It works!

One of my priest friends from 45 years ago has been active in a variety of protests and boycotts to promote social justice issues. At the time I said that I am not into "protests and boycotts" but do support solutions to the issues. My choice for support would be more private. I decided to abstain every Friday from meat as I did before the Church mitigated its ruling about abstaining from meat each Friday not just during Lent. Fasting and abstaining have become important habits in my life. Drinking alcohol has not been essential to my social life. I do need, however, to confess how I enjoyed a cold beer with my pizza, a whiskey sour, a gin and tonic, or a glass of wine with my meals. After a trip to Puerto Rico, I became quite good at mixing a pina colada during the summer months. With the scandal of sexual abuse and the need for forgiveness and healing in so many areas of the Church community, I made another pledge. I chose to abstain from drinking alcohol in reparation and for healing both for any hurt I may ever have caused during my life and for all who have been victims or perpetrators of the sexual abuse issue that has caused so much harm. Fasting and abstaining also benefit me because it keeps many people and causes regularly on my mind and in my heart.

An Aside

A PRIEST FRIEND OF MINE who read the first draft of this set of memoirs asked me, "Looking back over your years of ministry what have you seen change about the Church?" That was a tough question. I remember a few of my seminary professors told us to be sure to keep our textbooks. "When people come to you with a question, you can reach over to your bookcase, check the textbook, and you can give them the answer." We "professionals" would provide the answer. If I have learned anything else it is that many answers in science, psychology, history among other areas have changed to provide accuracy and/or a better understanding of the issue. Luckily, the Church community has many educated, articulate, faithful lay people along with men and women religious who have so much more knowledge and wisdom that it puts me to shame. Even my understanding and interpretation of Scripture, Church History, and Theology is still developing. "I don't have all the answers!" However, I am now looking at those topics through a bigger lens. We are all still learning and are not afraid to admit it.

One of the greatest blessings of my years as a priest has been the people I have met and who have been an important part of my life. I admire their commitment to their parish family even with its faults and failures. They remain devoted to a community of faith in need of continued healing. The people of God are the future of the Church because they are aware that they *are* the Church. If the institutional Church is to survive, it will be because of their life, sweat, tears, laughter, and deep faith in Jesus who is the Good News. It will not necessarily be the Jesus in the church building but the Jesus in the heart of each human being made in God's image. I often shared a secret with my students. "God is bigger than we think!"

I have lived under seven Popes. My favorites have been Pope John XXIII and Pope Francis. I respected the others and admired their varied gifts always in the service of the wider Church. One title they all shared was Supreme Pontiff. A "pontiff" is a bridge builder. Both John XXIII and Francis, in my mind, exemplified the art of building bridges between different groups. A few years ago the thought came to me that if the Pope is the "supreme" pontiff that means the rest of us Christians are also called to be "bridge builders." In recent years some groups seem to be committed to building walls not bridges. The walls do not necessarily need to be stone or wire fences but legal or economic. One of the differences I have noticed over the years is the many lay people's commitment to form a just society in which all can find dignity no matter their race, language, economic situation, sexual orientation, or even if they are not in our church pews on Sunday. Often these faithful lay leaders are ahead of the ordained leaders.

The thought about "building bridges not walls" came to me on one of my pilgrimages to the Holy Land. Our group travelled to the Holy Land to listen to the stories of Muslem, Jewish, Christian citizens about the mistrust, tension, and horrific actions that were deepening the divide in the area. The stories were heart-wrenching. For me, the visible sign was the "wall" that divides parts of the land. I became a member of a peaceful protest of the wall that can divide families, towns, and even private property. About eight of us were holding a Palestinian flag near a line of about 20 young, stern-faced Israeli soldiers with drawn rifles to our left, and a mounted machine gun about 25 feet from our faces. The Israeli captain ordered us to disperse, or we would be shot. I kept asking myself, "Is this going to make a difference? Am I willing to die today all because of a wall?" It did make a difference to me. I began to think of the walls in my own life that I need to take down. And, yes, I need to die to my own self-righteousness if those walls are to come down. How do I do that? Popes John and Francis both urged dialogue. Essential to dialogue is a willingness to listen. Listening would demand of me a willingness to tear down the walls of defensiveness and ridding myself of the arrogance "that Father knows best." Over my lifetime I have been working at more gentle listening. The recent Synod in Rome demonstrated that most visibly when the variety of participants sat at round tables where each could speak freely and listen patiently to each other face to face. By the way, the soldiers did not shoot. They and we backed away peacefully and, I think, gratefully.

The recent Synod reminded me of another image from another experience in the Holy Land. Our group was lunching out on one of the knolls. I saw a shepherd carrying a boombox on his shoulder with music blaring. He walked along next to a flock of sheep looking for a grazing spot. I could see his lips moving. I am not sure if he was singing along with the music or talking to the sheep. What struck me was the image of a shepherd walking along side, neither ahead nor behind; the shepherd gently talking/singing to encourage them on their search. That is another lesson I am still learning. Pope Francis called a variety of people to a Synod ("walk with") to search out better ways to accompany those seeking a safe space to "be." Over the past sixty years the good shepherds have listened to the many differing voices to meet the needs of a hungry flock some of whom have wandered off and, possibly, are lost. "Listen, Decide, Act."

So much for my thoughts about change in the Church. Has the Church succeeded? I keep going back to a decision I made years ago: Keep Jesus as the cornerstone and don't worry about the small stuff. I think more than one author has suggested that the need for change is an absolute for growth. Continued growth leads to a fuller life and expands our imagination. Jesus called us to conversion ("look at things differently") so that we might have a fuller life. Our chief shepherds have offered areas for change to attain a fuller life. Not everyone has listened, and some have listened to what they wanted to hear. I hope I have made the right choices.

If I were to choose one area of profound concern not just for the Church but for all institutions (and I mean "all"), it would be the growing deep mistrust within our communities and with those of other communities. Do we trust our leaders? Do they trust us? Do we trust a fragile church or state? Do we trust the law or those who make and enforce it? Do we trust business, educational institutions, and the list could go on? Do they trust us as critical thinkers? Erik Erikson posits the theory that trust is the basis to further development of the self and any relationship. Without trust we will fail in any worthwhile endeavor. I wonder, sometimes, whether many of us do not even trust ourselves. I do trust in the Good News and in the family and friends who have walked with me these many years. I pray for growth in trust for us all.

Working toward a Conclusion

When Covid hit the world initially seemed to go into a period of almost total isolation.

These past few years have become, for me, a time of extended reflection and retreat-like experiences. The Daily hour of prayer, daily journalling, and other devotional practices such as the "Chaplet of Reparation" for the sins of priests, for example, have been a source of strength for me. I have also been able to read much more extensively in areas I had not done before. Pope Benedict was not one of my favorite popes, but I read a two-volume biography of his life. I discovered that three of his favorite books were: *Animal Farm*, *1984*, and *Brave New World*. I reread all three to make a connection and added *Fahrenheit 451* as my own contribution to novels about a dystopian world, each of which gave me insight into Benedict's fears and decisions for the Church. Because of Benedict's Augustinian approach to theology, I reread the *Confessions of Saint Augustine*. It was my third reading of this classic and finally I began to understand it at a deeper level. This led me to read about the spirituality of Saint Augustine which led me to a book about his "quantum approach to theology" which forced me, in turn, to read a book called. *Quantum Theology*. The author of that book kept referring to the theories in quantum physics about which I knew very little. That led me to read a beginner's book as well as watch a DVD series of lectures about that topic. All of this has allowed me the time to look at my own journey as one of a lived "quantum" journey. All of this prompted writing my memoirs. Thanks, Pope Benedict!

Because of the isolation and restrictions set down by the Covid crisis to my pastoral ministry, as I have already mentioned, I chose to conduct classes/series at our independent living facility. Legacy at the Fairways about the Scriptures, the Spirituality of Aging, What Do Various Religions Say about Different Topics, and an annual talk about the need for memories of people who have helped us along our life's journey. These have also prompted me to do some soul-searching. Rereading Eric Metaxas' *7 Men and 7 Women and the Secret of Their Greatness* confirmed some of my own thinking about one's approach to the journey each of us needs to make to discover and enjoy the "good life." Hopefully, my reflections about my 88-year pilgrim journey will help others as much as they have helped me. To be happy, as many writers suggest, we need to trust in a healthy relationship with our core operating beliefs, our family, our true friends, and ourselves as well as the work we do in faithful service of others. I have been blessed with that set of gifts including a sense of humor. And, for all, I am very grateful.

I wrote most of this final entry on my 88th birthday two weeks before Easter. In case I died on Easter, as I pray to do some Easter, I wanted to express in writing what has kept me going then and now. Even today, almost two years later, I look back over the years in gratitude for "what was" and for the grace to have said "yes" (although sometimes it was difficult).

Thomas Merton summarized it beautifully for me in his *Thoughts in Solitude*. I cannot think of a better way to conclude this memoir.

> My Lord God, I have no for certain where I am going, I do not see the road ahead of me. I cannot know for certain where it will end. Nor do I really know myself, and the fact that I think I am following your will does not mean that I am actually doing so. But I believe that the desire to please you does in fact please you. And I hope that I have that desire in all that I am doing. I hope that I will never do anything apart from that desire. And I know that if I do this you will lead me by the right road, though I may know nothing about it. Therefore I will trust you always though I may seem to be lost and in the shadow of death. I will not fear, for you are ever with me, and you will never leave me to face my perils alone.

www.ingramcontent.com/pod-product-compliance
Lightning Source LLC
Chambersburg PA
CBHW071202160426
43196CB00011B/2166